Franklynn Peterson and Judi Kesselman-Turkel have written seventeen books, including *How to Fix Damn Near Everything, The Build-It-Yourself Furniture Catalog,* and *Children's Toys You Can Build Yourself.* They also write regularly for magazines like *McCall's, Popular Science,* and *Woman's World.* They have helped friends and neighbors improve their homes, and they live in a house they have extensively remodeled, improved, and increased in value.

HOW TO IMPROVE
damn
near
EVERYTHING
AROUND YOUR HOME

Franklynn Peterson
Judi Kesselman-Turkel

A SPECTRUM BOOK

Prentice-Hall, Inc., Englewood Cliffs, New Jersey 07632

Library of Congress Cataloging in Publication Data

Peterson, Franklynn.
  How to improve damn near everything around
your home.

  (A Spectrum Book)
  Includes index.
  1. Dwellings—Remodeling. 2. Dwellings—
Maintenance and repair. I. Kesselman-Turkel,
Judi. II. Title.
TH4816.P48   643'.7   81-11990
                                AACR2

ISBN 0-13-413013-8

ISBN 0-13-413005-7 {PBK.}

This Spectrum Book is available to businesses and organizations at a special discount when ordered in large quantities. For information, contact Prentice-Hall, Inc., General Book Marketing, Special Sales Division, Englewood Cliffs, N.J. 07632.

© 1982 by Prentice-Hall, Inc., Englewood Cliffs, New Jersey 07632

A SPECTRUM BOOK

All rights reserved. No part of this book
may be reproduced in any form or by any means
without permission in writing from the publisher.

10   9   8   7   6   5   4   3   2   1

Printed in the United States of America

Editorial/production supervision by Frank Moorman
Manufacturing buyer: Cathie Lenard

Material on pages 159–167 is adapted from the book *The Build-It-Yourself Furniture Catalog* by Franklynn Peterson, © 1976 by Franklynn Peterson. Published by Prentice-Hall, Inc., Englewood Cliffs, New Jersey 07632.

Prentice-Hall International, Inc., *London*
Prentice-Hall of Australia Pty. Limited, *Sydney*
Prentice-Hall of Canada, Ltd., *Toronto*
Prentice-Hall of India Private Limited, *New Delhi*
Prentice-Hall of Japan, Inc., *Tokyo*
Prentice-Hall of Southeast Asia Pte. Ltd., *Singapore*
Whitehall Books Limited, *Wellington, New Zealand*

Contents

v

HOW TO IMPROVE
damn
near EVERYTHING
AROUND YOUR HOME

I
THE BASICS

1
How to Plan
Your Home Improvement Jobs

Whether your home is cabin or castle, co-op, condo, or rented apartment, improving it can increase its monetary value, make living more comfortable, and even hide the wear and tear of age. But home improvement has to be fun, because the minute a project becomes a big hassle, its value —aesthetic as well as financial—tends to diminish rapidly.

Over our adult years, we've made major and minor improvements ourselves in a number of different homes. Even growing up, we helped our dads do likewise, so our interest in house-fixing is probably ingrained. We've helped other do-it-yourselfers through our other books, as well as on radio and TV, and our combined experience has led us to adopt a basic principle for this book: Home improvements—even the luxurious-looking alterations that are photographed in the pages of every month's *Beautiful This and That Magazine*—ought to fall within the budgets, lifestyles, and capabilities of average people. Therefore:

- All home improvements that we suggest require skills that are within the reach of motivated do-it-yourselfers.

FIGURE 1-1 The home on the left is owned and was designed by Allan Buchsbaum, noted designer. The glass brick wall and ceramic tile emphasized with dark grout may be too bold and stark for many tastes. On the other hand, the home on the right, with its three coordinated wall coverings, might seem unpleasant to Mr. Buchsbaum. *You* have to pick home improvements that you feel are beautiful; editors of *Beautiful This and That Magazine* cannot. (Photos courtesy Tile Council of America and Reed Wallcoverings.)

- *But,* if you'd rather hire an outsider to do any particular job, you will be able to (1) design your own tailor-made improvement; (2) turn the job over to a qualified pro; and (3) skillfully or economically supervise the project thanks to the know-how we've provided.

Before we go any further, our publisher insists on a word or two of warning. We have taken reasonable care in compiling this book, but we cannot possibly alert you to every conceivable hazard contained in the use of each tool, technique, or material discussed within these pages. Like most things in life, some can be dangerous if not used carefully. Neither we nor our publisher can assume any liability for anything that goes wrong. So please work carefully—and if you send us photos of your favorite home improvements once they're completed, maybe we can use them in our next book.

WHY IS THIS IMPROVEMENT BEING MADE? It's important that you decide early in your project exactly *why* you're undertaking the particular home improvement job you've chosen. You'll need this information to assess the cost-effectiveness of your many alternatives.

INCREASE THE VALUE OF YOUR HOME

Ask any real estate agent and she'll tell you that providing bathrooms and kitchens with modern appliances and attractive decors is one of the fastest ways to increase the monetary value of your home. That's why we've included entire chapters on how to improve your bathrooms and kitchens. In other chapters, we focus on walls, floors, ceilings, plumbing, and similar topics that will also help to increase the value of your investment, whether in the kichen, bathroom, or elsewhere.

On the other hand, improvements such as new furnaces, hot water heaters, paneled walls, and such do not always add greatly to the financial value of your home. If you have no idea whether the improvements you're contemplating will help pay for themselves if and when you sell your home, phone any local real estate broker. Better still, seek advice from several.

MAKE YOUR HOME MORE COMFORTABLE

We've found that most people don't make home improvements *only* for their investment value. In fact, often that doesn't figure in directly at all. Most people improve first for *comfort*. Over the long haul, making your home comfortable can make it more valuable, too.

For many people, comfort is tough to achieve except through trial and error—and that's expensive. How can you know in advance, for example, that a fireplace is really going to make your living room warmer and friendlier? You can't rely on ads as a source of objective input, and sales people are only a little better. But there are shortcuts, many of which we detail in this book. In the case of the fireplace, for example, you might rent or borrow an electric heater that puts out about the same number of BTUs. If you put the heater in the spot where you want the projected fireplace to go, you should get a reasonably accurate assessment, at little cost, of how much comfort you can expect.

For another example, take the garret-style attics that look so pretty in magazine pictures. Until you build one, how do you know that it will make a comfortable master bedroom for you? One way is to visit some already-built attic rooms in other homes. When we're planning home improvement projects, we walk through all the model homes and real estate agents' open houses we can find. Before too long, we've accumulated enough information about how our ideas might look in three dimensions to decide whether they really will be as comfortable as they look. And look at the inexpensive fun we've had in the meantime.

MAKE YOUR HOME BEAUTIFUL

No matter what the other reasons for home improvement, beauty is almost always one consideration. Even if it's something as mundane as a storm door, most people pick a style that not only does the job but looks good, too.

Even when beauty is the only motive for a particular home improvement, you still can't jump into the project without doing some research. First of all, unless you live alone you must make sure that everybody involved likes the planned improvement. Many people have trouble visualizing in advance how their improved walls, windows, wood shelves, or modernized kitchens will look when finished. Even those who can visualize just how something is going to look often have trouble describing it effectively for other people. The next section of this chapter shows several techniques you can use to help determine in advance whether your improvements will actually look lovely once they're finally in place.

PLAN AHEAD

The surest way to achieve the most pleasing results, with the least amount of frustration and the greatest economy, is to make careful written plans—in advance, not as you go along. Measure your "before" space carefully and make a good sketch of it. Then draw *all* of your "after" improvements on a similar sketch. Even if you're a long way from being a good artist, you can make perfectly adequate blueprints of all your home improvement jobs. Just follow the suggestions accompanying the nearby illustrations.

Once your preliminary plans and sketches are ready, calculate how much of the various building and decorating materials the job requires. Figure out how much all of that is going to cost. Then sit down and decide if you want to spend that much. If you don't, redo the sketches with economy in mind. Here are just a few hints to start you thinking for yourself.

• Expensive wall coverings don't have to be ruled out simply because you can't afford to use them on all four walls. Often the elegance is *enhanced* if you cover just one wall with the expensive stuff and then paint the remaining walls in a subdued color that accents the covering. A few odds and ends of the expensive stuff—framed on one plain wall, lining a knickknack cabinet, covering a table—adds that mix-and-match look that decorators strive for. (See Figure 1-5.)

• Some coverings work just as well on just half a wall. For example, a formal feeling can be achieved by paneling just the bottom half or one-third of a wall and then adding a molding across the top edge as a wainscot. That trick cuts your paneling costs in half.

• For covering floors, did you figure in even those portions of the room that will be under stoves, refrigerators, and cabinets? It's not generally necessary to cover those areas.

• Drapes don't have to hang from ceiling to floor in order to look custom-made. You can often afford the expensive fabric you really want by shortening drapery length or by using fewer panels, combining them with less expensive materials. Consider valances above windows, wall coverings below them, and inexpensive sheers combined with your drapes. Or look for alternatives like shades or shutters for casual rooms. But try them out on paper before you spend the money on your actual windows.

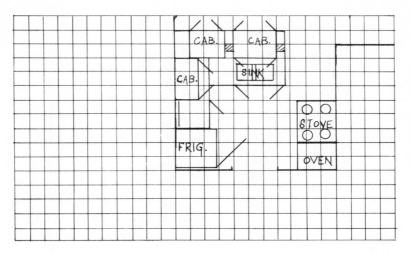

FIGURE 1-2 For most layouts of furniture and walls, a simple blueprint sketch on graph paper works fine. For almost all home improvements, allowing ¼ inch to equal 1 foot is standard. But for bathrooms, making ½ inch equal to 1 foot is preferred. Measure your space and your furniture or appliances carefully. This example shows a kitchen in the planning stages. The next two illustrations show the same kitchen drawn with two different techniques.

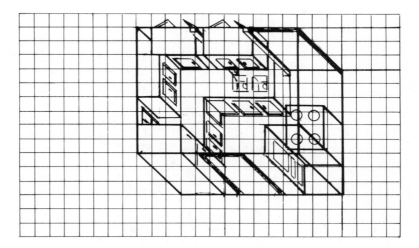

FIGURE 1-3 Kitchens and other rooms that require arrangement of cabinets and similar off-the-floor items are tough to lay out intelligently in simple blueprints. Here is one way to do three-dimensional views without studying art. Using ¼ inch equal to 1 foot, make an outline of the room's dimensions. Then draw a 45° line at each corner of the room, all lines pointing in the same direction. Go diagonally through three squares; then connect the four corners with straight lines. When the lines are completed, you will have a rough aerial view of your room, from a slight angle. This will let you plan wall as well as base cabinet placement.

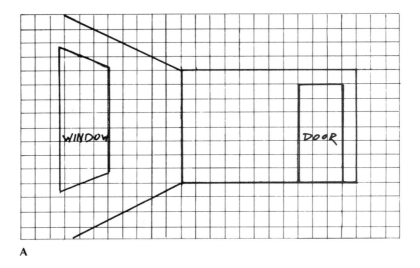

A

B

FIGURE 1-4 Even if you don't have art training, here's a way to draw simple perspective views to help you plan your kitchen or other room. (As with earlier drawings, ¼ inch equals 1 foot.) First sketch in the far wall of your room near the center of the right-hand side of your graph paper; then put in the lines that show the left-hand wall—and the right-hand wall if you want to visualize that at the same time. (See view A.) Then start filling in details for planned cabinets or other features; your dimensions, except along the far wall, will not be accurate, but strive to keep the various items approximately proportional. View B, as well as the earlier kitchen sketches, are from the authors' files, used when they were working out details for their own kitchen. Notice how, to help them visualize, they blacked in the doorway and pass-through areas, dotted in the ceiling tiles, and made rough designs to represent their tile pattern on the floor.

FIGURE 1-5 Don't despair if you can't afford to cover four walls of a room with the expensive wall covering that's caught your eye. One wall of it might give enough impact. Here the pattern is carried onto a pedestal covered with leftover pieces. (Photo courtesy Style-Tex.)

• Factory-built furniture is expensive, especially if it's unusual in design or well built. Consider making your own built-ins when it comes to cabinets and bookcases and putting the money you save into a few really striking conversation pieces. (For a guide to making your own shelves, chairs, desks, tables, cabinets, and even headboards we suggest Franklynn Peterson's *The Build-It-Yourself Furniture Catalog,* published by Prentice-Hall.)

Leaf through those tantalizing house, garden, and decoration magazines. Study other people's homes. Look for ideas you can adapt or improve on, and try them out on sketch paper. Compare your sketches to your budget, reconcile the two, and you're set for the next step. Start shopping for the materials you plan to use. Watch for sales. Better still, ask store managers about their plans for sales; in the home improvement and decorating supplies businesses, sales are often seasonal and it'd be a shame to buy all your materials only a week or two before the price drops 25 percent.

Many home improvement manufacturers provide comprehensive guides that show consumers how to figure how much of a product they'll need. Take home the booklets and study them with your sketches in hand. Ask the clerks for advice too. Many of them have been at their jobs long enough to save you money, time, and headaches.

FIGURE 1-6 Here's one way to cut the cost of expensive drapery material—don't run it all the way to the floor. You also might want to put in a bench, planter, or other eye-catcher to disguise the void. (Sketch courtesy Kirsch Company, © 1979.)

MEASURE UP TO YOUR JOB

One of the major sources of frustration for home improvement do-it-yourselfers stems from making imprecise measurements. The wallpaper ends up not quite reaching the ceiling; the paneling turns out to be a tiny bit too long and when you hammer it into place it chips the ceiling plaster and dents the panel; the countertop misses the edge of the cabinet by just enough that the kids' orange juice runs down into the flour bin. It's all enough to make you want to give up home improvement for life.

There once was a manual arts teacher in Port Edwards, Wisconsin, whose voice could be heard up and down the halls as he yelled at beginning students who were making their first wooden bread boards, "Make it precisely something. Make it exactly 10 inches or exactly 10⅛ inches, but make it exactly something." He knew the value of accuracy and this collection of home-improvement tips is compiled in part by a once-reluctant student of his. So we'll tell you right off that the first secret to successful measuring is to forget the words ". . . and a little bit." If you haul out the old ruler, slap it onto a piece of lumber, study the lines and sublines and sub-sublines and then say, "Hmmm, it's 4 inches and a little bit," your rooms will fit together the same way—a little bit.

Even when working with nonprecision home improvement projects, an error of 2 percent generally is the absolute maximum you should tolerate if your constructions and repairs are to hold their own. In a 1-foot-long piece of wood or steel, a 2 percent tolerance means that your measurements can be off no more than a mere ¼ inch. To attain that kind of precision, you must measure with an accuracy not of ¼ inch but of ⅛ inch. As a rule of thumb, figure that if you're measuring lengths of less than 2 inches, you should read your measurements in $^1/_{16}$ inches, and that

FIGURE 1-7 In home improvements, accurate measurements are vital. Forget the words ". . . and a little bit" when you're using a measuring device. For lengths under 2 inches, use $1/16$-inch markings; for lengths above 10 feet, use ¼-inch markings; in between, use ⅛-inch markings to obtain satisfactory precision. (Photo courtesy The Siesel Company, Inc.)

above 10 feet, the ¼-inch rulings are okay. (If sawing is involved, measurements finer than $1/16$ inch are practically meaningless since the precise thickness of a saw cut is tough to predict in advance.)

Accuracy is a virtue that's not always entirely achieved—neither by homemakers, carpenters, wallpaperers, or tilers. All that expensive molding and trim you see nailed or glued around the bottoms of walls, the middles of walls, the tops of walls, the sides of sinks, and all over everything else is not put there just to add beauty to jobs well done. Often, it's to cover up for big gaps caused, for the most part, by bad measurements. Spend a few extra seconds to measure each job just a bit more accurately. Then, if you find a practical need or an aesthetic beauty in a strip of decoration, tack it up. If not, leave it off—and point with pride to your super-professional home improvement.

2
How to Buy Lumber (and Other Supplies) and Haul It Home

Wood plays an important role in a great many home improvement projects, not only those that seem to involve it directly. Tile floors often require wood or hardboard underlays. Draperies often look best with a valance cut from wood. Paneled basements require furring strips behind the panels. New windows may need new wooden supports around them.

Later in this book we'll cover the important aspects to keep in mind as you shop for panels, floor tiles, ceiling tiles, bathroom fixtures, and similar improvements. For now, let's first concentrate on how you can effectively buy the kind of lumber and lumber-like products you may be needing; and then let's focus on how to carry it—and your other building supplies—safely home.

In the next few pages, we'll dispel some commonly held fears and misconceptions about lumber. You'll find that, with just a wee bit of book learning, it's easy to make sense out of sizes, grades, and descriptions of most products sold in those cavernous home improvement centers.

Since you're not likely to find a dealer who carries more than a couple grades of most kinds of wood, we don't have to cover every imaginable type. But we do want to wrestle briefly with understanding how that beautiful tree becomes the pieces of beautiful wood that you'll turn into a beautiful project.

If a tree is simply sliced into 1-inch or 2-inch pieces, we call that *lumber* or *boards.* It's one of the cheapest forms of wood, but not always the strongest. And the kind of tree is sometimes important. Pine trees, for example, are soft wood, and they're tall but seldom wide. So it's hard to buy pine boards wider than 12 inches. The 2-, 4-, 6-, and 8-inch widths are the most common and therefore the cheapest. You'll almost never find pine in odd-numbered widths such as 5, 7, 9, or 11 inches.

Hardwoods such as ash, walnut, oak, maple, and mahogany are cut more carefully and are more expensive. Here you do find odd-numbered widths. And since hardwood trees are generally wider than pine, you can often buy boards wider than 12 inches.

In addition to standard widths, boards come in standard thicknesses. Whether pine or hardwood, most boards used for decorative applications are nominally 1 inch thick. For heftier jobs you can buy boards which are 2 or more inches thick.

There are also standard lengths of board. The 8-, 10-, and 12-foot lengths are the most common. Some lumber retailers handle 6-foot lengths as well as 14- and 16-footers.

There's one catch to these easy measurements. What lumber dealers call a 1-inch board isn't actually 1 inch thick. It's about ¾ of an inch. A so-called 4-inch-wide board is really closer to 3¾ or even 3½ inches wide.

All of these measurements are based on dimensions at the sawmill, where the noble tree is sliced into long pieces. The saw that does the slicing is fast but rough. After the sawmill does its work, rough boards go through a plane or sander that takes away the roughness but also removes about ¼ inch of wood in every direction. Then, as freshly cut wet boards dry out, they shrink noticeably. If you're building a set of shelves entirely from 1-by-8-inch lumber, you can overlook a ¼-inch discrepancy. But as soon as you start to build or design projects which use all three dimensions—width, length, and thickness—you may have to account for the missing ¼ inch or so. So for accurate work, carefully measure the *real* size of your boards.

Figure 2-1 spells out the *actual* dimensions you're likely to find in the common boards you purchase. When you buy them, use the *nominal* figures to place your order, not the real, trimmed sizes. When you walk into a lumberyard, here's how you call for a board that is the size you need: To sound like a pro, first call out the number of pieces you want, then the nominal thickness, and then the nominal width. Finally, give the length. Boards 2 inches thick and 4 inches wide are usually called 2 by 4s. A 1-inch board 6 inches wide is called a 1 by 6. When lumber sizes are written in the

FIGURE 2-1 Lumber sizes: nominal vs. actual. When you shop for lumber, ask for the nominal size. But when you design projects requiring wood, assume that the lumber you buy will be sized according to the actual sizes given in this table. And then, for precise jobs, actually measure your boards before using them.

NOMINAL SIZE (inches)	ACTUAL DRY SIZE (inches)
1× 2	¾× 1½
1× 4	¾× 3½
1× 6	¾× 5½
1×10	¾× 9¼
1×12	¾×11¼
2× 4	1½× 3½
2× 6	1½× 5½
2×10	1½× 9¼
2×12	1½×11¼
3× 6	2½× 5½
4× 4	3½× 3½
4× 6	3½× 5½

dealer's catalog or in an advertisement, the *by* becomes the symbol *x,* as in *2 x 4.*

Ready to call confidently for some 1 × 6s in a lumberyard? If you want some boards that are 10 feet long, say, "I'd like half a dozen pieces of 1 by 6, 10 feet long."

The length you buy at a lumberyard won't always exactly match the length you plan to use in your project, since lengths are almost always stocked by even numbers such as 6 feet, 8 feet, 10 feet, and 12 feet. With few exceptions, there's no particular economy in buying longer or shorter lengths. But there is economy in planning *all* your needs ahead of time. A 10-foot board and a 12-footer should cost about the same per running foot. However, if you're making shelves about 5 feet wide, you'll waste 2 feet out of every 12-foot board, but zero feet out of every 10-footer. In that case, you'll be wasting money if you buy 12-footers.

On the other hand, you'll win few friends at the lumberyard or do-it-yourself center by asking for boards of a dozen different widths and lengths. You can buy a can of this and a box of that at a supermarket because you pick out the merchandise yourself. But the lumberyards we hope you'll deal with are set up to service small builders who buy a pickup truck full of only a few sizes. If someone does the picking for you, he might get downright testy if you buy only one piece each of 27 different kinds of lumber. He may retaliate by slipping you some pretty undesirable pieces of wood.

PINE BOARDS When most people hear you talk about lumber, they assume you mean *pine boards.* There are several different grades of lumber quality, even of pine boards. Most local lumber dealers stock no more than two of the grades. (There are also fir, hemlock, and other conifer woods on sale. We'll call them all pine for simplicity.)

Common or *number two* pine boards are the cheapest. They're solid enough for major construction work and suitable for most shelves you plan to build. You can even use common grade for highly visible areas in your projects if you intend to paint the end result of your efforts.

But if you plan to have a natural wood finish on pine, you should buy what's called *number one* (written *#1*) or *clear* grade. Clear pine should be stronger and look better than common, and the grain should be finer and more regular. It shouldn't have any loose knots or other defects that are found in common grade.

Ironically, much early Colonial furniture was made from common pine. The extra knots and coarser grain look more like the real pine to the eye of the novice. If you want to capture that early American feel, you'll be better off if you specify common grade.

But whether you're buying common or clear, beware of *green lumber.* Like green apples, green lumber can make you sick. It's hard to saw and it doesn't sand well. Paint, stain, and finishes don't stick well to it. As it dries, it shrinks and may pull away from other boards in a structure or piece of furniture. Green lumber simply hasn't been properly dried out. It has been rushed to the market too soon after cutting. You can tell if lumber is green by grabbing hold of a board: it actually feels damp. Sawdust clings tenaciously to green lumber. You can't blow it off.

Lumberyards know the problems builders have with green lumber. If they have some, they'll shove it off on strangers and unsophisticated buyers. So when you order lumber, add these few extra words: "Please make sure it's nice and dry."

FIGURE 2-2 Pick your woods carefully if you're buying them for use where they'll show. There's nothing finer than natural wood grain to catch visitors' eyes.

HARDWOOD

In addition to pine, which is a relatively soft wood, large lumberyards and specialty outlets stock various hardwood boards. Most common among them are walnut, oak, maple, mahogany, and birch.

Birch just barely qualifies as a hardwood. Even though it lacks the deep tones and hard surface common to most other hardwoods, many people enjoy its soft, subtle grain. These days, *oak* seems to be the favorite hardwood of home improvement do-it-yourselfers and builders. *Mahogany* is the second most popular. *Walnut* and some of the more exotic species are less popular, possibly because they're much harder to find in most lumberyards.

Some yards stock *ash*. If you simply walk in and say, "Gimmee some hardwood, please," the yard hand could give you ash and get away with it. Although plenty hard, ash is not considered pretty wood. It's reserved for use when strength, not beauty, is important, such as for use on the concealed frames inside upholstered furniture.

Even when you order carefully, no two boards will ever be exactly alike when it comes to color and grain. Often you can pick out the ones that you find most aesthetically pleasing.

The makers of vinyl and Formica-type plastics copy typical hardwood color and grain. For some projects, these plastics are excellent choices. But there are several advantages to working with genuine hardwood. In general, wood is tougher so you'll end up with a stronger product if the basic design and your handiwork utilize the material's inherent strength. Once it is well sanded and carefully finished, wood also looks superior to most materials.

Hardwood does have disadvantages, even over softwood. It's more expensive than pine, tougher to saw, and slower to sand. Nails will bend if you try to pound them into hardwood in the usual lackadaisical way. Hardwood also weighs more than comparable sizes of softwood or plywood. We once bought enough mahogany boards to build a huge headboard and a chest of drawers. Without thinking about the weight, we tossed the lumber on top of the old Dodge Dart and the springs compressed as far as they could go. That meant that we had to make two trips with the lumber—but you should see how our finished furniture looks.

Hardwood, like pine, comes in several quality grades, but you'll be lucky to find any at all in many lumber outlets. You may have to take whatever you can get.

PLYWOOD

So far we've been talking about boards—those long, thin slices of tree. But there are other types of lumber. For example, if the sawmill uses a different kind of blade, it can peel off an extremely thin, continuous *veneer* of wood. Most veneers are from $1/16$ to $1/8$ inch thick.

Thin veneers are understandably quite fragile. They're also hard to work with by themselves. However, modern science figured out how to glue several layers of veneer into a single, very solid, very strong piece of wood. That's *plywood.*

Plywood is sold in standard sheets almost always measuring 4′ × 8′. Sometimes you can buy them 4′ × 10′ or even 4′ × 7′. Don't count on finding odd sizes at a lumberyard. Some lumberyards and most do-it-yourself centers will cut up the larger 4′ × 8′s and sell you smaller pieces. Many outlets won't cut less than a 4-by-4-foot piece, but some—especially those catering to do-it-yourselfers—stock *pre-cuts.* If your supplier does, look for a bin chock full of pieces that have been carefully cut to many of the most commonly used sizes.

Plywood comes in four common thicknesses: ¼, ⅜, ½, and ¾ inch. Generally the ¼-inch size is used for a covering over a large, well-supported area. It is not strong enough or rigid enough to hold much of a load.

The ⅜-inch plywood starts to have some internal strength. It can be used for very small shelves, small doors, and sliding doors. You can glue two pieces together to form a fancy cabinet door.

There's plenty of strength in ½-inch plywood. It's suitable for most furniture applications, for larger doors, and for floor underlayment. It is substantially cheaper than ¾-inch plywood and works well wherever maximum strength and rigidity are not required. But after you've tackled a project or two, you may find that you don't have the patience it takes to drive nails into ½-inch plywood without their splitting the wood or sticking out from it in odd places. In that case, you'd better switch to ¾-inch plywood. That extra ¼ inch costs more, but it's also darned near impossible to split with nails no matter how carelessly they're aimed.

Plywood has various surface quality ratings: interior and exterior, smooth and rough, good 1 side and good 2 sides. It's rated by the letters A through D, although X is often used to refer to varieties designed for exterior use. Here's a brief guide to the types of good-1-side plywood stocked by many home improvement centers:

- *A–D interior:* For interior applications where the unpainted appearance of one side is important—paneling, built-ins, cabinet shelving.
- *B–D interior:* Utility panel with one smooth side made paintable by the filling of knots and cracks. Used for backing, sides of built-ins, utility shelving.
- *Decorative B–D interior:* Rough-sawn, brushed, grooved, or striated faces. Used for paneling, accent walls, counter facing, displays.
- *A–C exterior:* For outdoor applications where the unpainted appearance of one side is important—sidings, soffits, fencing.
- *B–C exterior:* Outdoor utility panel with one smooth, paintable side. For farm and work buildings, truck lining, containers, base for exterior coatings.
- *CDX:* A rough-on-both-sides, inexpensive sheet intended for covering walls or roofs that will be covered by shingles, siding, or similar materials.

The good-1-side grade is adequate for most applications, the only exception being if both sides of your project will be seen. As you might expect, it's less expensive than the good-2-sides grade.

Unlike boards, plywood measurements are based on *finished* size. A sheet of plywood sold as ½ inch thick is as close to ½ inch as most rulers can measure.

You'll almost never find a use for rough grade plywood unless both sides are going to be entirely hidden by some covering material. Most home improvement centers stock only smooth grades, although one or two kinds of unsanded plywood in an exterior grade may be available since it's used mostly for sheathing the sides of new buildings.

The plywood we've been discussing is often called *fir plywood* in the trade. Most of it does come from fir trees. Some is made from white pine, sugar pine, or a similar species; it costs about the same as fir plywood and has a similar appearance and workability, so don't worry whether you're getting fir or pine.

Other kinds of plywood are available, but cost substantially more. For instance, a softwood core may be embellished with an outer veneer of hardwood on one or both sides. This gives you the strength of plywood and the beauty of hardwood, without having to work with the relatively narrow hardwood boards available. For example, if you want to cover a large surface with genuine hardwood, the only alternative to using a veneered plywood is to equip a shop with enough tools to install veneers yourself.

Whenever you're considering using expensive hardwoods, substituting veneered plywood will save you some money. But don't expect to walk into just any lumberyard and find hardwood-veneered plywood in dozens of varieties. Few stock any at all unless they cater to the furniture or wholesale building trade.

PARTICLE-BOARD

As the price of lumber soars, more home carpenters are turning to the new *particleboards*. Lower cost isn't the only attraction. Lab research has developed some exciting new products, including the handsomely textured waferboards shown in Figure 2-3. Also, old standbys such as hardboard and the original pressed-sawdust type of particleboard are being used in a variety of new ways. These engineered boards are available in 4' × 8' sheets as well as in various sizes of pre-cuts. Available thicknesses are not as extensive as with plywood.

In today's construction industry, manufactured woods—hardboard, particleboard, and waferboard—are often used. But do-it-yourselfers who grew up knowing instinctively how to work with pine boards and plywood don't always know how to use these newer manufactured boards. Since the professional construction market consumes almost all of their existing output, particleboard manufacturers have not yet concentrated on supplying do-it-yourselfers with detailed information. We've surveyed the manufacturers and large users of particleboards and we've combined their knowledge with our own experience to offer the following tips.

FIGURE 2-3 Particleboards are gaining in attractiveness as well as in number sold. They're versatile, inexpensive, and when worked into your decor, make an eye-catching change of pace. (Photo courtesy U.S. Forest Products Laboratory.)

HARDBOARD IS VERSATILE

Often known as Masonite, one of its trade names, *hardboard* is a tough, economical, and easy-to-finish product. It's used for drawer bottoms and separators, cabinet backs, sliding cabinet doors, underlayment for rough but structurally sound floors, and wherever a relatively flexible material is called for. Tempered hardboard is suitable for exterior applications such as fences, windbreaks, and soffits.

Some hardboard siding panels are rated by local building codes as being suitable for nailing directly to studs without any additional sheathing. And the familiar prefinished wall panels are often adequately fire-rated and strong enough to use instead of plaster or gypsum board. Standard thicknesses are ⅛ inch and ¼ inch.

PARTICLE-BOARD IS ECONOMICAL

The original type of *particleboard* is a medium-strength, very inexpensive building material, and it is used almost exclusively for interior applications. The mobile home industry uses it extensively for floors and other structural units. Until recently, home crafters used it only for underlayment. Now many have discovered its value for shelves, cabinets, desks, and countertops. Because of its bland tan appearance, most people either paint it or cover it with Formica, vinyl, or wood veneers. Standard thicknesses are ⅝ inch and ¾ inch.

WAFERBOARD LOOKS WILD

The wild, though tamable, pattern of wood chips is not *waferboard's* only attraction. It's much less expensive than A–D interior plywood, and it's competitive with most exterior siding and interior wall paneling.

Most building codes have accepted waferboard as a substitute for plywood sheathing on roofs and walls. The price is steadier than that of always fluctuating plywood, which means waferboard is sometimes a dollar or two cheaper than CDX plywood, sometimes a bit more expensive. But it's always free of knots, edge gaps, and other imperfections found in CDX plywood.

Waferboard comes in 1/4-inch, 3/8-inch, and 7/16-inch exterior grade sheets. In some areas, it is also available with a lightly sanded surface for a softer look. There are also specialty products available such as paneling that is grooved every 8 inches and paneling that is grooved in reverse board-and-batten style. Both panels have exterior ratings but they are often used for dramatic interiors.

WORKING WITH PARTICLE-BOARDS

Ordinary saws, routers, sanders, and similar tools work well on all particleboards, but for extensive cutting or shaping, carbide-tipped tools are definitely a better choice. The gritty insides of particleboard can be murder on non-carbide-tipped tools. (The grits are equally hazardous to your eyes. Wear goggles.)

With power saws, it's important to expose only enough of the blade to penetrate the thickness of the board. Otherwise, you risk chipping the board's underside and ruining your project. Use a combination-type blade on your power saw. If you're working with prefinished products, saw from the *back* side with a power saw, but from the front by hand.

Before using waferboard structurally, check to make sure your locality has accepted the national building-code approval of waferboard. For roof or wall applications, some codes require that waferboard be 1/16 inch thicker than the required thickness for plywood sheathing. The Department of Housing and Urban Development (HUD) allows 3/8-inch Blandex on studs at 16 inches on center or 24 inches on center. For roof sheathing, 3/8 inch is accepted at 16 inches on center, but 7/16-inch Blandex is required for 24-inch-on-center spacing.

ASSEMBLY

Common nails are fine for waferboard construction, but don't use finishing nails—their heads pop through too easily. When using waferboard for cabinets or wall panels where the nails may show, use ring-shank nails coated in a color that will camouflage the nails among the flakes.

Both hardboard and particleboard have limited nail-holding powers and require ring-shank nails for most building construction. The best way to install hardboard or particleboard is to apply construction cement or a white glue (such as Elmer's) to the wooden supports before hammering in the nails. To assemble particleboard pieces into shelving and furniture, you can simply glue the pieces together after sandpapering edges to remove chemical impurities left over from pressing. Since the glue is doing most of the work, you can, in this case, hold the glued parts together with finishing nails. Set them slightly and fill the holes with a neutral wood paste.

Another way to assemble particleboard parts is with sheet-metal screws. Choose a size narrower but longer than you'd use on natural wood or plywood. You can countersink their heads, but do it only slightly. Unless you really need a knockdown capability, glue is really the best choice for assembly.

FINISHING THE BOARDS

Particleboard edges require some puttying but aside from that, finishing manufactured boards can be a joy. Most of them, in fact, require less sanding than pine, hardwood, or plywood.

Use a paste wood filler and a putty knife to plug any spongy-looking edge you've left exposed in your project. Then sandpaper the edge, making sure not to sand away too much of the filling. Now you can finish the edge along with the other surfaces. Another option: You can stick a strip of veneer or vinyl on the exposed edges.

Clear varnishes will leave particleboard tan-colored, but add a bit more character since the finish will penetrate more deeply into more porous areas. You can stain the project, too, before applying a clear finish. Stains penetrate deeper and faster into particleboard than into most wood, so always test your stain on scrap.

For best results with enamels first coat the whole surface with a wood filler. Otherwise you won't get the high sheen most people prefer in enameled finishes.

Hardboard requires a sealer for both clear and pigmented finishes, and clear finishes often work best after you use a filler as well. You can experiment with stains on hardboard, too, if you're looking for rich and unusual tones.

When you're working with freestanding pieces of hardboard or particleboard—such as doors, fences, and dividers—you have to apply the same finish to *both sides* even if one side won't normally be seen. Otherwise, one side may absorb more moisture than the other and become warped.

There are now three basic types of painted finishes for waferboard. For a solid-color finish, you can apply a good-quality paint according to directions. The result will be a slightly textured, matte look. Or you can do a wiped finish with a single color paint or resin. Or you can produce a handsome two-tone finish by wiping on a second color that lodges between flakes to give an exotic shaded effect. There are probably many more effects waiting to be discovered.

TRAVELING WITH BOARDS, BLOCKS, BRICKS, AND BAGS

Before leaving the subject of building materials, let's talk about how you get your purchases home. Many lumber dealers won't deliver the small quantities you buy. However, even sheets of plywood can be carried safely and conveniently on top of the family car. In fact, some station-wagon designers had the uncommon good sense to make their carrying platforms 4 feet wide to accomodate panels and plywood.

On short trips with narrow boards, a 30-foot length of rope is about all you need to secure your load. Spread an old blanket, sheet, or rug across the top of your car to protect the paint. Then lay the boards down as evenly as possible. Open any car doors you'll want to use before the lumber is unloaded again. At the very least, do open the driver's door. On the other doors, roll down the windows an inch or two.

Wrap your rope around the lumber and through the open back windows or doors. The rope makes a complete circle—over the top of the lumber, in the window or door, across the top of the passenger compartment inside your car, out the other window or door, and then up to the top of the lumber again. Repeat at the front seat next.

If you're apt to make quick stops or if you're going a long distance, even with narrow boards you should secure the back of the lumber in addition to the double straps you already tied through the windows or doors. That will keep the lumber from sliding forward in case you hit the brakes hard. (It won't slide *backwards* unless you hit the gas pedal very hard.) To tie down the back of your lumber, wrap a rope around it near the rear end and tie the rope in place. Run the long, loose end down below the rear bumper. You'll have to get down on your hands and knees in order to find some spot under the car where you can tie that end of the rope.

When you're traveling with 4-by-8-foot sheets of plywood, hardboard, chipboard, or similar materials, your car will feel like a kite as the wind gets under the sheets unless you rope down the front of your load. So find a spot under your rear bumper where you can tie one end of

FIGURE 2-4   Here's how to tie down your lumber and sheets of plywood or similar building material to help you reach your home safely. Don't worry if thin sheets of material bend; they'll straighten right out as soon as you untie the ropes. Beware of bending brittle items, such as insulation boards, or aluminum or thin iron conduit pipes which may not straighten out later.

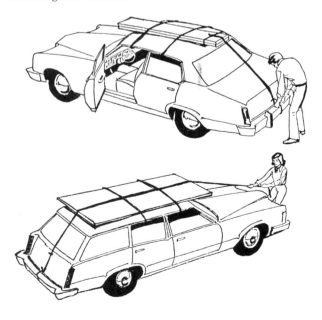

a rope. Toss the other end over the plywood sheets toward your front bumper. Tie that end under the front bumper, but first pull the rope as tight as you can. (See Figure 2-4.) Thin sheets of hardboard or plywood may actually start to bend. Let them. Unless you take weeks to get home, the wood will straighten right out as soon as you untie the ropes.

When you unload full sheets of plywood or paneling on a windy day, get help. One person should hold each end of the sheet. And keep the sheet slanted so the wind blows underneath or over the top. Otherwise you'll end up blowing down Main Street like Mary Poppins.

Wood, of course, is not the only building material you're likely to use as you improve your humble home. We now drive a van and can pile literally 1 ton of building supplies into it before the springs and tires reach their rated capacity. But we're amazed—and a bit distressed—to see how many cement blocks, bricks, bags of cement, and similar hefty objects some people cram into their cars before scraping away from a lumberyard. We hope they get home safely.

In general, most cars are designed to hold from four to six passengers weighing an average of 150 pounds each plus an additional 50 to 100 pounds in the trunk. Large station wagons typically can hold an additional 400 to 500 pounds. If you don't own or can't borrow a van or a pickup truck, you'd better calculate in advance both how much your car can safely carry and how much your planned purchases weigh. (Figure 2-5 will help you calculate the weight of your building materials.) If the weight of the materials is bigger than the capacity of the car, plan to make several trips.

FIGURE 2-5 Weight of common building materials.

MATERIAL	POUNDS PER CUBIC FOOT
Softwood lumber	30– 33
Hardwood lumber	35– 45
Bricks	110–140
Marble	155
Granite	155
Sand or gravel	100
Aluminum	165
Steel and iron	450–485
Lead	706
Glass	160
Hay (baled)	13
Straw (baled)	19

MATERIAL	POUNDS PER SQUARE FOOT
Acoustical tile	1.0
Linoleum	1.0
Plywood (½")	1.5
Vinyl tile (⅛")	1.4
Asphalt shingles	2.0
Plaster board	10.0

MATERIAL	POUNDS PER UNIT
Cement blocks	20–30 lb. each
2 × 4s, 8' long	9–10 lb. each
½" plywood (4' × 8' sheet)	50 lb. each
Asphalt shingles	65 lb. per bundle

3

How to Fasten Together
Your Home Improvement Projects

There's a confusing welter of hardware, glues, sealers, fillers, and similar products on the market for professionals and do-it-yourselfers. The trouble is, far too many of us don't know enough about all the helpful gadgets, cans, bottles, and tubes on the shelves to make good use of them. But if you become familiar with their uses, these products can make your home improvement jobs go smoothly and end up looking slick and well built.

You can discover these products for yourself if you take the time to browse inquisitively through the aisles of a well-stocked home improvement center. But you'll know what to look for if you first browse through the pages of this chapter, which covers some of the most commonly used supplies that you'll need. We'll start with the nails and screws you'll find most useful. Then we'll tell you what you need to know about choosing glues. For specialized projects, you'll need some of the less common gadgets and tools; we'll describe them in later chapters, as you need them. For a guide to all the attractive products that'll help you put the finishing touches on your improvements, see Chapter 11.

A nail is by far the fastest way to fasten two pieces of wood together. To make a strong joint you need several nails, but nails don't always make a strong enough bond for all purposes. There are several basic types of nails you're likely to use.

The *common nail* has a big, common-looking head. It drives into wood easily and holds tight once it's in place. But having all those big shiny heads poking out of soft, darkly-grained wood spoils the appearance of a fine finish. So for places that'll show, use a finishing nail.

Finishing nails are slender and have tiny heads. That makes them a bit trickier to pound. But when you're finished, the head can be camouflaged very easily. Sometimes the word *brad* is used instead of finishing nail. There are subtle distinctions between the two, but you won't have to worry about them.

A *sinker* is a bit thinner than a common nail, and the underside of its head is tapered to resemble a crude chisel so you can hammer the head flush with the surface of the wood. This feature makes it useful for installing siding, subflooring, and anything else that requires a very smooth, finished surface.

Roofing nails are short but have very large heads which are useful in fastening down thin but relatively soft materials such as shingles.

A *ring-shank nail* (sometimes called an *annular ring* or a *ring-groove* nail) is similar to a common nail except that it has concentric rings along most of its length—a feature that helps keep it from pulling loose from wood. Ring shanks are especially advised for installing plaster or gypsum boards, which otherwise have a tendency to wiggle loose from the studs and ceiling supports. We also prefer this nail when we install steel reinforcing plates to rafters and other critical supports in a house.

When nails are to be used outdoors where they'll be exposed to the weather, they have to be rust resistant. Most of the nails we've already

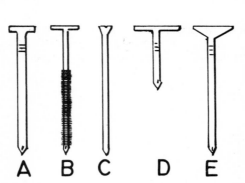

FIGURE 3-1 Five of the most common types of nails that you'll find useful for your home improvement projects: (A) the common nail with its big head and tough shank for easily (but not artistically) fastening wood together; (B) the ring-shank nail, which clings tenaciously once it's driven into gypsum board, siding, steel plate reinforcements, etc., (C) the finishing nail (or brad), which has a small head suitable for concealment in the surface of your fine woodworking; (D) the roofing nail for use on soft materials such as shingles without risk of tears; (E) the sinker, with a head designed like a chisel to penetrate the wood's surface and leave the nail head level with the wood.

A B C D E

discussed are available treated in one or more ways to make them rust resistant. Some are *galvanized* with rust-resistant metals such as zinc; others are *coated* with cement. Sinkers and ring shanks are often given an enamel-like coating. And some nails are made entirely of rust-resistant aluminum, although this is a relatively expensive alternative. None of these rust-proofing methods has particular advantage over other methods, so select whichever variety is available at the supplier of your choice.

The length of nail you should choose depends on the job you're working on. In general, select a nail about twice as long as the thickness of the wood or other product that you're nailing into place. For heavy use—such as in framing and support members of a house or addition—choose nails that are closer to three times the width of the wood. On the other hand, if you have to nail a ½-inch plywood board to another ½-inch board, you'll want to choose nails less than an inch long or the nail points will poke through. For such a job, you'll probably need ⅞-inch nails. That's why nails are available in so many sizes. (Though a one-inch nail no longer costs two pennies, nails are still sized as they were when this was true. So ask for your nails by their "penny" names—abbreviated "–d." See Figure 3-2 for a list of nail names, sizes and quantities per pound.)

HOW TO HIDE NAIL HOLES

Until now you probably thought that all you needed to drive in a nail was a hammer. But when you've finished hammering a finishing nail, either your nail sticks up a tiny bit or—to make it flush—you've risked pounding a dent in the wood. To avoid that, add a *nail set* to your tool list. Here's how to use it.

Pound the finishing nail with your hammer until its head is almost level with the wood. Then put a nail set onto the head and hit that with your hammer. (There are even dents in the heads of good finishing nails and brads so the nail set won't slip.) If you plan to paint your project or finish it with wallpaper, vinyl, Formica, or any other covering, you can stop hammering when the head is exactly flush with the wood. But for a professional appearance in the popular natural wood look that home remodelers often opt for, you'll need to disguise those nails. So pound the nail set until their heads are $1/16$ inch or even ⅛ inch below the surface.

FIGURE 3-2 Nail sizes and quantities per pound.

		NUMBER PER POUND (approximate)		
SIZE	LENGTH (inches)	COMMON	FINISHING	SHINGLE
2d	1	830		
3d	1¼	528		429
4d	1½	316	584	274
5d	1¾	271	500	235
6d	2	168	309	
8d	2½	106	189	
10d	3	69	121	
12d	3¼	63		
16d	3½	49	90	
20d	4	31	62	

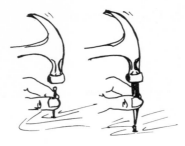

FIGURE 3-3 Here's how you can use a nail set to: (1) keep from denting your fine woodworking projects with the head of your hammer; and (2) sink the nail heads beneath the surface. Later you can fill the small void with Plastic Wood or a similar product.

There are several ways to camouflage nail holes. The first way, after all of your nails have been pounded into place, is to go back and fill each hole with wood dough, most often known by one of its trade names, Plastic Wood. Squeeze it into the nail hole carefully and level it off with a flat tool such as a putty knife, razor blade, or jackknife. If you're sanding your home improvement project, wait until the Plastic Wood is *thoroughly* dry. Then the sanding will smooth out almost all evidence of the nails. In pine boards, properly plugged nail holes will look like no more than tiny knots in the wood.

If you're working with dark-colored hardwood or hardwood plywood, the light, neutral color of ordinary Plastic Wood won't blend in so well. You can buy various brands of wood dough with color added. Theoretically, these products blend with walnut, oak, and the other popular hardwoods. But before you assume that the theory works for your practical project, test the color on one or two nail holes. Chances are it won't exactly match. So, even on dark hardwoods, you may want to plug your nail holes with ordinary neutral wood dough and then, after sanding your project thoroughly, take a very tiny artist's brush and stain the plugged holes. If you're using dark walnut wood, for example, buy a tiny can of walnut oil stain. Brush it carefully onto just a few nail holes and let it dry for 15 minutes (or whatever time the directions call for). Rub off excess stain with a soft cloth, rubbing a little beyond the plug to blend its color with the rest of your wood.

Assuming this technique works on your test spots, you can use it on all the other nail holes. If not, change the color and try again. If your nail spot is too dark, dilute the stain with turpentine (or any other solvent the instructions mention), or let it dry for a shorter time before you rub it. If the test color proves to be too light, there are at least two solutions. You can let the stain dry longer before you rub it, and then rub very gently. Or you can give the holes a second or third treatment with the same color oil.

There's still another way to camouflage nail holes. Many paint and wallpaper stores sell what are often called *putty sticks,* although they're not really putty at all. They're sticks of waxy, plastic-like stuff colored to match various types of natural hardwoods. Most of them are shaped somewhat like giant crayons. If you find a putty stick that closely matches your own wood finish, let nail holes go until almost the end of the project. Just before the final few coats of varnish, lacquer, or other finish, plug the nail holes with the putty stick. Make sure the final surface is very smooth.

Then add the last several layers of wood finish. The holes can't be seen unless you cheat and point them out to relatives and friends.

SCREWS

Screws take more time to use than nails, but you generally end up with a stronger product for your efforts. You should choose a screw that's about twice as long as your boards are thick.

Screws have their own distinct numbering system. A screw's length is signified simply by its actual length in inches from point to head, the head itself not included. The diameter is indicated by a code number such as 4, 6, or 10. The larger the number, the larger the diameter.

One commonly used screw is known in the trade as 1½ × 10. It's good for holding 1-inch pine boards together. (Those boards, as you learned in Chapter 2, are closer to ¾ inch thick than to a full 1 inch.) For ¼-inch plywood, a good size for screws is ½ × 4 or ½ × 6. Use ¾ × 4 or ¾ × 6 for ⅜-inch plywood. On ½-inch plywood, 1 × 4 or 1× 6 screws are satisfactory.

When you use ¾-inch plywood, something close to 1½ × 10 is called for. Pine boards are best screwed into place with 1½ × 10 or 1½ × 12. If you have clearance for them in your work, 1¾ × 10 are good, too.

Don't worry about memorizing all these numbers. When you want to buy screws, simply turn back to this part of the book and jot down the appropriate sizes you'll need. Then head for the hardware store.

There are two basic types of screws you are likely to use when making things that improve your home—the *wood screw*, which is most common, and the *sheet metal screw*, which is found most often in radios, TVs, refrigerators, and similar appliances that have metal chassis parts to hold together. Sheet metal screws should also be used when you're working with the new manufactured wood products discussed in Chapter 2. Sheet metal screws resemble bolts except that the threads are coarser and more spread out. A sheet metal screw requires only a hole of the appro-

FIGURE 3-4 Screws come in various types as well as sizes. Here, A–D are all wood screws while E is a sheet metal screw: (A) round head; (B) flat head; (C) oval head; (D) lag screw (which requires a wrench to turn in rather than a screwdriver); (E) pan head.

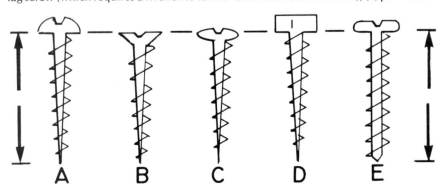

A   B   C   D   E

priate size to hold itself and two or more pieces of metal or particleboard tightly into place.

Both sheet metal and wood screws come with round, flat, oval, and lag heads, as well as with less commonly used kinds of heads. (To turn a *lag head* requires a wrench rather than a screwdriver.) For use in wood, always use flathead screws unless you want them to stand out as part of the design.

For using screws, it's almost imperative that you own an electric drill. They're inexpensive these days—and very handy. If you're planning a large project that will take plenty of abuse, your investment in a reasonably priced drill should pay for itself by the time that first project is completed.

Here's how to work with flathead screws.

First drill a slightly narrower *pilot hole* for every screw. Although some people skip this step in pine boards, it's not a good idea. Without a pilot hole you might as well use nails instead, since the results will be about as strong. A common wood screw exerts a tremendous mechanical force. If you simply knock it carelessly into place and twist on it, the threads can actually split some boards. The pilot hole permits the screws to twist into the wood with relative ease, without threatening to split the wood.

The easiest way to drill a pilot hole is with a set of drill accessories made specifically for this job. Such accessories not only drill pilot holes for the most popular screws in use, but also drill *countersink holes* in the same operation. The head on a flathead screw fits neatly into a countersink hole, just as nails fit neatly into their own hole after you tap them down with a nail set. Be careful when you drill a countersink hole. Make sure the hole is wide and deep enough for the screw head to fit completely. If you're going to camouflage the screw, you'll want it to fit beneath the surface with a little room for plastic wood to cover the head. But don't make the countersink hole so deep that you actually weaken the piece of wood. In very narrow wood, such as ¼- or ⅜-inch plywood, there is a very thin line between too little and too much countersink hole. That's why nails are used almost exclusively with plywood.

If you don't own a pilot hole countersink accessory, here's what to do. Choose a pilot hole drill bit that matches the size of the very tip of your chosen screw. Drill almost as deep a hole as your screw is long. Pick a drill bit for the countersink which is as big around as the head of your screw. Make the countersink hole deep enough to satisfy the requirements spelled out in the paragraph above.

Whether flat, oval, or round, screw heads are either *slotted* or *Phillips*. Slotted heads take a common, straight screwdriver blade. Phillips heads have openings that resemble Xs and require a screwdriver blade that's shaped like a three-dimensional X.

Most hardware stores stock only a limited variety of Phillips head screws. If your store has a good selection, they're worth using even if you have to buy a new screwdriver to accomodate them. With a Phillips head, your screwdriver is easier to keep under control.

Ideally, the blade thickness on your screwdriver should match the slot thickness in your screws. Otherwise, when you start twisting hard the screwdriver will slip out of the slot and chew up the metal. *Small* slots need *small-bladed* screwdrivers. *Large* slots require *large-bladed* screwdrivers. The same goes for Phillips heads.

If you plan to tackle a project that involves several dozen screws, you may be happy to know that for a pittance you can add to your electric drill an accessory that will twist screws into place within seconds. Variable-speed drills work best for turning in screws, but almost any electric drill will do the job if you're careful.

When you use a drill to turn in screws, protect the wood underneath unless you're planning to hide its surface. You're bound to slip at least once or twice, and without protection the screwdriver tip on your drill will gouge out a nasty scar.

A tin-can cover makes an adequate shield. Cut, poke, or drill a hole a little larger than the screwhead's size into the center of your cover. Then slip the hole over each screw *before* you twist it into place. That way, if you slip only the can cover gets scarred.

For screwing with an electric drill, you'll be especially happy if you use Phillips head screws. They were actually designed for use in automatic equipment.

After all the screws have been turned into their countersink holes, plug the holes and camouflage them, if needed, exactly as described in the section on nails.

MOLLY SCREWS AND SIMILAR FASTENERS

Molly screws are designed to anchor shelves and such to walls and other areas where you can't reach around behind to thread a nut onto a bolt. Those peculiar bits of hardware are, in essence, self-contained nuts and bolts with accordions in between.

First you have to drill a hole just big enough to slip in the Molly (the outer covering for the screw). Then shove that fastener all the way into the

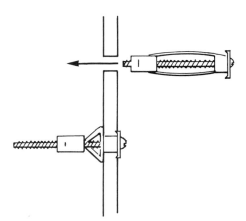

FIGURE 3-5 Molly screws are a convenient way to fasten items securely to a hollow wall. First drill a hole that matches the size of the Molly screw's shank. Then insert the device and turn the screw head which activates the "legs." Finally, mount your shelf or other gadget using the screw.

hole. Bang the exposed part of the Molly with a hammer or the flat of your hand so its two barbs dig into the surface of whatever material you're working with. Start twisting the screw inside the Molly, and its collapsible arms will elbow out against the inside of the wall. That anchors the entire device firmly in place. Then you can use the screw to fasten whatever you need fastened.

We prefer to use Molly screws whenever and wherever their use is practical. However, there are other fasteners available for holding things onto walls and ceilings, and some of them may be just right for a particular job you have planned.

Many lighting fixtures depend on *toggle bolts* to hold them onto ceilings. In using a toggle bolt, you simply drill a hole large enough to slip the toggle's fingers into the opening; when you do that, the fingers automatically spring open or simply flop open and grab hold of the top of the wallboard or other construction material. Then you can secure your lighting fixture (or other gadget) with the bolt that runs through the toggle mechanism.

We have two objections to toggle bolts: first, they're hard to find these days; second, they require substantially larger holes than Molly screws.

Other anchors are little more than specially designed plastic sleeves. To use them, first you must drill a hole just big enough for the sleeve to slip into the tile, cement block, wallboard, or other location. Then, when you use the proper-sized screw to fasten your shelf or other gadget into the plastic sleeve, the sleeve is forced to expand and grab relatively tightly to the surrounding building material. Plastic anchors have two major advantages over metal toggle bolts and Molly screws: they're cheaper and faster to use. But in most applications, they seldom provide as much brute holding strength. Where strength is not a major consideration, however, they make fast, inexpensive work of the job of holding things onto odd places on walls.

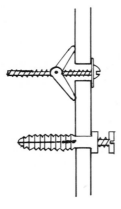

FIGURE 3-6   Toggle bolts (top of sketch) anchor lighting fixtures and other items to walls or ceilings. Simply drill a hole large enough to accommodate the hardware, shove it into the hole, and secure your lamp or whatever to the ceiling. However, don't ever remove the screw or the toggle will fall out of place. Plastic anchors (bottom of sketch) grasp many surfaces relatively securely, and they're fast and cheap. They work best in tough materials such as concrete.

GLUE AND OTHER ADHESIVES

When it comes to home improvement, there are a dozen or more different chemical *glues* and *cements* to know about. (Whatever difference there once was between a glue and a cement is all but nonexistent now.) Adhesives come in liquids, pastes, tapes, and even sprays. Many formulations have been created for all the specific sticking jobs you could think of.

For wood, glue is one of the toughest fasteners of all. It can be more durable than nails or screws, but there's a hitch or two in that promise. Most wood glues won't tolerate much motion after they've set. Glued joints aren't flexible enough to withstand a lot of bending and twisting.

When glues are first applied, they generally require a lot of pressure to create a strong, lasting joint. In other words, if you glue a table top to its sides, you have to find some way to put a lot of weight on the top so it will bond firmly and permanently to the sides. Professional cabinetmakers have expensive sets of clamps which hold onto odd-shaped pieces of wood and squeeze them together while the glue dries. It's unlikely that you just happen to have the right kind of clamps in your family junk drawer, and it isn't economical for you to buy any for a small project. But there's an alternative.

You can get the best of both worlds by using glue in combination with either nails or screws. The nails and screws are both easy to use, although neither is as tough on its own as a well-made, glued joint. But the nails and screws do serve as clamps while the glue dries. In most cases they work every bit as well as carpenter's clamps.

Screws or nails also provide a glued joint with some internal stiffness. That prevents the twisting or bending that might destroy the glue's grip on two pieces of wood. To make a good joint, first fit the appropriate pieces together so that you know for sure they're cut right. Then drill one pilot and countersink hole, if you're using screws. After that first screw is in place you can drill the others, confident now that your pieces won't slip out of place.

Squirt glue on all the pieces where they overlap. Even squirt a few drops of glue *into* the screw holes to hold them firmly. When you're sure everything fits well, cover the joint with glue and assemble the pieces immediately. Then nail or screw the pieces together firmly. Wipe away all of the excess glue which will get squeezed out of the joint. If you don't do it while the glue is wet, you'll have a heck of a mess to clean up later.

Put your work away while the glue sets. If you're continuously bending and twisting and hammering on a project while the glue is setting, the joints will never reach their full strength.

Some glues tell you on the label how much *set-up time* they can tolerate. That's simply the length of time, something like fifteen minutes or a half hour, during which you still can disturb the glue after applying it. Following the set-up time, the glue starts hardening quickly. In general, the faster the overall drying time, the less time you have to fool around during assembly. Glues strong enough to be used for cabinets and tables seldom take less than a few hours to dry.

There are many types of glue valuable to home improvers. Simplest of all is the white or tan sticky liquid glue that comes in plastic squeeze bottles. It is surprisingly tough, but some brands hold stronger than others. Read the labels. For working with wood, be sure you choose a glue that's specifically recommended for use with wood. Even better is a glue that's made *principally* for wood.

A second glue suitable for home projects is *contact cement.* Many different companies market this product. Buy the best your local store stocks.

Contact cement gets smeared onto both of the surfaces you want glued together. You should do the same with any other glue too, but with contact cement, the product is allowed to dry completely before you shove the two parts together.

After both surfaces of contact cement have dried, and after you shove them together, the surface areas bond together into an extremely tough, glued joint. That's assuming, of course, that you bring the two surfaces together tightly enough. Like other glues, contact cement requires a certain amount of pressure before it forms a tough bond.

Contact cement is best used on Formica and similar thin plastics. Because it grabs so well once the two glued layers are put together, you have to be very careful in aligning your pieces. With flexible, thin materials it's easy to make contact cement adhere well. Somehow it inevitably falls short of expectation when used on thicker pieces of wood.

When you're using contact cement, it's a good idea to make one piece oversized if at all possible. Then, in case the two are stuck together just a bit out of line, you can sand the oversized part to fit.

If working with oversized pieces isn't practical, line up the parts carefully while there's something between them such as waxed paper. (When dry, contact cement won't stick to anything but itself.) Make sure you use several short pieces of waxed paper even if one long piece will cover the entire surface. Then, when everything is in its proper place, hold one end of the joint very firmly while you slip one piece of waxed paper out from the other end. When it has been pulled out, a good firm push with your hand will stick the two surfaces together permanently. Then you can pull out the rest of the waxed paper leisurely, content in the knowledge that your pieces are well lined up for life.

To choose from the many other glues that are available for your home improvement projects, it helps to understand a bit of adhesive terminology.

Curing method is the technical term for what makes a glue harden. In selecting the right glue for a particular job, it is important to know whether it sets because water or solvents evaporate or because of a purely internal chemical reaction.

Porous materials such as wood or nonglazed ceramics can be bonded successfully with a solvent- or water-based adhesive because the material itself absorbs the solvent or water, allowing the glue to set in a reasonable length of time. But in bonding two pieces of metal or nonporous ceramic, you'll want to avoid a glue that sets by the evaporation of solvents or water.

If the two pieces to be glued are held as tightly together as they should be, there's no way for the solvent or water to evaporate, and the glue won't ever get hard enough to hold well.

Environmental factors also must be weighed when choosing an adhesive. A piece of outdoor furniture requires a waterproof glue. Tile near a fireplace demands a heat-resistant glue. Anything near a bar should receive an alcohol-resistant glue. And a workbench demands chemical- and heat-resistant adhesives.

For improvements in the bathroom or basement, stick to an adhesive that resists moisture, mold, and mildew. Not only is the growth of mold and mildew unsightly, it also can weaken the glued or sealed joint. Adhesives that are most susceptible to organic growths include silicone rubber and casein products, although some products have growth-resisting chemicals added, so check the labels.

Project materials themselves may dictate the types of adhesives that should be used. Solvent-based cements chemically attack many kinds of thin plastics, ruining their appearance. Water-based glues cause photographs to swell until the water dries up. A very thin, fluidy adhesive might be absorbed into a porous material, leaving too little glue in the glue line to hold the two parts together successfully.

Flexibility must be considered. In general, as we've pointed out, glues intended specifically for wood are very strong but not especially flexible. Many other adhesive formulations have been created with flexibility in mind. Rubber adhesives, for example, are rubbery and bendable. If you are working with an item that must flex and bend a lot, make sure that the label on the glue specifies the product's flexing qualities.

Whenever two pieces to be joined are made of different materials— such as wood to glass or glass to rubber—a flexible adhesive is vital. Dissimilar substances expand and contract at different rates when warmed or cooled. An inflexible glue is unable to absorb these slight variations caused even by weather changes, and may soon crack or break. Silicone rubber and cyanoacrylate glues are especially flexible, although rather expensive.

Glue line, in simple terms, means the amount of glue that must or can be applied between the two pieces being bonded. Most glues specifically intended for use with wood require a thin glue line for maximum strength; rubber adhesive compounds do best with a fairly thick glue line. When gluing wood with a glue requiring a thin glue line, therefore, it is important for both surfaces to be bonded to be smooth so that a thin layer of glue will successfully grab onto as much of the surface area as possible. In repairing a *broken* piece it may be impossible to obtain a truly thin glue line, so your needs might best be served by choosing an adhesive that reaches maximum strength with a wider glue line.

Set time, as we said before, is the length of time it takes an adhesive to become hard enough to support the glued joint. This term is almost synonymous with "drying time" and "cure time." An instant-setting glue, if you stop to think about it, is really not good for most applications. If you are trying to line up two matching pieces of anything, you'll want a glue that sets slowly enough to give you time to correct your alignment. On the other hand, if you are using an adhesive to stop a badly leaking pipe, the faster the set time the better.

Travel is linked closely with set time. Some adhesives, such as contact cements, clamp the glued materials tightly in place after they are laid together. Other materials allow for some movement until a certain percentage of the set time has elapsed. If alignment of two objects is important, you will want an adhesive with plenty of travel. If you are gluing heavy handles onto an erect piece of glass, however, more than likely you'll choose an adhesive with very little travel or you'll have to support the handles until it's finished setting.

Tack is almost synonymous with "sticky"—though it may have a little to do with set time. Thin, watery glues may end up forming powerful joints by the time they are hardened, whether an hour from now or tomorrow morning. But if you are forced to hold tile, cork, or wall covering onto a wall while the smooth glue sets, next time you'll look for an adhesive with lots of tack. A tacky adhesive, such as bituminous, silicone, rubber, and some epoxies, can hold even relatively heavy pieces in place before the glue has had time to set completely.

Figure 3-7 sums up the major attributes of popular glues on the market. But be advised that not all of them are found in all markets.

SEALANTS AND CAULKING AGENTS

For the most part, there is little basic chemical difference between the glues just described and sealants and caulkers. Only the way you apply them is different, and that means there must be subtle alterations in the specific formulations.

A glue does the best it can to hold together two pieces of something. Sealants and caulkers, however, generally don't have to provide any holding power. All they must do is grab firmly onto one or two surfaces, such as a crack or a joint, and provide a seal against the weather, water, chemicals, air, sound, or whatever other undesirables are to be sealed in or out.

In this area, no two manufacturers seem to use the same words for otherwise similar materials. *Caulk* and *sealant* commonly refer to the same thing, and *sealer* is a close third although it also is used when referring to materials that seal the entire surface of a wooden or concrete floor.

The first general type of caulking compound we'll discuss has been around since before chemists ever heard of silicone or synthetic rubber. Closely related to common putty, common caulking has a base of linseed oil or a related natural vegetable oil. The body of this caulking agent can be one of any number of minerals—most of them chemically and physically similar to the chalk that kids use in school.

Common caulking materials are cheap and easy to use. But permanance is not one of their virtues. Those on the commercial market are generally available only in professional sizes, large cans, and caulking-gun

FIGURE 3-7 Types of Glues.

	Bituminous & Mastics	Cyanoacrylate	Epoxy	Hot Melt Glues	Plastic Cements
Ingredients	Tarry chemicals, and sticky plastics.	Powerful chemicals.	Powerful chemicals.	Synthetic resins, often phenoxy plastics.	Plastics dissolved in volatile solvents.
Packaging	Cans. Caulking tubes.	Small tubes. Small bottles.	Tubes. Cans.	Sticks sized to fit heater.	Generally in small tubes.
Form	Paste.	Liquid.	Liquids or pastes, mixed at time of application.	Solid. Melts inside the heater compartment.	Liquid.
Strength	Low, but adequate for specified jobs.	Very high.	Very high.	Moderate.	Moderate at best.
Flexibility	Moderate, but adequate for specified jobs.	High.	Very low.	Low.	Moderate.
Set time	Slow (hours or days).	Few seconds.	Moderate (hours).	Very fast.	Very fast (minutes).
Setting method	Loss of solvents.	Internal chemical reaction.	Internal chemical reactions.	Cooling of glue resins.	Evaporation of solvents.
Travel permitted	Very high.	Low.	High.	Low.	Moderate.
Amount of tack	High.	None (but not vital due to very rapid set time).	Very high for pastes. High to moderate for liquids.	High.	Moderate.
Preferred glue line	Thick (1/16–1/8").	Very thin.	Thin for liquids. Thick for pastes.	Thin.	Thin, but can be made thicker by repeated applications.
RESISTANCE TO: Moisture	Low except for special formulations.	High.	Very high.	Moderate.	Moderate.
Mold & Mildew	Low, except for special formulations.	Very high.	Very high.	Moderate.	High.
Chemicals & Solvents	Low.	High.	High.	High.	Low.
Heat	Low.	Very high.	Very high.	Low.	Moderate.
Clamping required?	No.	No.	Very seldom.	No.	Very seldom.
Relative cost	Very low.	Very high.	High.	High.	Low.
Applications	Used for sticking floor tile to floor. Also for holding wall panels onto wall.	Repairs on smooth surfaces. Small constructions which require fast set time and high strength.	Repairs to wood, glass, tile, pottery, metal, most plastic, leather, fiberglass, etc.	Assembling wood, leather, some plastics, metal, paper, cardboard.	Light repairs or construction such as models, textiles, paper, etc.

	Polyvinyl Acetate	Resorcinol	Rubber Cement	Silicone Rubber	Urea-Formaldehyde Resins	Urethane
Ingredients	Plastics suspended in watery solvent.	Industrial chemicals.	Natural or synthetic rubbers dissolved in solvents.	Industrial chemicals.	Industrial chemicals.	Industrial chemicals.
Packaging	Bottles of many sizes.	Bottles. Cans.	Cans. Tubes. Jars.	Tubes. Caulking tubes.	Cans.	Tubes.
Form	Liquid (milky, white).	Liquids; two parts mixed at time of application.	Liquid.	Paste.	Powder which is mixed with water at time of application.	Viscous liquid.
Strength	Moderate.	High.	Low.	High to very high, depending upon items bonded.	Moderate.	High.
Flexibility	High.	Moderate.	Very high.	Very high.	Low.	Moderate.
Set time	Moderate (hours).	Slow.	Fast (generally in minutes).	Moderate (hours).	Slow (hours to days).	Moderate (hours).
Setting method	Evaporation of solvent and water.	Internal chemical reactions.	Evaporation of solvents.	Chemical reaction set off by moisture in the air.	Internal chemical reactions.	Evaporation of solvent.
Travel permitted	High.	High.	Very high.	Very high.	Very high.	Very high.
Amount of tack	Moderate.	Moderate.	High.	Very high.	Moderate to low.	High.
Preferred glue line	Thin to moderate.	Thin.	Thin, but specific products can use heavier glue lines.	Thick (⅛-¼").	Thin.	Thin to moderate.
RESISTANCE TO: Moisture	Moderate.	Excellent.	Fair.	Excellent.	Poor.	Excellent.
Mold & Mildew	High.	Excellent.	Low.	Poor unless label specifies additives are present.	Good.	Excellent.
Chemicals & Solvents	Moderate.	Good.	Very low.	Good.	Excellent.	Excellent.
Heat	Moderate.	Excellent.	Low.	Excellent.	Excellent.	Excellent.
Clamping required?	Often, when used for wood projects.	Yes.	No.	No.	Yes.	Seldom.
Relative cost	Low.	Moderate.	Low to moderate.	High.	Moderate.	Moderate.
Applications	Excellent for crafts since it dries colorless. Good for paper, textiles, some plastic, wood, photographs, etc. Most non-toxic of popular household adhesives.	Outdoor furniture, boats, toys, etc.	Used to bond flexible materials to other flexible materials or solids such as textiles or plastics to metal, wood, rigid plastic. Also rubber or leather to wood or metal. Can be used as one-shot glue or as contact cement.	Can bond most materials including glass and metal. Especially good for two solids of different composition subjected to heat, vibration and similar environmental abuses.	Indoor wood, furniture.	Repairs to wood, glass, tile, pottery, metal, most plastic, leather, fiberglass, etc.

cartridges. They're intended principally for exterior use around windows, doors, eaves, and such. As long as enough oil stays in the compound to keep it from drying out and cracking, the seal is okay. However, if you plan to live in your home for a long time, your laziest and most economical alternative over the long range is one of the more expensive synthetic products of rubber or silicone.

Many sealants available at hardware or paint stores are variations of the polyvinyl, rubber, and silicone rubber glues referred to earlier. Some can be used interchangeably as glues and sealants. The principal requirement for calling a glue a sealant is that it must have a high enough viscosity to bridge a gap of ⅛ inch or more without sagging or running off. To give added surface strength, more internal thickness, and color, many caulking materials have fillers such as powdered aluminum added to them.

There is a natural latex rubber sealant on the market. Most, however, are made from one of the synthetic rubbers—neoprene, nitrile, butyl, polysulfide, or silicone rubber. Some product descriptions mention "elastomer," simply a synonym for synthetic rubber.

Sealants must be flexible enough to withstand the slight motion or vibration that accompanies their bridging a gap between two walls or a tub and a wall or a window frame and a wall. Most of them are waterproof, and some say they can be applied under water or to wet surfaces—but don't do it if you can make a dry application instead.

Drying time for most ordinary sealants is quite slow. In as short a time as ten minutes, they may skin over and get tough at the very surface, but most remain unset underneath and require a day or more of relatively unmolested drying time. If the caulking around a bathtub has skinned over, chances are you'll be able to splash water onto the new seam. But read the instructions—especially the fine print—carefully before you take a stinging shower. If in doubt, stick to baths for at least a full day.

For most caulking materials, colors are limited. Generally you have to settle for white, clear, black, tan, or aluminum. Although some companies now offer decorator colors, few small stores stock a complete rainbow.

Some sealants can be painted over with good results. If painting is important, make sure you select one that specifically says it will accept a coat or two of paint. Silicone rubber sealers, in general, cannot be covered over with much of anything except more silicone rubber. There is an unwritten rule that the cheaper the sealant, the easier it is to paint over. That probably indicates that it has the least amount of rubber compound in it.

For home use, sealants generally come packed in tubes, often with spouts that can be cut to varying dimensions to create beads of caulking from about $1/16$ inch to ¼ inch wide. The size you select should be big enough to bridge whatever crack has to be filled, with some extra to adhere to solid tile or enamel. For economy, you don't want to squirt a ¼-inch bead when a ⅛-inch bead would have done just as well. Conversely, it will take still more of the stuff if you use too miserly a bead and have to redo the entire job.

Instinct seems to make folks use caulking tubes or caulking guns *backwards.* The sealant should not be squeezed out and allowed to fall free as you do with a tube of toothpaste. The nozzle of the tube must slowly *force* the oozing, sticky stuff firmly back onto the corner or crack, an art shown in Figure 3-8.

A small tube (about 4 ounces) handles a patch-up job around a tub or sink, renews putty around a window or two, or reseals a drain spout. For bigger jobs, a bigger squeeze tube is handy, but the next size in many brands is often a caulking-gun cartridge that holds $\frac{1}{10}$ of a gallon. The cartridge cannot be used by hand. Fortunately, the price of a caulking gun is so reasonable that the reusable gun and a disposable cartridge often can be purchased for the price of a comparable amount of the material packaged in smaller tubes.

FIGURE 3-8 Most people hold their caulking tube or gun backwards when they use it. The photo here shows the correct way. The caulking gun is being moved from right to left, and the nozzle forces the caulking material into the gap instead of simply laying it down gently atop the space between the two surfaces to be caulked.

MISCELLANEOUS HARDWARE MAGIC

Whenever you're beginning a new project that requires fastening together two or more pieces of anything, if ordinary nails, screws, or bolts are not perfect for the job, don't try to reinvent the wheel. Head for your hardware store or the hardware section of your home center to browse through the bins and shelves overflowing with handy stock items. The odds are very high that you'll find one or more ready-made gadgets that are just right.

To get your imagination started, you can browse through the last two illustrations of this chapter. There we've sketched some of the all-around handiest pieces of home improvement hardware. And if your browsing doesn't turn up what you need, ask one of the experienced hardware clerks for help. They may know where there's a whole shelf full of just what you're looking for.

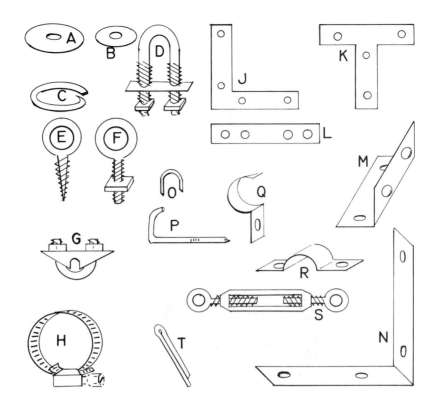

FIGURE 3-9 Miscellaneous hardware items that, if you know their names, can help you solve home improvement problems: (A) A fender washer has a much larger area around its hole than a common washer, so it resists slipping into overly large openings and more evenly distributes stress and strain than an ordinary washer. (B) A common washer should be slipped under every nut before you tighten it and under the head of every lag screw that otherwise might mar a wood surface. (C) A lock washer is used to keep nuts and bolts from vibrating loose on motors and similar mechanical gadgets. (D) A U-bolt can clamp around a rod or pipe through its curved end, or can be bolted into two holes through a board or other fixture (in which case you may turn a nut onto each leg first, then insert the support piece, then slip the U-bolt into place, and tighten down the final two nuts). (E) The screw-eye provides a steep "hoop" once you screw it into wood. (F) An eye-bolt functions like a screw-eye except you use one or more nuts to hold it in place after slipping it through a hole in wood or metal. (G) Cable clamps are intended to hold steel cables or ropes together, such as when you loop their ends around a pole or hook. (H) A hose clamp holds a hose or plastic tube onto a pipe. (J) An L-bracket is used for building or reinforcing wooden corners such as on doors, fences, or shelves. (K) The T-bracket serves the same purposes as the L-bracket. (L) Reinforcing plate serves the same purposes as the L-bracket. (M) Angle brackets reinforce inside or outside corners wherever two pieces of wood meet. (N) Corner reinforcement (sometimes called a shelf bracket) provides extra support for two joined pieces of wood, or support for small shelves. (O) Staples fasten wires to walls (in small sizes) or pipes to walls (in large sizes). (P) Pipe support fastens pipes to walls. (Q) Cable support fastens cables or conduits to walls. (R) A pipe strap secures pipes, cables, or conduits to walls, ceilings, etc. (S) Turn buckle provides adjustable tension for wires, ropes, etc. (T) A cotter pin secures wheels to axles, handles to rods, and similar functions; it slips through a small hole, then the two legs are bent in opposite directions for a semi-permanent installation.

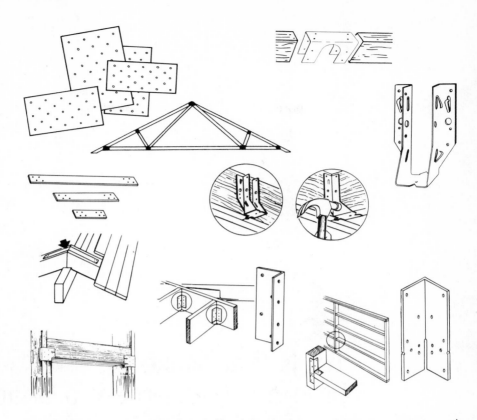

FIGURE 3-10 Kant-Sag brackets and hardware hit the contractor scene years ago and have saved tens of thousands of dollars in construction costs by now. Now the company is making them widely available to do-it-yourselfers. This potpourri of views from its catalog shows some of the versatile steel plates, brackets, and such, and how they're used. Many of them have sharpened barbs to hold onto your wood until you can pick up a handful of nails; all of them are punched-with nail holes. (Courtesy Kant-Sag division, United Steel Products.)

4
Tools that Make
Home Improvement a Snap

Sometimes the difference between being able to do it yourself, and spending a lot more money to hire someone to do the job, depends on whether or not you've got the tools that make it easy. If you pick the right tools, any home improvement task goes smoother. But with the wrong tools in your hand, you invite mayhem.

These days, lots of companies—dime stores, discount outlets, do-it-yourself centers, and others—sell all kinds of tools in a wide range of qualities. Overenthusiastic advertisements sometimes lead people to expect too much from certain tools and to forget all about some less glamorous oldtimers.

We won't try here to compile an encyclopedia of tools. We will touch on the ones most important to general home improvement, dig more deeply into those that we've seen misused by too many people, poke holes into a few advertising claims about some tools much-loved by mail order and discount peddlers, and resurrect interest in a few useful tools you might not have heard about. Mostly we'll stick to tools that have general uses around the home. As the need arises in later chapters, we'll discuss more specialized tools.

GUIDELINES FOR CHOOSING ELECTRIC TOOLS

Frankly, we're starting this chapter with data about power tools *not* because they are essential to home improvement, but because many people *think* they are. If you can afford them, *some* of the electric tools on the market will make your bigger home improvement projects go faster and conserve your energy and attention for more important concerns—such as working accurately. But some cheap electric power tools, such as inexpensive saws, are rarely useful enough to be worth even their low price. If you have a heavy job and a lightweight budget, consider renting a hefty tool instead of buying a puny one.

Here are some general guidelines for selecting electric tools like saws, drills, sanders, and routers.

• Never buy the bottom of the line. If a company makes six different saber saws, for example, you can count on its cheapest one or two models being what many hardware store personnel call throw-aways. The department head of one large tool retailer described part of one major brand name manufacturer's tool line this way: "Their yellow tools are part of their throwaway line—you take them home, open the box, and throw them away. Their green tools are also throwaways, except that you use them once or twice before you toss them out."

• Prefer tools with ball bearings and roller bearings to those with sleeve bearings. The latter just barely qualify as bearings at all.

• If you can afford it, buy a model that's more powerful than you think you'll need. First of all, you can't predict what kind of job you'll be tackling next. More important, tools last longer if they're not worked at or beyond their rated capacities too often. If your chosen saw is overpowered for your jobs, you'll get better and longer service out of it than with the opposite situation.

• Be sure you can easily buy replacement parts. You have to expect that your favorite power tool will break down when you need it the most. So buy from a retailer that has its own well-stocked service department—a rarity—or from a national chain with a reputation for prompt repairs or for supplying repair parts quickly to do-it-yourselfers who fix their own tools. (Our companion book, *How to Fix Damn Near Everything,* published by Prentice-Hall, will help you repair ailing tools.)

• Buy from a retailer whose clerks are ardent do-it-yourselfers or else well trained in tool specifications. Most general discount stores do not meet this important qualification. You might save five bucks on a particular model of saw at a discount store, but where's the saving if you buy a model that's totally unsuited to your work habits and your home improvement jobs?

• Be sure the tool either is marked prominently *double-insulated* or is equipped with a three-prong grounding plug that you'll always use correctly. Don't accept a tool if the words "double-insulated" are marked on the box but not on the tool itself. Such a tool may *not* actually be double-insulated—a method of construction that keeps *two* layers of plastic and not just one between your hands and live electrical wires. We'd rate the double-insulated and the traditionally insulated, properly grounded tool about equally safe.

• Be sure you get a written warranty. If you find a problem with any power tool within the first month after you buy it, you should be able to swap it for a new tool. And if it becomes defective within the first year, the manufacturer should repair it free. On tools that come with such a warranty, you can feel somewhat confident of getting your money's worth. Frankly, you'll probably find that cheaper tools aren't warranted adequately.

• Make certain your tool has an Underwriter's Laboratory (UL) marking on its label.

• If you want absolutely the best tool for the money, turn to a company's line of industrial products. They aren't always stocked at smaller stores, but they're worth looking for. In one manufacturer's line, for example, we compared ⅜-inch variable speed drills. The consumer model had a ⅜-hp motor and the industrial model a ½-hp motor. The motor housing on the consumer model was "thermoset polyester" whereas the industrial model's was "high-impact polymer." And the price tag on the industrial model was just 30 percent higher.

During our history as do-it-yourselfers, we've bought, used, abused, and cussed at a pulpit full of power tools. We've bought cheapos, brand names, and mail-order brands. You might save yourself some cash and clashes if we share with you the philosophy that's evolved over our many years. We don't buy a bargain basement offbrand *anything*—and that even includes the *hand* tools we buy for children. Top-of-the-line brand name tools are still worth about what they cost, but the same brand names' lower-end products keep getting flashier and more poorly constructed all the time.

We've settled on Sears' Craftsman line for most of our own tools, electric or hand-powered. (And Sears doesn't know we're writing this.) They are about as well built as their brand name counterparts; they ought to be since they're built for Sears by the same brand name companies. Some of the tools are minus a few frills. The prices are competitive in our book. And since we live near a Sears retail store, we never have to worry about what'll happen if a tool doesn't work out the way it's supposed to. If the balky tool is new, we swap it for a better one. If it's an old clunker that's gotten lots of use, we order replacement parts and in a few days it's back in service. That means a lot to us since we always seem to tackle the roof just before the first snow and fancy up the living room just before company's coming.

ELECTRIC SAWS

The *circular saw* is the electric counterpart to an ordinary handsaw. It's ideal for cutting straight lines through wood. With special cut-off type blades, the more powerful models can—in an occasional pinch—cut through modest amounts of asphalt shingles, asbestos board, and even concrete.

Basically a circular saw is a powerful electric motor with a handle on it and a frame for guiding it over the top of a piece of wood. A thin, steel, saw-toothed disc is attached to the motor, either directly or via gears.

When you set out to buy a circular saw, you'll have to choose from among blade sizes ranging from about 5 inches in circumference up to about 8 inches. And there are several motor sizes, from about ½ hp up to over 2 hp. The largest motor possible is an obvious advantage. Whichever

FIGURE 4-1 Circular saw. (Courtesy Sears, Roebuck and Co.)

FIGURE 4-2 Sabre saw. (Courtesy Sears, Roebuck and Co.)

FIGURE 4-3 Table saw. (Courtesy Sears, Roebuck and Co.)

FIGURE 4-4 Radial arm saw. (Courtesy Sears, Roebuck and Co.)

blade size you choose, it helps you cut through tough wood (and possibly other materials) without the stalling that may happen with smaller motors. If a motor stalls while you're cutting, you risk burning it out unless you shut it off quickly. Since circular saws employ trigger-like switches, turning them off fast is no problem. What is a problem, however, is keeping a stalled saw from jumping about while you stop it, pull it loose from the board, restart it, and tackle the tough wood one more time. *Every one of those situations is potentially hazardous.*

We do not believe that any circular saw that develops less than 1 hp is powerful enough to be safe doing most of the jobs we've seen people use them for around the home. But in the hands of a careful user who's made the effort to gain a bit of experience on easy jobs before tackling tough ones, a powerful, well-built circular saw is not a serious threat.

For most people, blade size is of less overall importance than motor size. If you want maximum versatility, select a large enough blade to cut through a 1½-inch thick piece of wood at a 45° angle; that requires a saw in which at least 2⅛ inches of the blade can be used in cutting. In general, most (but not all) saws with 6½-inch or larger blades can meet this criterion. Most people seldom cut 2 × 4s at angles, so if economy is important, choose a blade only big enough to cut straight through the narrow side of a 2 × 4. All the circular saws we've seen have that feature.

The *sabre saw,* smaller than most circular saws, is designed principally for cutting curved lines through relatively thin wood. It is named for the fact that its narrow saw blade resembles a sabre. It comes in sizes as narrow as ¼ inch and as long as 4 or more inches (although most blades are closer to 2 inches in length). Blades screw into the blade holder, which attaches to a set of gears driven by a small electric motor. Some sabre saws use a trigger-like switch; others have a simple, clicking on-off switch. Fancier models permit their users to instantly change the direction the blade points from frontwards—the traditional cutting direction—to sideways or even backwards, thus enabling easier cutting of scrollwork.

If you're going to use a sabre saw only occasionally, and then only for materials no tougher than ½-inch plywood, you could choose the cheapest model on the market, as long as it's adequately wired and insulated. Hazards in using a sabre saw come not from an underpowered tool so much as from not checking in advance to make sure that electric cord and fingers are not in the path of the advancing saw blade.

If you've bought one of the more powerful sabre saws to cut a large or ornate hole into a piece of wood, you can skip the preliminary step of having to drill an entry hole for the sabre saw blade. You can tilt the saw, turn it on, and use the sabre point to pierce the hole for you. *That,* however, can be hazardous unless you hold the saw securely, so practice the maneuver on scraps of wood before you try it on your real work.

The sabre saw is such a handy little tool that a lot of homeowners use it for a lot more than delicate little cuts now and then. They may cut fancy gingerbread for a roof line out of tough 2 × 12 timbers, as we did; or they may use a long, coarse blade to saw through 2 × 4s when knocking out a wall during remodeling, as we did; or they may use a metal-cutting blade to cut a 1-foot-square hole in the middle of a steel plate ¼ inch thick, as we did. Like us, they also may end up with a large collection of junked sabre saws.

Frankly, there isn't a great deal people like us can do to avoid having their sabre saws wear out, burn out, and fall apart. It's in the nature of a beast that jiggles up and down more than ½ inch per stroke some 2000 strokes every minute, using the smallest possible motor so it's easy to hold. If you know you're going to be rough on a sabre saw, look for one that has all ball bearings instead of sleeve bearings, a motor of at least ⅓ hp, a great guarantee, and a price tag reaching to perhaps a hundred dollars. Even then, don't expect a hard-run sabre saw to be a lifetime investment.

Table saws and *radial arm saws* are essentially simply bench-mounted models of the circular saw. In the table saw, a large metal table exposes part of the circular blade through a slot. You can tilt the motor or the table top and adjust various guides. On the radial arm saw, the motor with its circular blade is attached to an arm about 2 feet long. You can raise or lower the arm and pivot it; you can also tilt or rotate the motor and blade. Because of their noise and size, these large saws tend to intimidate novices into choosing hand-held electric saws; the fact is, both table and radial arm saws are much safer to use than the little ones—actually, they're much safer to use than a car, and you overcame your fear of that! Both types of bench saw can do about the same job, but beginners generally seem to learn how to use a radial arm saw's features faster than those of a table saw.

You can't carry either of these saws to your job. But if you can move parts of your job to the saw, and you can afford from $200 to $500 or more, then a table or radial arm saw provides greater versatility, greater safety, and greater precision than any other kind of electric saw. In addition to sawing, there are sundry other valuable jobs you can perform on a radial arm saw (which is more flexible in handling non-sawing jobs than a table saw): disc sanding, routing, milling, planing, grooving, slotting, mitering, and—to a limited degree—even drilling.

If you're going to buy a bench saw, don't skimp on quality. It'll do you no good if its various adjustments won't stay adjusted or its guides warp or twist. Buy a Sears, Wards, or brand name saw from a reputable dealer. And don't even consider a motor smaller than 1 hp.

HAND-POWERED SAWS

The fine old-fashioned *handsaw* is perfectly suited to most home improvements short of building garages and major additions. (In fact, Frank's dad built the family's two-story house in the early 1950s using only hand-powered tools.) There are two major reasons many people today look down on the lowly handsaw: they don't know how to use it well, and they seem to think that working up a sweat is taboo.

You can buy a good handsaw for under $20. You can't touch a comparable electric saw for double that price. There are two different kinds of saws to know about, a *crosscut saw* and a *ripsaw*. For cutting along the length of a board's grain, the rip saw is ideal. Typically, it has only 4 or 5 teeth per inch and they are cut and sharpened to deal most directly with the mechanics of cutting *with* the grain. For general use, in case your hardware store actually stocks both kinds, the crosscut saw is preferred. A blade with 8 teeth per inch (or 8 points, in carpenters' jargon) is satisfactory for the coarse work that most home handy people undertake. A finer crosscut saw generally features 11 or 12 points and cuts more slowly.

To cut correctly with a handsaw requires more care than strength. Lay the board you plan to saw onto something solid, preferably below waist-level. If you don't have a workbench, an old chair works well. If you're short, a wood or heavy cardboard box is good to use. Remember that it's hard to saw well when you're also struggling to keep a board from sliding around, or when you're more worried about cutting into the family's best piece of furniture.

If the end that's going to fall off, after your cut is completed, is more than just a few inches long, that part has to be supported separately. Otherwise the weight of that loose end may bend the board enough to bind against your saw; then, when you reach the end of your cut, it will break off and you'll get a messy-looking piece of wood.

FIGURE 4-5 A handsaw is a versatile, inexpensive tool—when used properly. With help from a friend, you can concentrate on sawing smoothly and on the line while your friend steadies the board. Near the end of the cut, your friend can hold onto the end piece so it doesn't crack away prematurely. Without help, your best bet is to work on a low surface, such as an old chair (or a not-so-old one protected by papers), and put one foot up on the board while you saw. Best for solo sawing, of course, is a sturdy vise clamped to a workbench.

After you've drawn the line you want to saw along, put the saw teeth against the line. Set your thumb firmly against the saw to hold the teeth right on that line. Pull the saw gently back and forth just a few inches on each stroke. This will start it sawing the wood exactly where you want.

When the saw cut is deep enough, the edges of the cut will act as a guide for the saw blade. Then pull your thumb away and gradually take longer and longer strokes. Ideally, you should use about three-quarters of the entire saw blade on each stroke, sawing all the way from your shoulder, not just from your elbow.

Once your saw is able to progress steadily without your thumb to guide it, you can also push harder on the saw. Most wood saws cut only on the *push* stroke. They coast on the *pull* stroke, and so should you.

Keep your eye on the line you want to follow. Once the saw has cut some way into the wood, you'll find that it is actually difficult to change direction even slightly. Therefore, once you're off to a good start the rest is easy. However, if you do go a bit off the line, you can alter the direction most easily by sawing only with the narrowest part of the saw blade while you progressively correct your course.

When you get close to the end of your saw cut, switch back to those slow, short strokes you used to start the cut. You'll have to treat the last fraction of an inch very carefully or it'll split off unevenly. If you find that ending a cut smoothly is hard for you—even after some practice—try this method. When you've cut to within an inch or two of the end, stop. Turn around and start sawing from the opposite side. This takes more time than sawing straight through in a single operation, but neatness is well worth waiting for. Besides, if you get a rough cut, you'll probably spend more time sanding the rough spots away.

Don't fight the saw. If it doesn't go smoothly, assuming that the wood is reasonably dry and the saw is reasonably sharp, it's because you're not keeping it lined up with the early part of your saw cut. (Sometimes binding and bad sawing is caused by poorly supported boards.) If you twist the blade either from left to right or from up to down, it will bind. Then you'll have to tilt the blade away from you and out of the cut. Begin sawing again with the same short, smooth strokes you used at the very beginning of the cut.

Once in a great while you may saw yourself into a real jam near the center of a board. Perhaps you've strayed off the line a bit too much, and a combination of factors foils all your efforts to get started again in the right place. Start over *on the other side of the board.* If you stay close to the line, your second cut will merge with your first one.

Nearly all this advice about how to saw successfully also applies to power saws. But forget about shoving your thumb near the blade to get a cut started!

Any saw has to be sharp or it's useless. When you buy it, it's sharp. If you don't cut nails with it, don't leave it to rust in a damp basement or woodshed, and don't try to sharpen it yourself, it should remain sharp almost indefinitely. We've been using our handsaw for 10 years, giving it plenty of use and a little abuse, and it still doesn't need sharpening.

You can tell that a saw needs sharpening when the wood you're working on seems to cut extra-hard and it's tough to keep the saw on your line. This can be caused by green lumber, too, so study the teeth of the saw. If their edges look more rounded than sharply squared off, take the saw to a pro and spend a few dollars to get it sharpened. You'll waste lumber and patience if you monkey around trying to sharpen the saw yourself.

A crosscut saw is designed to cut straight lines. Don't try to make it cut curves too. There are lots of very inexpensive and efficient small saws that are intended to make curved or wavy cuts through wood.

For very small circles and tight curves, the *coping saw* is useful. The trouble is, because of the way it's built, the darned thing doesn't work much deeper than about 6 inches from the edge of a board.

The second common saw for curved cuts is the *keyhole saw.* You can use this one at any distance away from the edge of your piece of wood. But it can't manipulate through extremely tight curves like its coping cousin.

When you begin cutting with either saw, put your thumb near the mark to steady it. Like the crosscut saw, begin with short, gentle strokes and then progress to more vigorous ones. As you change direction with a coping saw, you'll probably find it convenient to change the direction of the blade too. Loosen up the wing nut that tightens the blade, twist the top and the bottom ends of the frame, and then tighten the wing nut again.

Some people get carried away when they find out how easily the coping saw cuts curves. They saw faster and faster and that heats up the blade. Heat dulls and weakens it, and pretty soon the blade snaps. Coping saw blades aren't expensive and they're easy to install. If one snaps on you, it's not the end of the world. But if they snap too often, it's probably a sign that you're cutting too fast. And fast cuts are rarely clean or accurate.

If a curved line you want to cut doesn't begin or end at or touch the edge of your board, you'll have to drill a small hole somewhere along the line. The keyhole saw will slip right into the hole. You'll have to take a coping saw apart, fit its blade through the hole, then reassemble it. When the cutting is done, you'll have to go through the same procedure once more.

Small pieces of metal often can be cut by using only a *hacksaw blade.* Materials as thick and as hard as bolts can be handled nicely this way. Because a considerable amount of stiffness is built right into the blade, it is ideal for cutting off nails or other hardware in a very confined space.

Frames for the hacksaw blades are relatively inexpensive. Many are fixed in length, about 10 or 12 inches long, but most are adjustable to hold blades 8 to 16 inches in length. A hacksaw blade has a hole at each end to fit a matching pin in the frame. A thumbscrew tightens the blade. Position the blade so that the hacksaw teeth are pointed *away* from you when the saw is used.

In general, the thinner the metal you are cutting, the more teeth a hacksaw blade should have. There always should be a minimum of *two teeth* across the thickness of the material being sawed; that means that a

FIGURE 4-6 The hacksaw is ideal for cutting metal. Insert the blade in a hacksaw frame with the teeth pointing away from the handle. For small cutting jobs, the blade can cut through metal unaided.

sheet of metal $1/16$ inch thick requires a blade with at least 32 teeth per inch, and $1/8$-inch material can be cut with 16 teeth per inch—and cut faster.

A hacksaw blade, like a handsaw, cuts only on the *push* stroke. Its teeth all point in that direction. On the *pull* stroke, you should be coasting. The teeth should stay in contact with your work but the pressure should be off.

Don't rush a hacksaw. About 40 or 50 strokes per minute is the ideal speed. A faster rate heats up the blade and dulls it, slowing down your performance. To end up with straighter cuts and to minimize the danger of breaking the blade, firmly hold in place the piece of metal to be cut with a vise, clamps, vise grip pliers, or a similar tool.

The *rod saw* is a recent addition to the cutting field. The "blade" actually is a heavy wire coated with thousands of supertough tungsten carbide particles. The rod saw fits any adjustable hacksaw frame and many nonadjustable sizes as well. With it, you can cut through materials too hard for even a traditional hacksaw—hard steel, tough plastics, glass, and practically anything else short of diamonds. In fact, you'll gum up the works if you use your rod saw on soft materials. Like the hacksaw, this gadget must be used slowly, but it cuts on *both* the push stroke and the pull stroke.

DRILLS

Next to the hammer and the saw, the drill is one of the most used tools in home improvement projects. So many companies sell cheap $1/4$-inch *electric drills*, there's almost no excuse for not having one. But if you're doing some really serious home improving, shop carefully for yours.

Cheap $1/4$-inch drills typically have a one-speed nonreversible motor with about $1/6$ or $1/5$ hp. That's adequate for drilling small holes, for general maintenance, and maybe for an occasional use like wire-brushing rust off a porch railing. But it won't do for hefty or more exacting jobs. You'll need more than a cheap ¼-inch drill if: you're frequently going to drill holes larger than ¼ inch in diameter; you plan to scrape paint electrically off the siding of your house; you aim to make more than a few holes in concrete or tile; you want a tool that'll last at least half a lifetime.

For regular or heavy use, your drill should have at least a ¼ hp motor and only ball or roller bearings—no sleeve bearings. Cordless drills with built-in rechargeable batteries may be convenient, but they don't meet the test for power or durability.

The *chuck*—the part that holds the drill bits and other accessories—generally comes with a maximum opening of ¼ inch, ⅜ inch, or ½ inch. (There are metric-sized drills as well.) Since most drill bits and accessories these days are made with the smallest size drill chuck in mind, chuck size should not be a vital determinant. The more powerful drills used to come equipped with the larger chucks, but that's not true any longer; a few manufacturers stick the bigger chucks onto some of their smaller drills, apparently hoping to fool the unwary.

Variable speed motors are useful, although they can add something like $20 to the overall cost. If you're doing critical work and want to drill a hole precisely on your pencil mark, the variable speed motor is useful. With this feature you can drill at a slow speed until you've made certain that the hole will end up exactly where you want it, then squeeze the trigger harder for full speed. Frankly, before the advent of built-in variable speed controls, we used to accomplish the same effect simply by pulsing the motor. We'd squeeze the trigger once or twice a second until we were ready to switch into full speed.

A reversible motor adds about $10 to the overall price of a drill. It's valuable to have if you intend to electrically disassemble something that's screwed together. Occasionally the reversible feature comes in handy for helping to back out a drill bit that's stuck in something tough, but in such a situation we've often simply pulled hard on the drill and then flicked the trigger switch on—which backed out the drill bit too. Reversible switches tend to be chintzy in construction and can cause annoying little problems unless you choose your drill carefully.

A *drill press* is little more than an elecric drill with a heavier motor, mounted on a sturdy stand. That results in greater precision and a great deal more power. It also means you can't tote the drill around to job sites. Now that manufacturers have started to design—and price—this tool for home workshop use, a serious do-it-yourselfer might like to own one. They're definitely valuable for working in heavy metal; for making dozens of big, deep holes at precise locations in wood; and for similar demanding jobs. Our drill press has practically paid for itself in saving the price of drill bits heretofore broken by pushing too hard and with too wobbly a hand on very tough jobs.

Many companies sell inexpensive, lightweight stands that seem to turn ordinary small electric drills into drill presses. We've tried a number

FIGURE 4-7 Electric drill. (Courtesy Sears, Roebuck and Co.)

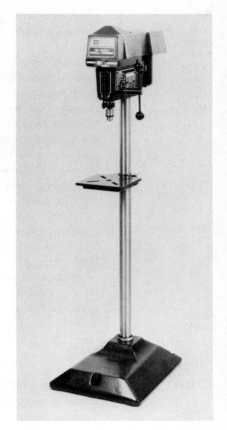

FIGURE 4-8 Drill press designed with home workshops in mind. (Courtesy Sears, Roebuck and Co.)

of them and have yet to find one we consider worth the price. They're not accurate, sturdy, versatile, or able to stand up to much use or abuse.

When shopping for a drill press, put your money into the motor. Anything smaller than ½ hp is too small, and ¾ hp is none too large.

Many models come with solid state speed controls that offer continuously variable speeds; that's nice, but not necessary. If you're on a budget, and who isn't, settle for the oldstyle speed control that matches sets of pulleys of varying diameters. In order to slow down or speed up your drill, you (1) turn off the motor; (2) flip open the top cover; (3) loosen the tension handle; (4) slip the belt upwards or downwards on the first pulley; (5) do the same on the second pulley; and (6) flip the cover closed. It takes as long to do in real life as to read about.

Don't get the idea that electric drills are used only for drilling. They're valuable for myriad other chores important to fine home-improvement work. We'll list just some of the accessories that expand the versatility of both electric drills and their hefty cousins, drill presses.

• Drilling small holes requires a set of *drill bits.* A ¼-inch drill holds bits with shanks up to ¼ inch diameter, and ⅜-inch and ½-inch models hold proportionately larger-shanked bits. However, you can buy drill bits that make up to about 1-inch holes yet have reduced shanks to fit into ¼-inch drills.

• Drilling large holes is accomplished with one of two accessories: a hole cutter or a spade drill. A *hole cutter* resembles a cookie cutter with saw teeth cut into it. It comes in several sizes and clamps into your drill's chuck. A *spade drill,* so named because it resembles a spade, is a flat, sharpened wood-boring tool that cuts smooth holes quickly through wood. Spade drills come in sizes up to about 1½ inches, whereas hole cutters range to 4 inches and beyond. Some hole cutters are made of high-speed steel or are tipped with super-tough carbide so you can cut through plastic and metal with them—but we'd recommend a good drill with *at least* a ¼ hp motor for that kind of work.

• It's handy to be able to drive screws with an electric drill when you're building something major with wood or sheetmetal screws. *Screwdriver accessories* are very inexpensive. When using your drill to drive screws, however, we recommend strongly that you use Phillips head screws. They were created with exactly this function in mind.

• Wire-brushing rusty metal and the like goes quickly with a *wire-brush attachment* in your drill.

• *Polishing and buffing attachments* help you wax the car, polish furniture, etc.

CHISELS

There are wood chisels, metal chisels, masonry chisels, brick chisels, and more. Each is designed for a specific job. It does that job well but becomes a nuisance—and even a hazard—if used for any other type of work.

No chisel, whether for wood, masonry, or metal, is prohibitive in cost if you legitimately need it.

At one time, *wood chisels* were meant to be struck by a wooden mallet. So many carpenters, pro and otherwise, used the common metal-headed carpenter's hammer that most manufacturers now design even their wood chisels so that they can withstand the rigors of being hit by steel hammerheads. The mark of such a tool is an iron button at the end of the handle.

A *flat chisel,* which generally ranges in width from ¼ inch up to 3 inches, is used to remove relatively large amounts of wood to create a rough shape. More than likely you will find one handy when installing a lock or a hinge. It comes in handy elsewhere too. For example, if you've slipped up in your measurements and find that the already-nailed-into-place molding is too large, a chisel removes the excess. In knocking out walls or moldings for remodeling, call on a heavy wood chisel to chip away unwanted bits of wood.

The *gouge* is a wood chisel best suited to create grooves or clean them out. It is the chisel that woodcarvers most often use to chip away at statues. Some of the varieties of wood chisel you can choose from are shown in the illustration.

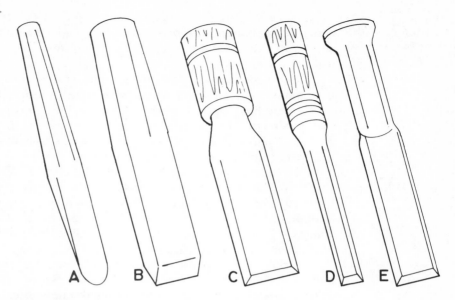

FIGURE 4-9 Chisels come in many sizes and shapes for specific uses on specific materials: (A) metal chisel for knocking away bolt or rivet heads; (B) metal chisel for general metal-working jobs; (C) wood chisel, often with handle made of wood or plastic, for mortising out hinge spaces or lock openings in doors; (D) wood chisel, also with wooden or plastic handle, for daintier jobs—only in wood; (E) wood chisel made entirely from steel so it will withstand frequent pounding with a metal hammer.

The *cold chisel* is the major tool you will have occasion to use on metal. Like the wood chisel, it comes in a variety of sizes and shapes, many of which you can see in the illustration.

It is important to protect your eyes when using a cold chisel. Pieces of metal can fly off the work or the chisel itself. If you already wear glasses (assuming that they were made after federal regulations required that all eyeglass lenses be hardened), they should be sufficient. If not, an inexpensive pair of protective goggles is needed.

A cold chisel must be struck with a hammer of the proper size. You cannot accomplish much by tapping at a big chisel with a tiny hammer, and a tiny chisel slugged by a massive hammer is so uncontrolled that you invite damage to your work or your body. Still, the head of a hammer should always be considerably larger than the cold chisel it strikes. A ½-inch chisel, for example, needs a hammer with at least a 1-inch head. Although the striking end of a hatchet is properly hardened so that it can be used for driving nails, it *cannot* be used against a cold chisel without the risk of splitting the hatchet head.

When the head of an all-metal chisel (whether intended for use on wood, metal, masonry, or brick) mushrooms over, the likelihood of its tossing off shards of sharp metal is great. The mushroomed portion of the head must be ground away, or the chisel must be replaced.

The typical home improver has to resist the temptation to say,

"Hmm, a cold chisel cuts metal easily. It should cut through stone and concrete like butter." Not so! A chisel designed for cutting metal will do a very slow, tedious, and unpredictable job on concrete or stone—and ruin its cutting edge as well.

There are several kinds of masonry chisels. The *star drill* is most often seen. It's not a drill at all in the usual sense, but a chisel designed to cut a round hole into a concrete floor or wall. One manufacturer's reference guide says, "Popular sizes range from ¼ inch to 1¾ inches in length." Actually, "popular" is not the best choice of adjective. When you use a star drill, you cannot help but work up a hearty sweat.

To use one, first locate the precise site for the hole you need in the concrete. Then select a star drill that is close to the size required. If you are fluctuating between two different sizes, you may be happier in the end to have picked the larger one. You will not enjoy going back over the hole to enlarge it. And should the hole come out a trifle too large, a bit of concrete patcher or epoxy glue will fill the void.

A star drill is struck with the largest hammer practical. The drill must be twisted slightly after each blow so that its four cutting edges create a round opening and not a four-pronged indentation.

Chisels can be, and should be, sharpened periodically, probably just before their next use. (For sharpening instructions, see Chapter 14 of the companion volume, *How to Fix Damn Near Everything.)*

HAMMERS

Pound for pound, the hammer is one of the most widely used tools in the home—and perhaps the most misused and abused. You may be surprised at how many different kinds of hammers there are. *Carpenter's hammers, nail hammers,* or *claw hammers*—all common names for the same tool— generally come in sizes ranging from a head that weighs 7 ounces to one that's a hefty 20 ounces. For home use, unless the muscles in your arms are as strong as iron bands, a hammer with a 13- or 16-ounce head is preferred.

The part of the hammer that pulls out nails is called the *claw* and comes either curved or straight. Novices generally find that the curved claw pulls better for them. The driving end of the head is labeled the *face,* and a *bell-faced hammer* is the one you are most likely to find in hardware or department stores.

A carpenter's hammer is designed to hammer on soft steel items such as common nails, finishing nails, nail sets, and the soft metal caps on some wood chisels. It is dangerous to use the hardened head of a carpenter's hammer to pound on other hard steel objects such as cold chisels, masonry nails, concrete nails, and other hammers. Pounding hard steel against hard steel could crack the hammer head or cause pieces of it to fly off.

When you must pound against hard steel, a *ball pein hammer* is called for. The head on this tool ranges in weight from about 4 ounces to 2½ pounds. (The words *pein* and *peen* are interchangeable, although man-

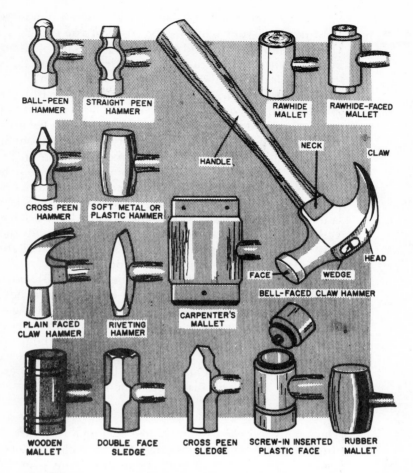

FIGURE 4-10 A potpourri of hammer types to choose from. You won't find all of them stocked at smaller hardware stores, but if you need a specialized pounding tool, most of these are hidden in dark recesses of big hardware or home improvement stores.

ufacturers now lean toward the former. It means the striking surface opposite the hammer's face.) Although they're not expensive, you are not likely to buy a handful of ball peins. The 1- to 1½-pound range is most suitable for simple home applications. If you buy two, a 12-ounce and a 1½-pound hammer are good choices.

Whenever you use a hammer to do any task other than driving soft nails, you're well advised to wear glasses to protect your eyes. Even the coated nails commonly used to install wood paneling frequently split and send sharp missiles flying off in unpredictable orbits.

To protect your hands, the nail, chisel, punch, or whatever other tool you're hammering should be grasped lightly. That way, if you accidentally miss the target your fingers will slip quickly away—although not necessarily all the way out of the way—instead of absorbing the full blow.

If the hammered object is big enough, hold it in a loose fist so that the fleshy part of your hand will be struck if you slip.

A hammer's face and pein are designed for hammering. The side of its head is *not*. Neither are the claws. Using these surfaces probably won't accomplish the job and may damage the hammer.

Hammer handles come in a variety of materials. Unless you intend to put a hammer to rugged or constant use, a plain wooden handle is satisfactory and nominally priced. Fiberglass handles are becoming popular despite their somewhat higher price. Deluxe models come with steel handles, either solid or tubular. Handles come in different thicknesses and lengths, so choose one that's comfortable in your hand.

Wood hammer handles are priced so low that if one shows signs of wear, cracks, or any other damage, discard it. Even if the handle is sound, it must fit into the head very solidly. Any shake or wobble, no matter how little, is too much. If a steel hammer head accidentally flies off the handle as you pound a nail, its force is sufficient to send it all the way through a plate glass window—or partway through a skull.

Hardware stores sell replacement handles. Removing the old head and installing it on a new handle is a 5-minute job. Pry out the metal wedge that holds it in, using a chisel, punch, or screwdriver to get it started. Pliers help tug the wedge loose once it has been started on its way. With the wedge gone but not forgotten, tug, twist, or tap the handle or head until the two pieces separate. The new handle fills the void just created. Be sure to drive the wedge tightly into the handle again to expand the wood enough so that it will firmly grab the metal head.

PLIERS AND WRENCHES

Having a good *pliers* is almost like owning a third arm. Guide manuals dutifully tell the novice never, never to use a pliers to loosen a nut—and it really *shouldn't* be done. But what if there isn't any wrench around that can tackle the particular nut in question? Almost any mechanic whips out a pliers without a moment's hesitation. If the slot of a screw has been so badly chewed up that a screwdriver no longer works, a pliers saves the day. If you are going to tackle a plumbing job but have only one pipe wrench, a large pliers holds onto the pipe while your pipe wrench twists away at the fittings.

The granddaddy in this tool family is the *slipjoint pliers.* Like all types of pliers, this one comes in sizes ranging from a few inches up to a foot long. An 8-inch model is good for all-around use. The frontmost parts of the jaws are straight to accommodate flat pieces; the hind portions are rounded to accept pipes or other circular shapes. The pliers' joint can be slipped into one of two positions depending upon the thickness of whatever you're holding onto.

A *slipjoint combination pliers* simply adds one refinement to the ordinary slipjoint pliers. Just ahead of the joint in each leg is a notch that can be used to cut wire—not well and not heavy wire, but it can cut.

Also related to the slipjoint pliers is the *water pump pliers,* which grabs

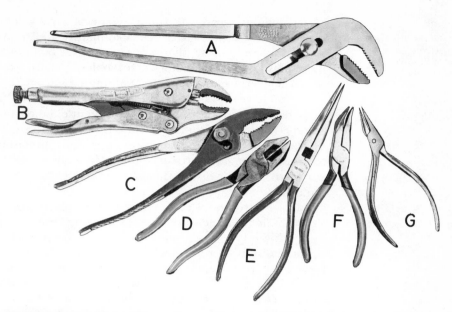

FIGURE 4-11 Pliers are like owning an extra hand in tackling certain jobs. Here are some of the most useful pliers: (A) channel-lock, ideal for balky jobs since it has long handles and is fully adjustable to clamp securely around pipes, nuts, and other hardware of varying sizes from tiny to huge; (B) vise grip, fully adjustable via the screw at the end of one leg, locks onto any job to free your hand for other chores; (C) slip joint, the common pliers that adjusts to two different jaw settings; (D) electrician's, which acts as wire cutter and pliers; (E) large needlenose, ideal for reaching into remote areas for small parts; (F) bent needlenose, for behind around corners to reach dropped parts and other remote jobs; (G) small needlenose.

to the side instead of directly to the front. Instead of only two positions in the jaws, this tool has about seven. The *channel-lock pliers* is more refined. It may have more than seven positions, and its handles are considerably longer than almost any other pliers, making it able to exert a very powerful grip.

Second only to slipjoint pliers in popularity and usefulness is the *vise grip pliers,* often known as *lock grip pliers.* Its jaws are hinged to multiply the pressure of your hand many times over, resulting in more leverage (squeezing power) than probably any other hand tool of this sort. That power is both a blessing and a curse. If someone has accidentally twisted off a cup hook, for example, and wants to screw out the broken-off stub, a vise grip pliers will grab firmly onto even the tiny remaining piece of hook. However, if the job calls for twisting a thin, hollow chrome pipe, the vise grip pliers may very well squeeze too hard, collapsing or at least scratching and denting the pipe.

Electrician's pliers or *side-cutting pliers* are extremely handy for anyone undertaking rewiring. Its jaws form a small pliers, and a cutting surface on its side enables you to cut a small wire with ease and then to strip it of insulation.

Anybody faced with fine mechanical work will appreciate the delicate touch of *needle-nose pliers,* a miniature tool that comes in several varieties. Needle-nose pliers are valuable for bending and locating wires in small electronic assemblies, for holding nails too tiny for hands to steady while they are first being hammered into place, and for retrieving parts that have slipped into tiny spaces. Some varieties' jaws are serrated to grip hard, and others are flat for gentle holds on delicate objects. Needle-nose pliers themselves should be treated with a certain amount of delicacy. Their joints are small and, hopefully, precision-made. If you try to squeeze them too hard on an unyielding object, the excess pressure can spring the joint or distort the jaws and there's little hope of repairing the damage.

The word *wrench* makes most people think of a single tool that can be successfully adjusted to twist on everything from a peanut-sized nut to a bulky drainpipe. That misconception has been the ruination of many a simple household renovation. Except for its value with plumbing (discussed in a later chapter), an adjustable wrench should be used only when nothing better is available. The most common of adjustable wrenches, the *crescent wrench,* is infinitely variable over the entire range for which it is designed. But it never fits quite perfectly. And if you try to loosen an especially tight nut or bolt with a wrench that doesn't fit well, the result may be a damaged bolt and a set of bruised knuckles as the wrench slips.

A crescent wrench has a fixed jaw and an adjustable jaw. The wrench always must be turned so that the fixed jaw receives the greatest share of the pressure. It must be adjusted to fit as snugly as possible around any nut or bolt it's used on, with the nut's head positioned as far back into the jaws' opening as possible. That brings the wrench and the nut into firm contact on three of the nut's four sides. This three-out-of-four rule also applies to nonadjustable wrenches, which we'll get to later.

When using either an adjustable or a nonadjustable wrench, it is

FIGURE 4-12 The crescent adjustable wrench has to be used so the fixed jaw forces the adjustable jaw tightly against the nut (or other hardware). If you reverse this position, the adjustable jaw is likely to slip loose from the nut.

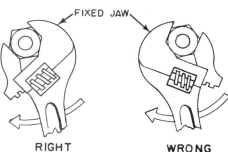

RIGHT   WRONG

highly advisable to *pull* on it and not to push. Your arm muscles are in much better control when you exert pressure towards your body. Should the wrench slip off the job, a pushing motion could send your hand into a nest of sharp nuts or the edges of exposed metal. A pulling motion results in a tap on the tummy at worst.

If you *must* push, do it with the palm of your open hand.

For practically every application short of big plumbing pipes, the nonadjustable *socket wrench* is nearly ideal. A complete set of well-made socket wrenches is expensive. But instead of falling for one of the cheap but shiny sets you see advertised, invest in a few pieces of well-made equipment at a time.

A socket wrench set consists of sockets (with 6, 8, or 12 points ground into their faces) that slip snugly over nuts and bolts of specific sizes. A variety of handles is available for the sockets. Most common is the *ratchet handle,* ideal for quick work and for use in confined spaces. *Extension bars* in various lengths are available to reach out-of-the-way places, and a *universal joint* snaps into any part of the socket wrench system to provide turning power at odd angles.

One good way to afford the cost of the full range of socket wrench equipment is to buy pieces as they are needed. The ratchet handle is the most expensive single piece. Individual sockets are relatively inexpensive, cost varying with size. There are three standard sizes, ¼ inch, ⅜ inch, and ½ inch. Choose the size that permits your handle to slip into the back of each socket for your particular set. The smallest size is used almost exclusively for very small nuts and bolts. Of the two larger sizes, the ⅜ inch is a bit less expensive than the ½ inch and offers practically as much power and scope for household chores. You also can eventually buy an adapter so that ½ inch and ⅜ inch drive sockets can be used on the same handle.

Less versatile than the socket wrench but not less effective, the *box wrench* generally comes in sets that accept 8 or 10 common sizes of nut. Box wrenches can be bought with 6, 8, 12, or 16 points ground into the face. The 12-point is the most adaptable.

Closely related to the box wrench is the *open-end wrench,* which is faster to use and occasionally reaches into less accessible areas. A single open-end or box wrench has a wrench at each end of its handle and thereby covers two sizes of bolt. Trying to combine the best of both worlds results in the *combination wrench,* a box wrench at one end and open-end at the other. Each individual combination wrench works on one size only.

Open-end wrenches purposely are rarely laid out in straight lines. Their ends are displaced by 10°, 15°, 45°, and even 90°. A 15° *displacement* is common. That's because in very tight quarters it is often impossible to twist a nut more than maybe ⅛ of a turn. But with a six-sided *hex nut* or a square nut, a full ¹/₆ or ¼ of a turn is necessary before the wrench can grab the next set of faces. With a 15° displacement, you need simply turn over the wrench after every twist.

Some wrenches, aside from featuring a displacement, also offer an

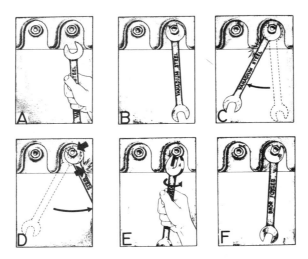

FIGURE 4-13 Box wrenches have displaced jaws to overcome obstructions found in many jobs. After this wrench has twisted to the left as much as possible (C) and can't be fitted back on the nut for an additional twist (D), it is flipped over (E) and can once again grasp the nut (F).

angled arrangement from top to bottom, an *offset*. Here again, 15° is typical. Figure 4-13 shows how a 15° offset in a wrench is used to clear nearby obstructions that otherwise make twisting a nut very difficult.

There is one other wrench that is of some importance to home improvers, the *allen wrench*. Some call it a *hex wrench* because it is six-sided (hexagonal).

It is hard to predict where you may next encounter a hex head bolt. They hold pulleys onto shafts, knobs onto TV and stereo sets, fan blades onto motor shafts. Even your car mirror may have a bolt with an allen head. Using a screwdriver in the recessed space of an allen head does no good to the bolt or the screwdriver—or to the job you're doing. For less

FIGURE 4-14 Most box and open-end wrenches have an offset built in to clear obstructions such as this one.

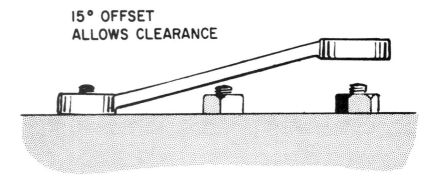

15° OFFSET
ALLOWS CLEARANCE

than $2 you can buy a set of imported allen wrenches in a plastic case that's usually clear on one side and red on the other. People always seem to lose one or two pieces from the set, and always the most useful ones. So be smart when you need allen wrenches; spend a little extra change on a set that's mounted permanently in a single case.

SANDPAPER, ELECTRIC SANDERS, AND SURFORM TOOLS

Sandpaper is one of the most overlooked tools in home improvement. It—or more precisely, its lack—has been the ruin of many otherwise well-executed projects. Like almost every other tool, sandpaper comes in a big selection.

Sand—or flint, as it's often called—is just about obsolete in the manufacture of what we call sandpaper. Sand just doesn't cut wood quickly or hold up well. But it is inexpensive. If you're not going to do much sanding, flint paper is fine.

Garnet paper is next hardest. It costs more but lasts longer and cuts faster.

Alumina and *carbide* are about the best sandpapers in common use. They cost the most, but you get what you pay for. Sheets of them last longer, if used well, and they sand substantially faster than cheaper tools.

For fine wood finishing, you may want to wet-sand between coats of paint, varnish, or lacquer. Look for a sandpaper label that says it's especially made to withstand being wet.

Too many people use sandpaper only to get rid of obvious surface defects. The secret of a professional looking remodeling job is often how well the wood is sanded. To sand correctly, you have to invest in several sheets of good sandpaper in at least medium, fine, and superfine grades. You also need a *sanding block.* Buy one if you like, or simply look around for a scrap of lumber about an inch thick, 5 or 6 inches long, and 3 or 4 inches wide.

Wrap sandpaper around the sanding block whenever you work on flat surfaces. That will keep them flat. Bare fingers press unevenly on sandpaper and cause problems on flat wood. Even if your wood looks clean and smooth, begin sanding with medium-grade sandpaper. Any wood that lies around in a lumber yard picks up a layer of dirt in the grain. A gentle once-over with medium sandpaper cleans that dirt away.

After you've kicked up a bit of dust with your sandpaper, stop and pound it against the palm of your hand. Do this at least every minute or so. That knocks the sawdust loose. If it stays there, the sandpaper grains get plugged up quickly, the paper cuts more slowly, and you have to replace it more frequently.

Switch to the fine grade next. Keep sanding until the wood looks smooth and the grain sparkles. Periodically wipe the sawdust off the wood with a soft rag or paper towel. If you blow it away, make sure your mouth is dry. Saliva or water raises the grain, and you'll end up with uneven spots.

Just before you're ready to apply your first coat of wood filler, finisher, or paint, use your superfine or extra-fine grade of sandpaper. When you've finished with it, your wood will look satiny smooth.

No matter what grade of sandpaper you work with, and no matter what you're trying to accomplish, always move in the same direction as the grain. Otherwise, the sandpaper will etch scratches into the wood instead of removing them. Even the edges of boards have direction to their grain. If the edges are going to show, they have to be sanded until they look just as stunning as the top surfaces. Along the long edge of a board the grain moves the long way. On the short edge it moves up and down but not always at a perfect right angle to the surface. For most boards, the short edge needs more sanding than any other part of the wood. But with enough elbow grease and patience, even that pesky edge looks handsome.

Makers of moldings, legs, and other decorative wood products often advertise that their products come ready to finish. People are led to believe that they're ready to be painted. Actually, they're just ready to be rubbed with fine sandpaper—always with the grain. With odd-shaped items you may have to forgo the sanding block.

Electric sanders can turn the tedious chore of hand sanding into something as easy as brushing your teeth—that is, if you choose a big enough sander. Basically there are two types of hand-held electric sanders, belt and pad.

You also can use sandpaper discs in an inexpensive attachment to your electric drill. The *disc sander* is most valuable for smoothing out tough but small irregularities in surfaces. If you ever patch large areas of broken plaster or mend a dented fender, you'll find this devise handy. Beyond that, it's too crude for most home improvement jobs.

The *belt sander* is a powerful tool intended to be used when power and brute strength are important. It's ideal if you've built a large project out of coarse lumber, or if there are plenty of not-entirely-even joints that have to be smoothed out. Used with medium or coarse sandpaper, large belt sanders remove large chunks of wood as efficiently as wind blowing sand. Really big ones can be used in refinishing hardwood floors. A well-built belt sander runs in the $100 price range, and belts cost from $1 to $5 apiece. Unless you're a serious do-it-yourselfer, you'll probably find that renting a belt sander is your best bet.

Pad sanders are perfect for home improvement chores. They smooth down blemishes in wood, plasterboard, and such; they clean up surfaces prior to painting and staining; and they bring out the finest grain possible from the wood you're using. To work a pad sander you clamp a ½- or ⅓-sheet of ordinary sandpaper into its padded holder. Its motor vibrates the sand-covered pad approximately 4000 times per minute. Some sanders vibrate with an orbital action, others with a straight-line movement. Still others offer a switch so you can choose between the two—the orbital for tougher jobs and the straight-line for fine finishing. Frankly, in most sanders the real difference between the two is too subtle for most people to detect. Faced with a choice, we'd select the straight-line action, the mode used in most larger pad sanders.

FIGURE 4-15 The belt sander is intended to make quick work of rough sanding jobs. For fine finishing of wood, the pad sander is the tool of choice. (Photos courtesy Sears, Roebuck and Co.)

In choosing a sander for substantial work, don't pick one with a motor smaller than ¼ hp or you might as well sand by hand. For durability, buy one with roller or ball bearings and a ½ hp motor or larger. For faster operation, pick one that uses ½-sheets instead of ⅓-sheets or smaller pieces. With the former, you get about 45 square inches of useful sanding area; with ⅓-sheets you get 29 square inches.

SurForm tools (a trade name derived from *Sur*face *Form*ing) are hand-held wood-working devices that are like saws in some respects. They're full of tiny points just like saw blades. They're used like coarse sandpaper, for shaping pieces of wood. Most oldtimers like to think of a SurForm tool as a super file. Think whatever you like. Then look at Figure 4-16 if you've never seen one.

FIGURE 4-16 SurForm tools are convenient and effective for removing roughness from wood, planing away edges, forming rounded corners, and similar jobs. They come in diverse shapes.

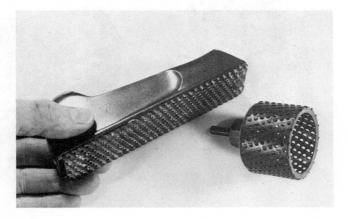

To use a SurForm tool, gently stroke it across the surface of whatever wood you want to shape. If you have a bumpy piece of wood you need flattened out, run a flat SurForm tool over its surface. If you have a flat piece of wood you want rounded or cambered or beveled, run the same flat SurForm tool over its edge. You can create curves with curved SurForm tools, and there are round ones which fit into electric drills. To avoid sharp corners on a home improvement, run a SurForm tool evenly along every edge. You could get the same effect with a sanding block and sandpaper, or with an electric sander, but it takes longer.

OTHER MAJOR HOME IMPROVEMENT TOOLS

A *router* is one of the most heavily advertised of all power tools, yet in the hands of most home improvement people it's of limited value. True, routers in well-equipped workshops can put fancy edges onto cabinets and shelves, make mortise and tenon joints for drawers and furniture, groove shelf supports, engrave signs, carve spindles and legs, and impress the neighbors. The trouble is, each and every task mentioned above—along with everything else you might want to do with a router—requires painstaking preparation with jigs and guides or expensive accessories to avoid some of the preparation.

Before you succumb to an on-sale router, be sure you have a specific use for it. Then be sure either that it will perform what you want without needing accessories or precisely concocted jigs, or that you're prepared to buy the proper accessories.

A *welder* frightens most people. They envision high voltages, high temperatures, sparks, and other mystical hazards. In truth, a properly installed, properly used welder is no more dangerous than your ordinary

FIGURE 4-17 A router. (Courtesy Sears, Roebuck and Co.)

FIGURE 4-18 One welder intended for home workshop use. (Courtesy Sears, Roebuck and Co.)

circular saw. For puttering around with metal-joining projects, a $50 to $75 welder is adequate. For hefty jobs, you have to plan on spending $100 or more.

Welding is a skill as easily acquired as knitting, baking cakes, or roller skating. Most welders come with instruction booklets detailed enough to get you started.

Bench grinders are useful for restoring sharp edges to heavily used tools and for grinding away sharp edges and corners from hacksawed metal. You can count on spending about $50 for a small grinder and over $200 for an industrial type model. The $1/5$ hp model with 5-inch grinding wheels is adequate for sharpening tools and tackling small household chores—as long as you're patient with it. Its small motor won't tolerate much abuse. With a 1 hp motor attached to 8-inch wheels, you can tackle almost any metal-working job.

Vises are very useful to hold onto work that's in progress. If you permanently clamp or screw a vise onto your workbench, you won't have to wrestle with a slippery board with one hand while attempting to guide a saw through it with the other hand, while wishing all the while that you had a third or fourth hand to hold it down. The vise can be your third hand. Convenience aside, using a vice can keep your fingers farther from saw blades than they are when you simply hold the work with one hand while you saw. You'll be more accurate, too, if your work is held absolutely steady in a vise.

There are two basic types of vises: metal-working and wood-working. The former is more powerful and more versatile, while the latter has smooth jaws to keep from marring fine wood surfaces. If you can't buy both, choose the metal-working vise and protect the surface of your wood with scraps or rags before twisting the jaws tightly closed.

FIGURE 4-19 Bench grinder. (Courtesy Sears, Roebuck and Co.)

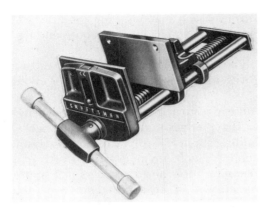 

FIGURE 4-20 The woodworking vise has flat jaws, generally protected by wood overlays, so your fine woodworking will not get marred when you clamp it tightly into the jaws. The metalworking vise has narrower jaws to better accommodate odd-shaped pieces of metal as well as to offer greater holding power. If you cannot afford both, buy the metalworker's vise but protect your wooden projects by slipping scraps of wood between your board and the jaws. (Photos courtesy Sears, Roebuck and Co.)

Clamps are the portable equivalent of the vise. They come in various sizes and shapes, as the illustration shows. They're intended mainly to clamp pieces of wood together while glue dries, but nobody will arrest you for using clamps to hold pieces of wood or pipe steady while you saw, sand, or drill them.

Catalogs, discount stores, hardware and building supply stores, and similar retailers have shelves of shiny tools that we haven't mentioned. We've covered just the basics. We'll deal with specialized tools as they're needed, chapter by chapter. For now, we're all set to get started on improving your home.

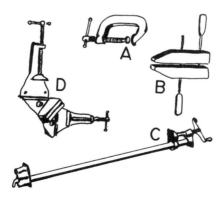

FIGURE 4-21 Clamps can hold onto your projects while you're working on them, squeeze glued pieces together firmly while the glue sets, and perform hundreds of other useful functions. They come in sundry shapes, such as: (A) C clamp; (B) glueing clamp, primarily for woodworking; (C) pipe clamp, ideal for clamping large glued pieces of wood (you buy separately the clamp elements and whatever length of pipe you choose); (D) mitrebox clamp, for holding two pieces of work at right angles, such as picture frames. (These sketches are not drawn to scale.)

II
INTERIOR IMPROVEMENTS

5
Ways to Save Energy

Over the past several years, a lot of hot air has been blown over the subject of energy, and how expensive it is, and why we have to start conserving it. But there's been little real guidance for homeowners or renters who want to improve their surroundings with energy-saving in mind.

Oh, there are lots of new products filling the shelves of home improvement centers and hardware stores, and lots of ads filled with impressive-sounding catchwords that attempt to sell these products. But they're not all cost-effective or even very energy-saving. And there are a number of oldtime, unheralded products on the shelves that do the same job easier and with less cost.

Since energy efficiency is one of the prime considerations nowadays in tackling any home improvement, we'll begin this unit with a brief but basic overview of the facts about home energy-savers, so that you can make your own wise decisions whenever energy efficiency figures into a project. To keep our thinking down-to-earth, we've kept within the following parameters:

- Our suggestions can be followed by any motivated do-it-yourselfer.
- The hardware we recommend is inexpensive enough not to require financing.
- The gadgets we mention are endorsed not just by their manufacturers or retailers but by independent experts such as the U.S. Forest Products Laboratory, the Department of Housing and Urban Development (HUD), the National Center for Appropriate Technology, and university researchers.
- Each item is able to pay for itself within a year in cold climes, two years in more temperate zones.

UNDERSTANDING HOME ENERGY LOSS

There are four major ways that your energy dollars get wasted. You can't totally stop any of the four, but you can control each of them.

1. *Heat rises.* Never forget that, as you decide which energy-saver to spend your money on first. If it's a form of insulation that goes on top of heated rooms or heated pipes, it's probably a better investment than if it tries to retain your precious heat from the sides or bottom.
2. *Hot air and hot surfaces give up energy to cold air and surfaces.* That's why you have to keep some space—air or insulation—between your warmed rooms and the cold outdoors or unheated attics. The bigger the space, the better.
3. *Hot air blows away easily.* Drafts, even small ones, rob homes of more energy than most consumers realize.
4. *Comfortable lifestyles and bad energy habits consume immense amounts of energy— probably needlessly.* Fortunately there's some hardware that can help modify and monitor habits acquired in the days of cheap energy, without causing discomfort or inconvenience.

INSULATION

Most novices believe that insulation is the first thing an energy-conscious homeowner should look to for big savings. That's because the insulation industry has spent millions of dollars to get you to believe it. We're not suggesting you forget about insulation entirely, but only rarely can it provide the biggest and fastest energy pay-backs.

If the tops of your heated living areas are not protected by more than six inches of insulation, do add some quickly. As cold weather approaches, and all your neighbors go shopping for insulation too, the price will go up and the supply will go down.

If there's an unheated attic over your living space, the floor of the attic is the most logical place for insulation; you can just pour in one of the loose filler types which are among the cheapest available. If you don't have an unheated attic, staple rolled fiberglass or rockwool onto exposed knee walls and rafters. It's not a difficult chore. The instructions we've seen in building centers for do-it-yourselfers have been quite adequate.

In buying insulation, give most consideration to the R-value you can get per dollar. R is a measurement of insulation's *resistance* to heat passing through it. The higher the R-value, the greater the insulation's power to keep heat from escaping. For attics, R-19 is considered the bare minimum. R-38 is preferred if you use oil or electric heat, or if you live in a

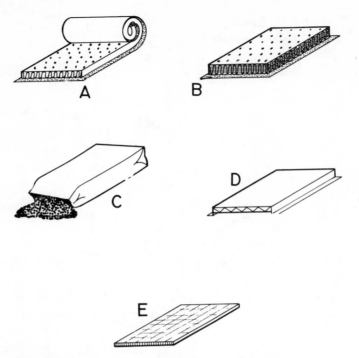

FIGURE 5-1 These are common types of do-it-yourself insulation: (A) Blanket, usually of fiberglass or mineral wool, comes in large rolls, as a rule; it may have a vapor barrier installed on the blanket (as shown here) or not. (B) Batt, with or without vapor barrier attached, is generally made from fiberglass or mineral wool. (C) Loose fill can be cellulose, mineral wool, fiberglass, or other mineral such as vermiculite. (D) Reflective insulation is used in building cavities to keep radiant heat from leaving the building (in winter) or entering it (in summer). (E) Rigid boards, such as Styrofoam.

very cold climate. Insulating your roof area can cut heating bills by 30 percent, enough to pay back your investment before the first year is up.

In working with loose insulation or batts, wear a face mask. With fiberglass and mineral wool, wear gloves as well as washable clothes with long sleeves and long pants-legs to keep you from getting an allergic reaction. (Wash the clothes in a machine several times, and then run the empty washer through a wash cycle to clean it thoroughly.)

Sheets of polystyrene and polyurethane are the handy person's favorite for ease of application, but they should never be left exposed in or under living areas. A minimum of ½ inch of gypsum board or its equivalent in fire-stopping ability must cover the plastic insulation totally, as it gives off toxic gases in even a small fire. Because of this danger, HUD's manual on energy-saving home improvements advises: "Polystyrene and urethane rigid board insulation should only be installed by a contractor."

If your walls are uninsulated, insulating them generally pays off in

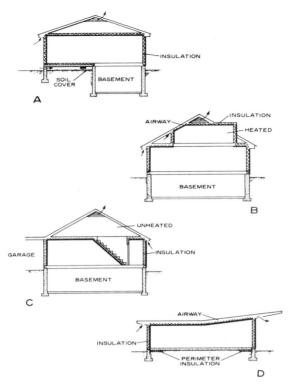

FIGURE 5-2 Here are typical places where the U.S. government recommends insulation. Notice that they suggest lots of insulation above living spaces, plus some to the sides, and that they allow ventilation room above the insulation. Ventilation removes moisture so that it doesn't accumulate and soak into the wood or insulation.

under two years only in extremely cold and windy climates, or in pockets of higher-than-average energy cost, such as New York City. Unless you're very handy, it's a job for contractors. There are several basic approaches.

First, if you are planning to add new siding anyway, your contractor can add an inch or two of polyfoam boards over your old outside walls, and then apply the new siding. The skinny touch of insulation that comes already bonded to many of the aluminum and vinyl siding products touted by high-powered salespeople is barely R-1 and not worth its weight in natural gas. (Chapter 18 tells about new siding.)

As a second alternative, you can have a contractor blow in cellulose or foam insulation. Both have problems. The ureaformaldehyde foam inevitably releases toxic formaldehyde gas. If enough of it gets into your home, it can severely endanger or cause discomfort to people with respiratory maladies or allergies. Although properly prepared cellulose is among the most effective and economical insulation products, some fly-by-nighters have been using improperly fireproofed cellulose. We'd take a sample of any contractor's product to our local fire or building inspector before blowing it into our walls. Both types of blown-in insulation *require* vapor barriers in northern states (a fact that contractors who are selling price instead of quality like to overlook), and that means every room in your house with outside walls will have to be repainted with low-permeability paint.

A third alternative is our choice if you're planning to remodel your home's interior. You can add an inch or two of polyfoam insulation to the interior sides of your outside walls, and then cover the insulation with new walls of ½-inch-thick gypsum board or with wood paneling that has the proper fire rating.

Insulating basement walls, crawl spaces, floors, and other areas may be valuable to comfort, and may pay dividends over the long run, but it seldom returns your investment within two years.

WINDOWS AND DOORS

Right behind uninsulated roofs and ceilings, windows and doors are most homes' second biggest heat-wasters. The best time to conduct a do-it-yourself audit of your windows and doors is on the first cold and windy day after you've put on the storm windows.

If you don't have storm windows, buy them. When it's 0°F outside and you have only single windows, the inside of the glass stays at only 17° and absorbs heat just as fast as it can. With storm windows, the inside glass will be closer to 40°, absorbing much less of your valuable heat. (In summertime the reverse is true. The hot outside air taxes your inside air conditioning. This is a fine excuse for you to leave on as many storm windows as possible year-round.)

An investment in plastic or glass storm windows that cost about $4 to $5 each will repay you in fuel savings the first year. Even makeshift thin plastic storm windows keep Mother Nature's chilly outside air well separated from your warm inside air—if you just make the fit as airtight as possible.

To check for fit on windows and storm windows, run your hand along all four inside edges of all your windows. *Any* chilly breezes you feel are robbing you of heat as well as comfort. Defeat them with caulking or weatherstripping.

On the outside, plug up all gaps between windows and siding with caulking material. Even the least expensive oil-base caulk-in-a-tube will do its job for many years, and an investment of 50 cents per window will be repaid your first year.

On the inside, another 50 cents' worth of weatherstripping or rope caulking material on each window gets repaid in a year. The putty-like rope caulk is simplest to use and most effective at stopping air leaks of all kinds, but it has to be replaced annually (unless you don't ever open the window) and it may look unsightly. Among permanent weatherstrips, the adhesive-backed foam kind is easiest to install, but the metal-stripped

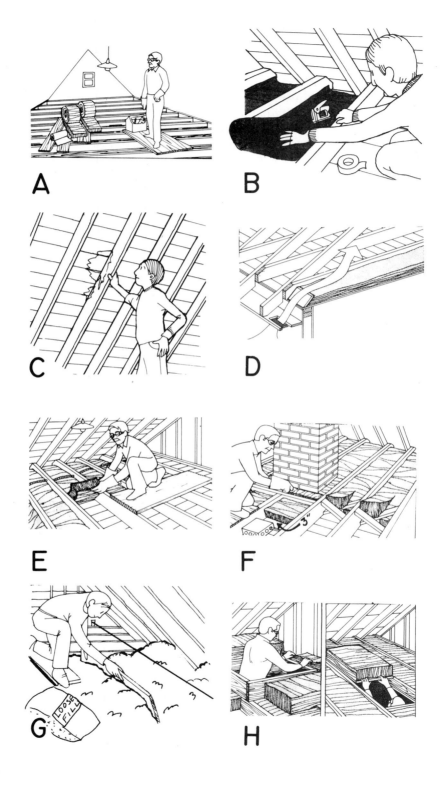

A

B

C

D

E

F

G

H

version that you nail on is somewhat more effective and considerably more permanent.

Even with effective weatherstripping and caulking, windows let a lot of winter heat out and summer heat in. Though the minimum recommended insulation for new walls is R-11, even windows that are double-glazed and insulated, or that are covered with good storms, have ratings of less than R-2. Conservation Consultants, an energy think tank, estimates that an average-sized single-glazed window facing north in Boston wastes 12 gallons of fuel oil per heating season; at 95 cents per gallon, that's a waste of $11.50 per window every year. A window facing south in Boston wastes only about 2½ gallons per heating season. So if your budget is tight, it's the north-facing windows you should tend to first.

Tight-fitting roller shades or heavy drapes (especially if they're lined) can save $4 to $5 per average-sized window every year, assuming you remember to close them every evening. The saving on north-facing windows is more, on south-facing less. You can boost the saving by keeping north-facing shades closed whenever light from their windows is not needed.

To save closer to $10 per window, make shutters from sheets of 1-inch polystyrene and fit them tightly into your window cavities. The simplest way is to carefully measure each window frame and cut a piece of insulation board to fit. Then cut a matching piece of wood paneling, glue the paneling to the insulation, and add a handle. Your "shutter" is complete. Store the shutters in a closet by day and slip them into your window

FIGURE 5-3 Typical do-it-yourself insulation jobs involve all of the following: (A) Install temporary flooring and lights. Keep insulation in wrappers until you are ready to install. It comes wrapped in a compressed state and expands when the wrappers are removed. (B) Install separate vapor barrier if needed. Lay in polyethylene strips between joists or trusses. Staple or tack in place. Seal seams and holes with tape. (Instead of taping, seams may be overlapped 6 inches.) (C) Check for roof leaks, looking for water stains or marks. If you find leakage, make repairs before you insulate. Wet insulation is ineffective and can damage the structure of your home. (D) If you're using loose fill, install baffles at the inside of the eave vents so that the insulation won't block the flow of air from the vents into the attic. Be sure that insulation extends out far enough to cover the top plate. (E) Lay in blankets or batts between joists or trusses. (Note: batts and blankets are slightly wider than joist spacing so they'll fit snugly.) If blankets are used, cut long runs first to conserve material, using leftovers for shorter spaces. Slide insulation under wiring wherever possible. (F) The space between the chimney and the wood framing should be filled with *non-combustible* material, preferably unfaced batts or blankets. Also, the National Electric Code requires that insulation be kept 3″ away from light fixtures. (G) Pour in loose fill insulation to the depth required. If you are covering the tops of the joists, a good way to get uniform depth is to stretch two or three strings the length of the attic at the desired height, and level the insulation to the strings. Use a board or garden rake. Fill all the nooks and crannies, but don't cover recessed light fixtures, exhaust fans, or attic ventilation. (H) Cut ends of batts or blankets to fit snugly around cross bracing. Cut the next batt in a similar way to allow the ends to butt tightly together. If you want an R-value that requires a second layer, place it at right angles to the joists. (Courtesy U.S. Department of Housing and Urban Development.)

FIGURE 5-4 Here's one do-it-yourselfer's answer to blocking the substantial wintertime heat loss that occurs even through triple-glazed windows. Fashion a Styrofoam "shutter" and cover that with an attractive finishing material such as the paneling shown here. Add a handle for easy in, easy out operation. When the sun goes down, slide your shutters into the window frames.

frames by night. In a cold climate, these two-dollar shutters should pay for themselves during the month of December alone.

Audit your doors for air leaks the same way you do your windows. All of the caulking and most of the weatherstripping devices for windows work well on doors too, and give the same general savings. Don't overlook the threshold. Heat leaks in and out there too. Your hardware store or building supply outlet can recommend several different draft-inhibiting gadgets. Some fasten onto the threshold, others onto the bottom of the door itself.

A storm door purports to be the equivalent of a storm window, but it seldom pays for itself in less than 5 or 6 years. Especially if you have a family that runs in and out, you might consider investing in a vestibule. The large air space that separates the outside and inside doors of a vestibule keeps cold outside air from blowing into your warm house. (The reverse is true in summer.) Exact figures for savings depend on how often your door opens and shuts and which direction it faces, but you can generally get a vestibule-building investment back in about 5 years (less if you do it yourself), and after that your savings are substantially greater than if you just added a storm door.

FURNACES, HEATING SYSTEMS, AND HOT WATER HEATERS

The simplest way to save money immediately, with no investment, is to turn down the thermostat in wintertime—and turn it up in summer if you have central air conditioning. HUD estimates that if you turn down your winter thermostat by 6°, you can save from $27 to $87 a year. But 6° may result in more spartan living than many people are willing or able to tolerate. An alternate is to cut the heat while you're asleep.

One expert estimates you can save over 20 percent on your fuel costs during the winter by keeping temperatures at 68° by day and 58° by night. That's enough to make a handy clock-controlled thermostat pay for itself before the first year is up, even if you have a contractor install it. It's even more cost-effective to remember to turn down the thermostat yourself every evening, but very few people are as easy to program as that tiny electronic box.

The next step in fuel-energy saving is to insulate heat ducts that run through nonliving areas that don't need heating or cooling. You can buy 2-inch-thick blankets of fiberglass designed specifically for this job. In addition, change your furnace filters *at least* as regularly as your furnace manual recommends: it will be well worth the cost.

If you turn back the control on your water heater to 120° (140° if you have a dishwasher), you can save from $5 to $45 a year. To cut heat loss, blanket the sides of an older water heater in 3 inches of fiberglass and wrap hot water pipes in special insulating sleeves.

If your lifestyle permits, you might consider turning off your electric water heater for most of the day. Let's say you need hot water when you get up in the morning, but don't have to use any again until late in the afternoon. It isn't hard to install a timer to turn on the water heater an hour or two before you need it and turn it off at the end of a pre-set period of time. Timers can be set for several "on" periods a day, and they have manual override switches in case company drops in. The simplest timers pay for themselves well within a year. After that they can save well upwards of $40 a year.

VENTS AND RANGE HOODS

Every time you flip on the switch that activates your range hood (unless it has a charcoal filter and no vent to the outdoors), you're sucking out a lot of air that you've already paid to heat or to cool. Bathroom vents pull out

FIGURE 5-5 You can save $5 to $45 a year by blanketing your old water heater with three inches of fiberglass and by wrapping hot water pipes in special insulating sleeves. The blanket is available in many do-it-yourself centers and hardware stores. (Photo courtesy Thermo Saver division of S & S Gasket Co., Inc.)

only 50 to 70 cubic feet per minute (cfm), but kitchen vents draw up to 300 cfm, which means they can empty between 2 and 3 percent of all the air inside your house in 1 minute of use. Run the kitchen vent for 15 minutes and you've pulled out over one-third of your home's heated and humidified, or cooled and dehumidified air. Then you'll have to pay for heating or cooling the outside air that gets sucked in while all this is going on.

Very few cooks are willing to give up their range hoods, but they don't have to run at full blast unless that pan of fried chicken is really smoking and spattering. A motor speed control, which looks very much like a light dimmer (but has different internal protective circuits) is a modest investment that will pay for itself within a year. With it, the cook can dial an infinite number of speed settings tailored to do the job with the least air wastage.

FIGURE 5-6 This motor speed control can lower your energy bill subtly but noticeably, if you now have a motorized kitchen vent. It wires easily into existing circuits and comes with installation directions. (Photo courtesy Lutron Corporation.)

FIREPLACES

Fireplaces and most woodburning stoves waste more energy than they create unless they're the only source of heat or are specially built and installed. When it's burning, the typical home fireplace chases more of your expensively heated air up the chimney than it replaces. So it pulls cool air into your room from the outside. Even when a fire's not burning, any opening in your fireplace's damper is equivalent to having an open hole in your wall *double* that size.

Most of the fancy and expensive hardware that's reputed to increase the efficiency of your fireplace *doesn't*. Forget blowers and hollow andirons. Concentrate on properly fitted dampers that are permanently kept tightly closed except when there's a fire going. The *only* way to make a fireplace or auxiliary wood stove *save* energy rather than *consume* it, is to pipe unheated outside air directly into the firebox. Then you must also separate the fire from your room with an airtight glass fireplace screen. Finally, a woodburning stove is only cost-effective if you have access to cheap wood.

For specific guidance in buying and installing an energy-efficient fireplace, see Chapter 7.

For some people, simple modifications in lifestyle can bring substantial energy savings. They're worth considering when you plan your home improvements. For instance, if the kids are grown and gone, do you still need a separate freezer that costs $5 a month to run? Is the dishwasher still worth $5 a month? Does the finished basement need to be heated to 70° every day of the week?

Do you use every upstairs room in the house often enough that it pays to heat or air-condition it? If you find one or two that are seldom used, close them off. Weather-strip their doors that lead to the rest of the house, totally turn off their heat (and air conditioning) ducts, put insulated shutters over their windows, and thereby pare as much as 10 percent off your heating and cooling bills while the rooms are out of use. It only takes an hour or two to get a closed-off room back up to temperature.

Study your habits. Do you spend most of the day in a room at the north side of your house? Switch your wintertime room uses so that you're in a south-facing room during the sunny time of day. You'll probably be able to turn down your thermostat a degree or two and live on less energy as comfortably as before.

Don't get swept up in the high-powered pitches of the energy sellers and energy-saving device manufacturers. Decide how important you consider energy-saving aspects to be in *your* home improvement plans; budget realistically in terms of what *you* can reasonably afford in energy-saving hardware; figure out how much time *you* can devote to doing it yourself; and then zero in on only the energy savers that are best for *you*.

6

Home Heating and Central Air Conditioning Systems

There's very little you really need to learn, factually, in order to understand how home heating and central air conditioning systems work and what you can do to make them work better. With the little bit of information you'll find in this chapter, you will be able to make substantial improvements in your home. There are some you may not want to tackle yourself, but you'll learn enough here to supervise a heating contractor's handling of those jobs.

Along with presenting the basic information you'll need, we'll also reproduce parts of some manuals that accompany projects that we feel are well within most do-it-yourselfers' competence. So many people these days do tackle their own improvements to their heating and air conditioning systems, manufacturers of equipment in this field have started to pack in comprehensive, illustrated installation manuals. Mail-order houses such as Sears and Wards even prepare their own installation manuals to accompany equipment they sell if they feel that the original manufacturers' manuals are not adequate for the needs of do-it-yourselfers. Read the representative selections we've included, and decide for yourself which are within your range of skills and which you ought to have done—under your supervision—by outsiders.

HOW YOU FEEL WARM IN YOUR HOME

There are many kinds of heating fuels and many ways to distribute their heat throughout a home, but they all have essentially one purpose: to keep you feeling warm. The fuel may be gas, coal, oil, wood, or electricity. The heat is distributed via forced air through ducts, steam pipes, or radiators—or radiated directly from the stove or electric heater to you. Whichever fuel and whichever delivery vehicle, your heating system's efforts to keep you feeling warm either succeed or fail depending on how well it achieves three things: radiation, conduction, and convection.

• *Radiation* is the movement of heat through air (or a transparent medium like glass) from a warm object to a colder object. That warm glow that you feel as you sit alongside an open fire comes from heat waves that *radiate* from the fire directly to you. Most people know that fires and other heated devices give off radiant heat, but few realize how important radiant heat really is to their comfort at home. (You do if you happen to have one of those electric radiant heat systems in which heating elements, strategically placed in walls, radiate heat into rooms. You feel the heat whenever you get very close.)

Unless you do stand close to a radiant heater, you scarcely notice any difference in temperature as you walk from one end of the room to the other, or from near the heat source to far away from it. The reason for that is the same reason you feel comfortable at home even though your furnace—no matter what kind—is not running continuously: the floors, curtains, walls, chairs, tables, and books are sources of radiant heat, too. When somebody comes in from a long trek through sub-zero weather, everybody inside feels cooler until that person's clothing warms up to room temperature and can radiate its share of heat back into the room. Your furnishings—and you—don't radiate self-generated heat like a stove, but absorbed heat that your furnace has supplied through its system. The fact that so much of your comfort comes from heat radiated indirectly by your room's walls, floors, and contents explains why you can't turn up your thermostat six degrees on arising and feel immediately comfortable. It takes half an hour or so for your home's furnishings to be brought up to "room temperature" even though the air temperature climbs quickly.

• *Conduction* is the movement of heat directly from one object to another, touching object. If you grab onto a hot pot, your fingers feel the heat instantly. You know *that* for sure, but do you know why? It's conduction. The heat of the hot pot *conducts* quickly to your fingers in much the same way the pot's heat conducts to the water or beans inside it. Conduction adds to—or subtracts from—the warmth you feel inside your home.

For an example, walk barefoot on a cold floor; your feet will feel cold. That's due to the fact that their heat is conducted away to the cold floor. (If you want to be unscientific but practical, you can say that the floor's coldness is conducted into your toes.) Likewise, if your walls are uninsulated and your storm windows are still sitting in the garage, the heat that should remain inside your home is quickly being conducted into the cold air outside, and your walls and windows therefore feel quite cold.

The obvious way to avoid heat loss due to excessive conduction through ceilings, walls, and windows is to upgrade the windows (see Chapter 9) and insulate the walls and ceilings (see Chapter 5).

Conduction is the principle underlying forced-air heating systems. Gas, electricity, or oil heats air inside the furnace's heat exchanger and a blower forces the heated air into all parts of the house via ducts. The heated air leaving the ducts spreads out to all parts of the room via the network of channels on the surface of the duct's covering grille. The heated air, by conduction, transfers its heat to all the objects in the room. (The heated objects then keep the room warm via radiation, as we discussed.) If you stand in the path of the heated air being blown out of a duct, you'll find that it's not a particularly effective way of getting warmed. That's because moving air feels cooler than air standing still.

- *Convection* is the movement of heated air. Warm air rises and cold air falls. That happens as a matter of course unless you overpower or block the air current. Years ago, almost every modest-sized farmhouse in the north was heated by a single woodburning stove, often set in the kitchen. In order to get heat into the upstairs bedrooms, the carpenter—generally the farmer himself—simply cut holes for grilles that would allow the kitchen's heated air to rise into the bedrooms. It got the job done—but boy, did it cut down on privacy.

Even modern homeowners have to take convection into account when they evaluate—or reevaluate—a heating system. Warm air naturally rises to the very top of high ceilings, where it doesn't do anybody much good. What's worse, the room's colder air falls down and accumulates near the floor where you are. You can keep recirculating the air if you have return air ducts where the hot air collects. Or you can lower your ceilings using, for example, suspended accoustical tile systems (see Chapter 12). Or you can install a fan, separate from the rest of your heating system, that overpowers the rising hot air—something like the paddle fans that kept Humphrey Bogart comfortable in so many of his movies. (You have to use a fan judiciously, however, since moving air makes people feel cooler. More about that later.)

Convection is the principle behind heating systems that use baseboard heaters. Typically, such heaters employ long pipes full of hot water or steam or long electric heating elements covered by small metal fins. Heat inside the heaters *conducts* to the fins, but the fins are spaced about ½ inch apart so that air between them can be heated (also by conduction). Then, however, the heated air rises—by *convection*—and is replaced by the cooler air that has fallen to the floor. Since free movement of air is necessary if such a system is to work well, people who own convection-powered heating systems must make certain that furniture and draperies do not block easy movement of air to and from their convecting baseboard units.

Big old-fashioned steam-heated radiators *radiate* heat into a room once they're heated to their normal operating temperature. But while they're heating up, and also while they're cooling down again, they are warm enough to also be quite effective convection heaters. So people with radiators ought to heed the same warning and keep their radiators uncovered by drapes and other insulators.

WHY AIR CONDITIONING AND HEAT-PUMP SYSTEMS WORK

The major principle behind today's central air conditioners was explained in the subsection on radiation—only now we'll turn it backwards because chilled air coming through your air conditioning ducts chills all the objects in your room—the walls, floors, lamps, tables, and such—to keep them from radiating heat. The cooler the objects become, the less heat they radiate, and the cooler you feel.

There's a secondary principle at work during the air conditioning time of year: moving air chills. When a breeze passes over your body it evaporates a bit of the perspiration that's there even when you're not noticeably wet, and that evaporation takes heat out of you. It's that evaporation-by-cooling bonus that makes air conditioner engineers attempt to keep your central air conditioner's blower on as much as possible.

Fans utilize the cooling effect of moving air. They're a low-cost alternative to air conditioning. Most summer days in Wisconsin, it's cool in the shade. When our home's temperature gets warmer than we like, we close windows on the hot, sunny side of the house, open windows on the shady side, and turn on a large fan installed in an upstairs window. That's generally enough to keep everybody comfortable. (An attic fan achieves the same goal.) When the day's a scorcher and even the shady air is uncomfortably hot, that's when we flick on the air conditioner's switch.

When you evaluate your air conditioning system, it is helpful to know how air conditioners cool air in the first place. Actually it's similar to how your refrigerator cools food. They both work on the principle that evaporating liquid absorbs heat from its surroundings. To boil away some water, you have to put it on the stove and supply heat. If you want to evaporate rubbing alcohol you've spilled on your hand, you need simply wave your hand a few times—but your hand will be left feeling very cool because the "boiling" alcohol has absorbed its heat.

In a central air conditioning system, a very anxious-to-evaporate (volatile) liquid called Freon is inside the centrally located coils. (The coils are placed inside the furnace's housing so that its blower can send air through them.) As the liquid Freon evaporates, it takes out heat from the air surrounding the coils and the very cold air is blown to all parts of your home. The hot Freon gas is sucked into a compressor. The compressor turns the Freon back into a liquid, and in doing so releases all the heat the gas picked up. (That's why the compressor is placed outdoors; the last thing you want in your home is the heat you've just paid to pull out.) A fan in the compressor unit blows away the heat. And the liquefied Freon flows back again into the cooling coils. (In room air conditioners, the compressor and cooling coils are contained in a single unit, the compressor in the outside half and the coils in the inside half.)

The *heat pump* is a new kind of heating-and-cooling system being installed in many new homes, sometimes as the only heat supply, other times as a supplemental source. It works exactly like an air conditioner, except that it uses a somewhat more sophisticated network of liquid, coils, and compressor. In hot months it is an air cooler; in cool months it works in reverse, taking heat from outside and transferring it to the coils inside the house. That may sound contradictory, but in reality even when the outside temperature is below zero, the volatile liquid in a heat pump can still absorb enough heat from the frigid air to transfer 70° warmth into your heat ducts.

The two big mail order houses, Sears and Wards, supply kits that enable do-it-yourselfers to install central air conditioning systems. There are four or five basic steps you have to take when you install one:

1. You have to open up the sheet metal—called the plenum—that links your furnace to its warm air ducts, so that you can insert the air conditioning coil. Then you have to close the plenum again. Alternately, you can buy a new plenum designed specifically to accommodate your air conditioner coil.
2. You have to run two copper tubes from your air conditioner coil to the exterior site you've chosen for the condensing unit. This involves making about a 3-inch hole in one wall, stuffing it with insulation, and waterproofing it.
3. In many parts of the country, local codes require the condenser unit to be placed on a small concrete slab. You can learn how to pour one yourself in Chapter 19. (Our code permitted us to put ours on the roof—a job for two strong men and a rented hoist. But now it's rarely noticed and its noise is high above ear level.)
4. You have to connect the condensing unit's motor to a 230-volt line. If you don't want to tackle that job, you can hire an electrician for just that part of your project.
5. You may have to install a new relay in your furnace and a new thermostat or air conditioner adapter on your thermostat. Nowadays many furnaces come with relays in them that are suited to air conditioning. If not, replacing yours is a simple task, and it's explained adequately in instructions that come with each device.

THERMOSTATS A thermostat measures the air temperature in whichever room it's located and, when the heat drops a degree or two below a pre-set level, it switches on the furnace. If the thermostat is set to control an air conditioner, it switches *that* on whenever the temperature rises a degree or two.

More elaborate thermostats also allow you to lower the house tem-

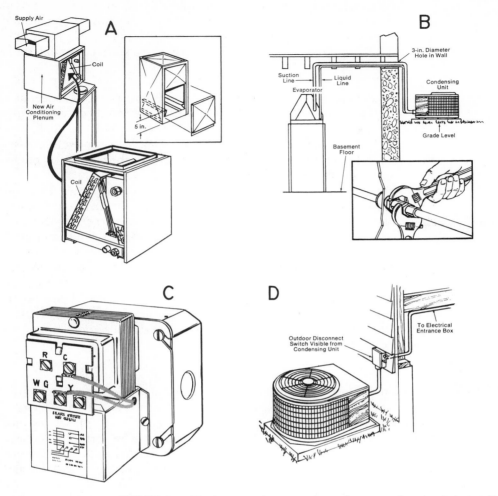

FIGURE 6-1 To show you how easy it can be to attach central air conditioning to your forced air furnace, here's a selection of diagrams from Sears's manual for do-it-yourselfers. (A) You can either cut a hole into your existing plenum (top right-hand box of this drawing) or replace the plenum with a new one made just for this job (the major part of this sketch). (B) Place the condensing unit outdoors and run the two copper lines through a hole in your house. The lines come with ready-to-connect fittings, as the small box in this drawing shows. (C) The new relay hooks up to your furnace by connecting color-coded wires to both the furnace's electrical system and your thermostat. (D) The electrical hook-up is simple if you're willing to install a new circuit breaker into your existing main. (Courtesy Sears, Roebuck and Co.)

perature automatically at night by way of a built-in clock. You can set a daytime temperature of 70° and a nighttime one of 60°. At a chosen time, let's say 11 PM, the thermostat will let the temperature drop to the lower setting; at another pre-selected hour, let's say 6 AM, it'll start bringing the heat back up to the higher setting. (You can get a combination thermostat that'll also work in reverse for air conditioning.)

Nearby illustrations show how simple the job of installing a new thermostat can be. Don't assume that you have to replace *all* of an older one, however. Check first with the company that supplies your particular brand. You may be able to buy and attach a new backing that updates it.

FILTERS

The filters on most older furnaces do not, as most people erroneously believe, strain out tiny particles from the air in order to keep your lungs and furniture dust-free. If your filters are only an inch or two thick, they were put there primarily to keep the *blower motor* clean, not your house. Nonetheless you ought to replace them regularly or the blower will not be able to draw air through them efficiently.

Modern filter systems *can* clean your room air of from 65 to 99 percent of its particulate material such as dust and pollen. Some of them employ large folds of filter paper. Others rely on electrically charged plates to trap dust and dirt that passes through the filters. The latter kind is accused by many medical people of putting ozone into your home's air system, and ozone has been implicated in a number of health problems.

Both kinds of air cleaning filters, filter-paper and electronic, are available for do-it-yourselfers to update their old systems. Their dimensions are usually bigger than the old motor-cleaning filters they're replacing, but the large mail order houses sell adapters that accomodate them to most cold air return ducts.

HUMIDIFIERS

Low humidity—dry air—can make people feel cool at otherwise comfortable temperatures. That's why air conditioners are designed to extract summertime moisture. But in many parts of the country, wintertime humidity inside homes gets so low there's actual discomfort. Fortunately, there are many humidifiers that do-it-yourselfers can install directly onto the furnace ductwork. That way, the humidity will be kept automatically at a pre-selected level.

Fancier models keep track of outside temperatures as well as inside air moisture, since the two have to be considered to arrive at a proper humidity setting. However, people who use humidifiers that don't monitor outside temperatures generally find that they have to adjust their controls only a few times during the year.

Nearby we've reprinted the simple steps required to install a typical humidifier kit into a typical furnace, so you can decide whether you'd like to take on the job. We put ours in last winter, and our working space—both inside and outside the furnace—was pretty tight. Still, the job went smoother than even we had expected it would.

FIGURE 6-2 A simple frame holds dozens of folds of soft filter paper that trap particles of dust filtered from the air inside your home. Shown here is an air filter made by one major supplier of improved filter systems. (Courtesy Research Products Corporation.)

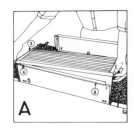

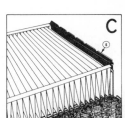

FIGURE 6-3 Here's how Sears explains what's involved in installing one of its electronic air filters in the existing cold air return plenum of your forced air furnace. It's just about that easy to do! (Courtesy Sears, Roebuck and Co.)

Measure your return air duct at the place of installation.

Cut the duct. Install the cell and power pack mounting plate.

Attach power pack. Slide in cell assembly and pre-filter.

Attach the cover and plug it in . . . That's all there is to it!

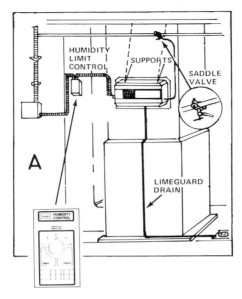

A

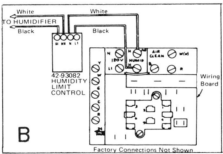

B

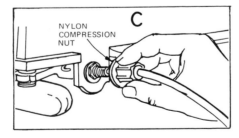

C

FIGURE 6-4 Here's a condensed view of how a typical humidifier can be installed in your furnace on a Saturday morning. By following a template supplied with the unit, you cut a small hole in the plenum above your furnace and mount the unit. On newer furnaces, to make the electrical connection, simply hook up two color-coded wires to the furnace relay and make a simple electrical hook-up to a house wiring box that's located nearby. Then you can tap the water supply into the closest water pipe without having to disconnect or turn off any pipes. (Courtesy Sears, Roebuck and Co.)

7

An Energy-Efficient Fireplace or Wood-Burning Stove

Fireplaces and woodburning stoves are fun. Everybody knows that. But few people know that an improperly installed fireplace or other wood-burner is a serious health and fire hazard. Installing one properly isn't difficult once you understand the rationale behind each of its components.

Even fewer people realize how energy-inefficient most fireplaces and woodburning stoves really are. Since there's an entire counterculture now of wood choppers, splitters, and burners, that's tough news. To help you folks, we've gathered together a great deal of factual information that homeowners ordinarily don't have access to. Some comes from engineering and wood use manuals that are normally available only at engineering laboratories and libraries. Much comes from a pioneering scientific investigation of fireplaces that was undertaken by Harrison Edwards, an outstanding inventor, while he was president of Norwich Laboratory Inc.

You may want to improve your home with a fireplace just for the fun of it, energy savings aside. If so, simply read our installation advice and go

FIGURE 7-1 Most fireplaces these days are made of metal at a distant factory. People often decorate them with brick to keep that old-fashioned look. (Courtesy Heatilator Fireplace.)

FIGURE 7-2 Glass fireplace doors keep this couple warm and their fuel bill from soaring. Any fireplace that burns inside air consumes 2 to 5 times more heat (from your furnace) than it produces. (Courtesy Heatilator Fireplace.)

ahead. But if you hope to burn wood to conserve other sources of energy, including money, pay close attention to the entire chapter.

THE THEORY OF WOOD FIRES IN FIREPLACES

When wood burns inside a completely efficient fireplace, a mere 10 to 20 percent of its heat is radiated directly into the room. The remaining 80 to 90 percent goes straight up the chimney in the hot gas and smoke that's given off by the combustion. And few ordinary fireplaces achieve even that optimum efficiency.

The hotter the fire, the more efficient it is. Metal grates that enclose a fire take heat away from it—especially those hollow grates that circulate cold air *into* the bottom openings of the grate tubes and draw out heated air from the top openings. These new devices actually create less efficient fires than used to take place in old-fashioned unadorned fireplaces.

It's true that old-fashioned fireplaces, constructed of brick and then lined with firebrick, initially draw a lot of heat from the fire as they warm themselves up. But once they reach their maximum temperature, they actually enhance fire efficiency by keeping temperatures as high as possible right near the burning wood. Additionally, the firebrick sides of such fireplaces radiate a lot of heat back to the fire. Some of it helps to keep the fire as hot as possible; some of it radiates past the fire into the room to warm its occupants.

Nowadays, instead of installing brick fireplaces, many people choose less expensive and quicker-to-install prefab metal models. In order to get the most efficient fire possible inside a wall-mounted steel fireplace, you'd better choose the largest one you can comfortably manage. Unless a metal fireplace is specially designed, heat that's absorbed by its sides goes right on outside the house. The larger the fireplace, the further removed its absorbing rear is from the fire. A small firebox robs your fire of heat in much the same way that a hollow tubular grate network sucks heat from it.

There's another reason that the hottest fire is the most efficient fire, in addition to the fact that you're tapping its maximum energy. Cold-burning fires don't burn the wood cleanly. Wood fires send large amounts of tar and creosote up your chimney. The force of a really hot fire pushes the contaminants right on through, but a cool fire lets them build up *inside* your chimney. Eventually the creosote can flame up, resulting in a chimney fire—a terrifying experience. (We'll talk more about chimney safety later in this chapter.)

Since radiant heat is one of the steadiest and most dependable sources of warmth from burning wood, any fireplace you choose should have the largest possible height and width dimensions for its firebox opening. That will help you obtain as much heat as possible from that 10 to 20 percent of radiated energy that *doesn't* go up the chimney.

But you needn't write off as a total loss all the remaining 80 to 90 percent of heat that's contained in the smoke and hot gases. That's true only if your fireplace has the classic hole in its top that leads directly up the chimney. Nowadays, many factory-built fireplaces incorporate baffles that force the rising gases and smoke to pass through heat-absorbing mazes on the way to the chimney. Room air is then passed through heat exchangers to draw off as much of that trapped heat as possible. Frankly, none of these devices captures anywhere near the full amount of heat that escapes up most chimneys. But you do retrieve enough heat to pay for their added cost.

In considering heat exchange systems, keep in mind fire hazards as well as energy savings. Every time you cool down the products of your fire's combustion, you risk condensing out that dangerous creosote and the other flammables. If the heat exchanger is right inside the firebox, then the flammables can be burned up right there where, by design, any fire is safe. When the heat exchangers attach to chimneys—as several add-on systems do—the condensed-out creosote can accumulate in either the chimney or the heat exchanger where, eventually, it may catch fire and cause possible damage.

So far we've only talked about getting heat *out* of a fireplace. An important consideration, in evaluating any fireplace or woodburning stove, is the fact that the air burned in its fire can be *robbing* your home of heat faster than the fire replaces it. This is especially true if your wood-burner is an auxiliary heat source, simply taking some of the load off your primary furnace. When an ordinary fireplace, one that has no doors, is in use it is pulling in *heated* air to use for combustion. Worse, it is pulling additional heated air straight up the chimney, sucked along in the fire's draft. The net result is substantial heat loss. Estimates conclude that an open fire wastes two to five times more heat than it produces.

There's another sobering statistic about what a fireplace can do to a heat bill. Even when it's *not* in use, the ordinary heat loss is equal to the heat you'd lose if you lived with a wall that's got, knocked into it, an open hole *double* the size of your chimney's opening—unless you've got a chimney damper that closes absolutely airtight.

The answer to this heat loss is to enclose the front of your fireplace. Stoves have doors that do the trick; now there are plenty of glass fireplace screens on the market, and most of them can do an efficient job of keeping room air from entering the fireplace. If you love the sound of a crackling fire, you're going to have to choose between that pleasure and energy savings. Our solution has been to open the glass once in a while and indulge our senses in measured quantities.

A glass barrier, however, is only a partial answer to heat loss, since fires need to burn air from somewhere. Ordinary glass fireplace screens incorporate dampers that permit small amounts of already-heated room air to sift through. *If* you remember to close off both that damper and the chimney damper whenever the fireplace is not in use, you've stopped most up-the-chimney heat loss.

When you've got a fire roaring, though, you're still suffering a net *loss* of heat. Just one more modification will transform that loss into an energy gain for your home heating system: a mechanism that permits you to pipe air in from the chilly outdoors and burn *that* air, instead of your heated home air, inside your glass-screened fireplace or door-equipped woodburning stove. Since you haven't already paid once to heat Mother Nature's sub-zero air, when your oak logs burn it up you'll experience your first genuine gain in heat energy. Some pre-fab fireplaces and woodburning stoves offer accessory kits that connect the fireboxes to outside air, and the instructions that come with them are easy to follow.

Let's sum up all the hints we've scattered through the last few pages.

- Most heat from a fire comes through radiant energy; therefore the maximum firebox opening allows the maximum heat radiation.
- Heat exchangers placed inside the firebox region will safely squeeze out additional heat from the fire's hot gases and smoke.

FIGURE 7-3 This cutaway view shows an energy-efficient type of factory-built fireplace. It burns outside air, not already heated air. Baffles capture as much heat as possible from the hot gasses created by the fire and pass that heat into the room. (Note: due to design, this fireplace can safely draw outside air from *above* it. Not all fireplaces can. Before you draw air from *above* your fireplace, be sure your owner's manual recommends it.) (Courtesy Heatilator Fireplace.)

- To make an energy-efficient system, you must stop room air from entering the fireplace or woodburning stove.
- For energy efficiency, you must burn outside air instead of heated room air.
- For greater savings, you must be able to close both the outside air damper and the chimney damper when your fireplace or woodburning stove is not in use.

CHIMNEYS ARE NOT JUST FOR SANTA CLAUS

Grandpa knew the value of a good chimney for his woodburning stove, but Junior doesn't seem to. During one recent, especially cold winter, people in and around Madison, Wisconsin, stuck in such quickly erected fireplaces and wood-burning stoves that there were more than double the normal number of fire department calls for chimney and fireplace accidents, two deaths-by-asphyxiation due to faulty chimney installation, and several close brushes with death.

But that destruction was all needless. Several manufacturers make perfectly safe, reasonably priced, easy-to-install chimney kits. They even come with easy-to-follow installation instructions. The trick is to go to a reputable dealer and to take along all of the necessary information she'll need to help you pick out the right chimney type, size, and hardware; to follow all instructions and measurements fastidiously; to ask questions if

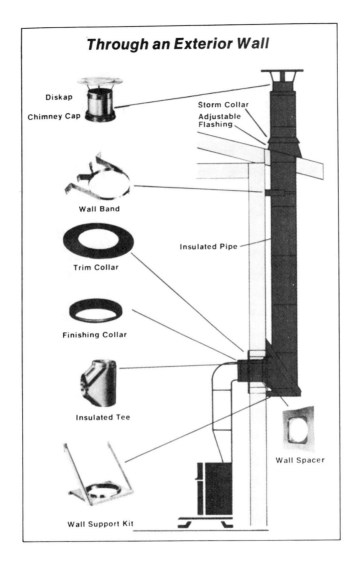

Through an Exterior Wall

Diskap
Chimney Cap

Wall Band

Trim Collar

Finishing Collar

Insulated Tee

Wall Support Kit

Storm Collar
Adjustable Flashing

Insulated Pipe

Wall Spacer

FIGURE 7-4 These are sketches from a brochure showing *typical* chimney installations. Your requirements may vary. Ask your local building code authorities and reputable suppliers of chimney materials for help in figuring out exactly what type of chimney materials to use for your wood burner. The ABCs of good chimney installation are: (A) Adequate support; (B) Proper clearance; (C) Sturdy roof assembly. And once it's installed, keep it clean. (Courtesy Metalbestos Systems by Wallace Murray.)

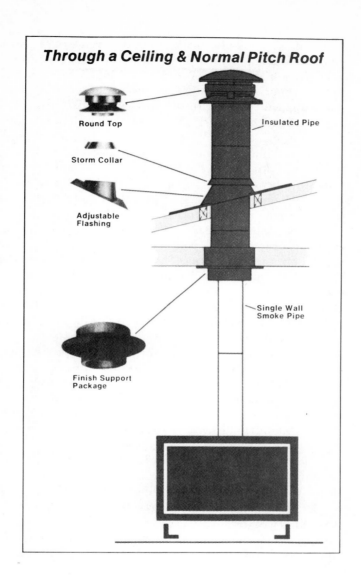

Through a Ceiling & Normal Pitch Roof

Round Top

Storm Collar

Adjustable Flashing

Finish Support Package

Insulated Pipe

Single Wall Smoke Pipe

you're in doubt about anything; and to relax once you know that your chimney is adequate for the woodburner you plan to stoke.

To help you plan your trip to a chimney supplier, we've reproduced nearby some sketches showing the variety of ways you can connect a prefabricated chimney to your stove or fireplace. Major elements generally come in lengths of 18, 24, or 30 inches depending on the manufacturer. Fittings are available to help you run the chimney through just about any kind of ceiling or roof, and even through a wall and then upwards. Your factory-built fireplace will probably come with instructions for the size of opening your chimney must have. For informal guidance on that, Figure 7-5 shows the figures that are supplied by one metal-chimney manufacturer.

Unless your factory-built chimney comes with instructions to the contrary, or includes a secure system for interlocking all its parts, secure the various elements together with sheetmetal screws. Drill four evenly spaced holes around each joint and into each hole screw a ½-inch-long sheet metal screw. This provides protection in case you ever do have a chimney fire; at such a time, the heat and turbulence inside a chimney can cause so much vibration, the pipes could shake loose from one another unless they've been securely screwed together.

Do make sure to follow *all* the manufacturer's recommendations for how far from combustibles the chimney must be located. Assuming it's listed with Underwriters Laboratory, local building code enforcers accept its recommendations. (If it's *not* UL approved, use your building code regulations as your guide, not the manufacturer's.) If you've never operated a woodburning stove or fireplace that's connected to a metal chimney, you have *no* idea how hot the pipes can get.

The manufacturer of your fireplace or stove and the manufacturer of your chimney parts will probably both advise you to keep the chimney clean. We'll add our own warning to theirs. Invest in the brushes that scour soot and creosote from inside the chimney flue and *use* them once a year; otherwise, be sure to use the annual services of a top-hatted chimney sweep. Don't scrimp on this important clean-up if you hope to sit back and enjoy your woodsy fire in the security that you and your home are totally safe as well as cozily warm.

WHAT SHOULD YOU BURN?

There's a lot of folklore about what kinds of tree make the best fireplace logs. Let's puncture a bit of that lore. We asked three well-respected, degree-laden wood scientists to tell us what are the best fireplace logs. Their independent responses: whatever somebody else has cut down and split for you. Beyond that, the consensus is that the *species* of wood you burn is less important than *how dry* the wood is. Dollar for dollar, they explain, woods all give approximately the same number of BTUs when burned.

A ton of pine logs does provide about 10 percent more BTUs than a ton of oak, but since oak is denser than pine, a cord of oak logs gives close

FIGURE 7-5 Guide to wood-burning capacity of a fireplace or stove. Based on Underwriters Laboratory tests.

CHIMNEY DIAMETER (in inches)	BTU/HR OF HEAT	LBS/HR OF WOOD
6	97,000	12.1
7	131,600	16.5
8	172,400	21.6
9	218,000	27.3
10	270,000	33.8

to double the number of BTUs than a cord of pine. Since oak (as well as similar hardwoods) is more expensive and tougher to cut and split than pine, and oak logs are heavier to toss around, it costs more to buy. On the other hand, as we pointed out, each oak log burns almost twice as long as pine of comparable size, so the choice is usually a toss-up.

Figure 7-6 compares the relative heating capacities of various wood species. But notice, in that chart, how much more effective well-dried wood is compared to green logs. A pound of properly air-dried oak provides almost 5600 BTUs, whereas a pound of green oak gives barely 4000 BTUs.

Wood that's been stored indoors, such as in a heated garage, may have only 8 percent water content. Wood that's been stored under cover outdoors for at least 6 months may contain 12 to 15 percent water. Green wood can contain as much as 30 percent water.

The water in green firewood produces several contradictory problems. On the one hand, the fire has to be hotter than normal in order to dry out the green logs so they'll burn. On the other hand, their moisture chills the fire noticeably, so it's tough to get them fired up to the high temperature you need.

In buying wood, then, pay at least as much attention to how green it is as to its species. If you're planning to burn it right away, look for wood that has been cut six months to a year ago and then stored well enough to have lost at least half its original moisture. You can get a very rough gauge of a wood's dryness by checking its weight per cord against the figures in the nearby table.

A *cord* of wood, in case you're not familiar with the term, is a specific unit of measure. It's defined as a stack of wood 8 feet long, 4 feet high, and 4 feet wide; that results in 128 cubic feet of wood. Since logs for fireplaces

FIGURE 7-6 Heating properties of wood. Based on data in Kents Mechanical Engineer Handbook, 12th Edition, Wiley Handbook Series.

SPECIES	HEATING VALUE (BTUs/lb) Air Dried	Green	WEIGHT/CORD (lbs) Air Dried	Green	HEATING VALUE (BTUs/cord) Air Dried
Oak, white	5,558	3,972	4,300	5,600	23,899,400
Elm, white	5,710	3,591	3,100	4,400	17,701,000
Beech	5,359	3,940	3,900	5,000	20,900,100
Birch, yellow	5,225	3,804	4,000	5,100	20,900,000
Pine	5,864	4,226	2,200	3,300	12,900,800

and woodburning stoves are seldom cut in 4-foot lengths, the unit called *face cord* has developed.

A face cord is defined as a stack of wood 8 feet long and 4 feet high. The width is not considered, nor is the overall number of cubic feet. If you're comparing prices on face cords of firewood, ask what size logs are involved. A face cord of 1-foot logs obviously provides only half as much heat as a face cord of 2-foot logs of the same wood.

Another point to consider is that logs of small diameter provide more overall wood in a cord than logs of huge diameter; in the latter you're paying for a lot of air space between logs. Likewise, straight logs yield more wood per cord than crooked ones—for the same reason.

There's just one figure we can't provide you with: how many BTUs it takes to warm your heart when you see those birch or oak or pine logs flickering on your hearth.

8
How to Wire Like a Pro

If you can use a screwdriver and pliers, you're skilled enough to tackle most home rewiring and electrical updating projects. What's probably kept you from all those jobs you'd like to get at is, first of all, fear of electricity and, second of all, unfamiliarity with the hardware and specialized gadgets that make electrical jobs so easy for the pros.

To counter the first, we'll familiarize you with the simple rules that not only govern installations that must meet electrical code approval, but that also make wiring practically foolproof. To eliminate the second, we'll name and picture for you all the items that are useful in most home wiring projects. Armed with our information, you should be able to wire as easily and as well as the pros.

Buying all the electrical supplies you'll need isn't as hard as you'd think. Both Sears and Montgomery Ward stock a great many of these items in their mail order catalogs (but not in their retail stores). Local hardware stores may have added to their stock since you last looked, because General Electric and other manufacturers are now pushing them to put up displays of wiring equipment for do-it-yourselfers. If those sources fail you, look for a supplier in your Yellow Pages under *Electrical Equipment and Supplies—Wholesale.* If you have the proper trade name for what you want, its appropriate dimensions, and money to pay for it, they'll usually take care of you.

The rest is easy: Mount the equipment securely. Turn off the circuit breaker or unscrew the fuse. Connect the color-coded wires to the color-coded connecting screws: just remember *white* wire to *white* screw, *green* wire (the bare one) to *green* screw. Stick on the decorative plate that covers up most wired gadgets. Then flick the circuit breaker back on. If you *have* done something drastically wrong, the breaker will trip instantly with no damage to anything but maybe your patience, and you can try again.

So you see, once you've read this chapter, there should be no reason at all to put off your do-it-yourself wiring projects.

THEORY OF HOME WIRING

Unless your home had its last wiring job back before World War II, or you live in a rural area, your house more than likely has three wires running into it from the power company's pole or underground cable. You can probably tell at once whether you are served by two or three wires if you'll take a look near your outside electric meter or at the spot where the wires from the pole enter your house. (First look on your meter. It often says "three wire" or "two wire" in the written description inside the glass cover.) If you see three insulated wires entering the meter or your house, then you most likely have the modern three-wire system. But if you count only two wires, you may have the older system.

Sometimes the electrical wires are loosely wrapped around a steel cable that provides support—usually when the wires have to span a long distance; don't count that shiny, silver-colored support cable as an electrical wire. Your wiring system is also grounded, generally by a bare copper wire about as thick as a ballpoint pen; don't add this grounding wire to your tally either. Often such a ground wire runs directly from your electric meter to a nearby water pipe or to a pipe driven into the ground.

If your connection to the power company is underground, your cables probably run to the meter in an enclosed conduit. In that case, you probably won't be able to add up your service wires so easily. A phone call to your electric company may tell what you need to know.

For some homes, the major difference between a two-wire hook-up and a three-wire one is whether you can get the 230 volts needed to run heavy appliances such as electric stoves, dryers, furnaces, and such. But for some that have two-wire service, it may mean that the electrical wiring lacks a separate ground connection at each and every installation throughout the house. The individual ground is a very important modern safety feature and a must for every home improver to add to her list. So if you discover that you've got a two-wire meter, we suggest you consult a local agency—*before* you attempt any other improvements suggested in this chapter—and find out both what your local electrical code requires, and also whether or not you should take our advice (or that in any other book) when it comes to grounding connections. At the same time, find out the cost of having your home updated. Agencies that can help include: building inspection department, power company, a local *licensed* electrician.

In the three-wire system, two wires are *hot*—they each bring 115 volts of electricity into your home. The third wire, often color-coded white or yellow, is a neutral connection that returns unused power to the main line and helps balance your own system. However, even the neutral carries sufficient power to hurt you, so treat it with the respect (not fear) due hot wires. In a two-wire system, one is hot (115 volts) and one neutral. The way most two-wire systems are set up, you can't get the 230 volts that run heavy-power users. That's how simple your basic wiring is.

In both systems, the power company's supply lines lead directly or indirectly to your own fuse box or circuit breaker box and through a main shutoff switch. Then, via the protective fuses or circuit breakers, the power gets divided up and smaller-sized branch circuits run it to all the parts of your house. You can find out which fuse or breaker goes with which room's line by simply unscrewing the fuse or switching off the breaker. (Often, the outlets of a room are divided between two lines so that even if one breaker blows, some parts of the room will have power.)

Even if a three-wire system brings power into the house, most of your branch circuits use one hot lead and one neutral, providing you with 115 volts at your lights, outlets, and such. Heavy-power users that require 230 volts are connected to *both* hot wires plus the neutral.

(Some people get confused at what seems to be a disparity of numbers for voltages. There are two or three generating systems in use throughout the United States, and each system results in its own peculiar voltages. In one, the low voltage is 110 volts and the high 220 volts. In another, the low is 115 and the high 230. In yet another, the low is 120 but the high is 208 volts. For most purposes, these differences between 110, 115, and 120 volts, or between 208, 220, and 230 are of little consequence. In some major appliances, such as electric ranges, the difference can be important enough that manufacturers specify the proper voltage for their particular products; even then, many makers provide separate wiring connections to accommodate 208, 220, or 230 volts. Though we use 115 and 230 for convenience throughout the book, if your local wiring is one of the others the information applies to you nonetheless.)

The wiring inside your home is coded to make work simple. In a 115-volt two-wire branch circuit, neutral is *always* white and the hot wire is *always* black. In a 230-volt three-wire hookup, you'll either find two black wires and one white one, or black and red for the two hot leads along with the white neutral. Grounding wires are always green or uninsulated. To help you along, we'll provide nine simple rules.

• Rule 1: Always connect white wire to white, black to black. In a three-wire set-up, connect the red to red or, if there is no other red, to a separate black lead. Make sure you don't hook two wires on the same cable or one another even indirectly; that'll cause a short. (If you make the mistake you'll know it because the fuse or breaker will blow the instant you try to turn it back on.)

• Rule 2: Always connect white wires to silver-colored terminals and black wires to brass-colored terminals. (Mnemonic device: white to white.) To keep wiring simple, manufacturers of all the switches, outlets, appliances, and other gadgets that you're likely to wire have standardized the wiring hardware so electricians and do-it-yourselfers can't help but install the proper wires to the proper parts of their equipment.

• Rule 3: Always connect ground to green. (Mnemonic device: gr to gr.) To insure that installations are always properly grounded, manufacturers have standardized on green as the color for the grounding connections. Although the ground wire inside the cable you're likely to use for rewiring or updating the wiring inside your house is probably bare (and it'll be the *only* bare wire), ground wires in appliances and grounding screws in all sorts of electrical gadgets are colored green.

• Rule 4: If you encounter aluminum wires (silvery instead of copper-colored), be sure everything you connect them to is marked: "AL-CU" or "CO-ALR." In using aluminum wire, apply to every connection an oxide inhibitor that's designed for aluminum wiring—*before* you hook it up.

Many older homes, mobile homes in particular, use aluminum wire instead of copper. Even today, the main wires coming into your home from the power company's pole may be made of lighter weight, less expensive aluminum. Aluminum wires require special appliance connections, or corrosion can cause serious fire hazards. To let electricians and others know if any particular electrical equipment has been designed to accommodate aluminum wires, manufacturers mark the approved ones "AL-CU" or "CO-ALR." Most modern electrical connectors are rated to handle aluminum. So if you have doubts about an older one, and your house is aluminum wired, your safest alternative is to replace the questionable one if it's modestly priced. If it's expensive, seek counsel from your power company, building department, or a licensed electrician—*now*.

• Rule 5: Make all electrical connections inside metal or approved plastic boxes. Every electrical connection (except a low-voltage application like a doorbell) has to be enclosed within a metal box. This is part of the electrical code's fail-safe system. When you use proper materials and wire everything properly, nothing should go wrong. But in case it does, it goes wrong inside the metal box where it causes a minimum of damage. We'll show you typical boxes in a later section. Many companies are making electrical boxes out of plastic these days, and they are approved for most uses and in most parts of the country. But we've found that inexperienced people have more problems with plastic boxes than metal ones; unless you're undertaking a very large project where cost is a major factor, stick to metal.

• Rule 6: Don't overcrowd electrical boxes. The electrical code is so thorough, it even specifies how many connections are safe for the electrical boxes of various sizes. We've summed up these limitations for the most popular boxes in Figure 8-7.

In tackling rewiring jobs, you'll often encounter a box that's filled to its maximum rated capacity. Fortunately that doesn't mean you have to stop. You can add a box extender, which we'll explain more thoroughly later. We'll also show you how to use the electrical code's method to tally the number of connections you've got.

• Rule 7: Be sure the cable you buy is rated for the proper application. Not only do the connections between wires, or between wires and appliances, have to be kept inside approved enclosures, but the wires themselves have to be covered with approved insulation. Professional electricians, who have lots of skill and the right tools, often snake simple wires through metal or plastic conduits that make very effective insulators. But it's quite a chore for most do-it-yourselfers to tackle. In fact, many electricians avoid it these days, too, because several pre-insulated cables are now available. (*Cable,* incidentally, is a term used in the industry—and we'll use it here, too—that refers to the collection of two or more individually insulated wires all inside a further insulating sheath.) We'll discuss the various cables in a later section. Some are rated for use only indoors, others for outside applications or for burial in the ground.

• Rule 8: Make your connections as tight as possible. Once you've chosen all of the right materials, your fittings should mate well. The right wire should slip easily into the right terminal of an electrical outlet, that outlet should slip neatly into the metal outlet box of the proper size, and the cover plate should fit over all of *that* without shoving and prodding. But if you haven't made tight connections between wires or between wires and terminals, then all of the electrical industry's well-laid plans have been for nought. Your wiring won't work well (or at all), and it won't be as safe as it should be. Figure 8-1 shows some tips for making connections that are as foolproof as possible.

• Rule 9: Don't improvise. Use approved materials for approved purposes so your job will proceed smoothly and safely. It doesn't pay to try to get around the standardized requirements and manufacturing details of the electrical industry. Over the years the National Electrical Code and related regulations have served to make all the equipment and hardware from the various manufacturers compatible with each other, in order to make electrical installations of all sorts as safe as possible. If you find that you can't make a particular outlet fit into a particular metal box, the two probably were not intended to work together. Don't improvise. Find a box that's compatible with your outlet. And be sure that all of your major hardware and cable bear the Underwriters Laboratory (UL) approval mark.

If you run into a snag, ask for guidance from someone knowledgeable in code-approved electrical work. Building departments in most cities and counties are helpful; many hardware and building supply outlets have staff members who can offer assistance; electric power com-

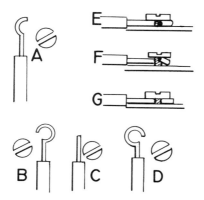

FIGURE 8-1 There are only two correctly installed connections here, one side view and one top view. You'd better know how to find them before tackling home wiring jobs. Which are the 2? Hints: In (A) through D), the poor connections either are not curled the proper ⅔ to ¾ distance around the screw, or are curled in the wrong direction. In the end views you can see that one wire is not curled far enough and the other is twisted so that the screw cannot grab onto the maximum surface of the wire. The proper connections are shown in (D) and (E). In (D), the wire curls about ¾ around the screw, leaving just enough space to slip the loop over the screw's shank. It's curled tightly enough to fit almost entirely under the screw's head. As you can see in (E), the curl is flat and allows maximum contact with the screw head. The curl is clockwise so that when you tighten the screw (clockwise), you also tighten the wire's curl.

panies often accommodate consumer inquiries. If you can't fix your problem any other way, please do not hesitate to call on a licensed electrician. Their hourly rates may seem steep, but they get a lot done in one hour. And whatever it might cost, it's far cheaper than jeopardizing your family and your house by trying to invent your own electrical technology.

TOOLS TO MAKE EASY WORK OF ELECTRICAL JOBS

Most wiring jobs involve a fairly standard regimen:

1. Locate the chosen position for your new gadget.
2. Run wire from an existing source of power to the new location, using approved cable.
3. Install a metal box to enclose the connections.
4. Strip away about 6 inches of outer insulation from the cable.
5. Strip away the proper amount of insulation from each individual wire—this can be ½–¾ inch to attach to a screw terminal, or 1–1½ inches for intertwining with other wires.
6. Bend the wire's end to fit neatly under the screw terminal, or twist together the wires to be intertwined.
7. Fit an insulated wire connector on your intertwined wires, or tighten the screw terminal.

You can cut insulation with a knife, intertwine wires with a pliers, trim wires to size with a side-cutting pliers or a wire-cutter, loop wire ends with a pliers, and tighten screws with a screwdriver. You probably already own all these tools. However, if you're undertaking a lot of wiring, you might want to invest in one or more of the tools designed specifically to make wiring jobs go quickly and easily.

STRIPPERS

On small jobs, a large side-cutter pliers can snip wires to size, a small sharp knife can strip away insulation, and small pliers can bend wires to fit screw connectors. But on lengthy projects the three-tool cutting, stripping, and bending process seems to take forever and, as the job stretches on, more and more wires get damaged. That's dangerous if they have to carry close to their full capacity. Do-it-yourselfers can overcome the cut-strip-and-bend blues with one of the following inexpensive tools.

The Romex stripper and ripper is many times more valuable than its one-dollar price might lead you to believe. With the ripper's sharpened tooth, you rip open the plastic that covers your Romex cable. Next you insert the end of each wire in turn into the stripper's hole. Twist, pull, and the insulation is stripped away faster than it takes to write about it.

For a slightly larger investment, you can buy one of the many pliers-shaped electrician's tools. The best of them perform all the cores essential to wiring: cutting, stripping, crimping, and forming the wire loop that fits snugly around connector screws.

CIRCUIT TESTERS

Even if you're pretty sure you've shut off the correct circuit breaker, it's reassuring to have visual proof that the juice is off before you reach into an outlet box. For a dollar or two you can buy a neon circuit tester that tells you "all clear." The tester is also helpful when you're troubleshooting balky circuits.

FIGURE 8-2 All models of Romex strippers are designed to rip the outer plastic insulation from the cable most commonly used in home wiring jobs. Some models then strip the ends of insulation off the electrical wires, as shown, and many also help you put a proper curl to the wire end. (Courtesy Holub Industries.)

FIGURE 8-3 For larger wiring jobs (or for lazier do-it-yourselfers), you can invest in an electricians' tool that does darned near everything from stripping to measuring the size of wires and hardware. (Courtesy Holub Industries.)

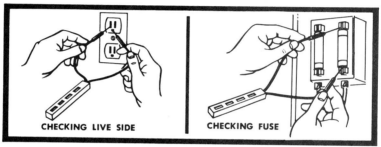

CHECKING LIVE SIDE   CHECKING FUSE

FIGURE 8-4 A simple neon tester is worth its weight in copper. On the left, it's being used to analyze a recently installed outlet. The light *should* glow: (1) when one terminal is in the hot (small) slot and the other terminal is in the neutral (larger) slot; (2) when one terminal is in the hot slot and the other is in the grounding (round, third) slot. The light *should not* glow when one terminal is in the neutral slot and the other in the grounding slot. In the right-hand view, the circuit tester is troubleshooting a fusebox: the light will glow if the fuse is *blown*. (The light itself will make the connection across the blow-out fuse; if the fuse were OK, the current would be flowing through the low-resistance fuse wire and would not flow through the high-resistance neon light inside the circuit tester.) (Courtesy Holub Industries.)

After you've wired a new outlet, you can plug in a circuit analyzer. With its battery of tiny lights, it reports whether all the connections have been properly made, whether polarity is okay (connect positive wires—the black ones—to positive; connect negative wires—the white ones—to negative), and whether the gound connection really is grounded properly. Such a test is especially valuable in older houses where ground connections may have deteriorated or wires may have gotten turned around, and in newly wired outlets that are to serve TVs and other small appliances that have the new polarized plugs. (Without this device, you can run the same tests by following the caption to Figure 8-4.)

THE RIGHT MATERIAL FOR SAFE AND CERTAIN ELECTRICAL JOBS

Wiring electrical circuits is a lot like playing with Lincoln Logs or Legos, those popular children's building toys. If you choose the proper materials, they fit together like greased lightning. For example, if you're installing a switch or outlet, you have to select a box that's designed with its screw-holes in the proper place to accept the two mounting screws that are on the switch or outlet. A hanging lamp calls for different configurations of electrical box and fittings that match lamp-hanging hardware. Most well-stocked building suppliers and home improvement suppliers have ample stock to meet every popular electrical job's requirement.

CABLE

Cable, as we said, is the wrapped-up package of wires that runs from your fuse or circuit breaker to your electrical outlet or fixture. The modern cable choice of home improvers is called Romex cable. Typically, it consists of two or three insulated wires and an uninsulated ground wire inside a loose-fitting plastic sheath. (Usually, your choice of two-wire or three-wire depends on whether you're running a 115-volt or 230-volt line.)

If a fuse or circuit breaker is rated at 20 amps on a 115-volt circuit, all the wires in that circuit should be #12 in size. If the circuit has a 15-amp fuse or breaker, the wire can be the smaller size, #14. Approved house wires have the size marked on the cable's outer wrappings. For example, the marking 12/2 means that the wires are #12 in size and that there are two of them *plus* an additional ground wire of the same size; 12/3 means that there are three wires, each #12 in size. With 12/3 (and 14/3) there is not always a separate grounding wire.

Ordinary Romex cable (called in the trade *Type NM*) is suited for interior use in dry locations. For wet places or for outside use and burial, Type UF Romex is required.

Romex cable has to be protected from careless carpenters who might drive nails through it. Therefore, most codes require that whenever Romex cable passes through a stud or other wooden structural member,

FIGURE 8-5 This steel plate is designed for protecting your Romex cable from carpenters who might happen along and not realize there are hot wires in the path of his nails. Electrical and building supply centers stock them. Use 'em. (Courtesy United Steel Products Company.)

you must either protect it with at least 2 inches of wood on both wall-facing sides of it (which you can do in a 6-inch wide board but not in the 3½ inches of wood found in a common 2 × 4), or else shield it with a metal plate. Building suppliers stock metal plates that are designed specifically for protecting Romex cable. Since they have built-in prongs, you don't even have to use nails to put them up. (See Figure 8-5.)

If you're working underground, most codes require that you bury your UF Type Romex just one foot beneath ground level and then cover it with stones, steel, wood, or something to keep errant shovels from tearing into it. We live in Wisconsin, where the ground heaves every spring thaw and winter frost. Concerned that the protective covering could shift one way while the cable shifted another, last time we buried UF Romex we dug down three feet—but then, we used slave labor: a 16-year-old son.

Older building codes required the steel-sheathed cable known as *BX cable*. You're likely to find some of it in your walls. You probably will not choose BX cable for your own jobs, but there are a couple of features to bear in mind if you encounter it.

1. To cut BX, carefully hacksaw away the metal sheath so as not to slice into the wires incased in the steel.
2. Before hooking up cut BX cable, you must insert a red fiber bushing between the steel and the wires to keep the metal from gradually wearing through insulation. Dealers who stock BX cable also stock the bushings.
3. The cable clamp at your metal box must be made for BX cable. Usually it has a *single* screw that you tighten directly against the steel exterior. Using other kinds of cable clamp for BX seldom works well. Using BX clamps for other kinds of cable is also dangerous. (Romex clamps usually use two screws to tighten a flat steel clamp against the cable.)
4. In older wiring installations, the steel sheathing material acted as the ground. If you remove BX and then reinstall it, be certain that you maintain a good electrical connection between the sheathing and the metal box, as well as between the metal box and any new switches or outlets you install. (The metal screw that holds your new switch or outlet onto the box can serve as that connection. However, a more dependable method has been developed; most electrical suppliers stock grounding leads, green wires connected to green-colored screws. Fasten the screw end into a convenient screwhole in the metal box, and fasten the bared wire end to the green grounding screw of your new switch or outlet.

UTILITY BOXES

Utility boxes (also called junction boxes) are those metal (or plastic) boxes behind your walls that enclose and protect all your cables' black, white, and ground leads that are hooked up to your switches, outlets, lighting fixtures, and similar appliances. They come in dozens of different sizes and shapes. In the illustration, we've sketched what the major utility boxes look like, showing their approximate dimensions and how many connections the national electrical code permits inside each of them.

In Figure 8-8, we've illustrated some of the major ways to fasten utility boxes into place. For new construction, you have more options than for remodeling: you can nail them directly to 2 × 4s, on braces between 2 × 4s, or almost anywhere else where you can screw a brace or nail the

FIGURE 8-6 These are some of the most widely used utility boxes for home wiring jobs. All of these boxes come in varying depths; Figure 8-7 guides you in choosing the proper depth. They also require varying methods for fastening into place; some common ways are shown here.

FIGURE 8-7 Capacity of standard-sized electric utility boxes. Boxes for wiring purposes are rated by the National Electrical Code for the maximum number of wires and devices they can safely accommodate. The larger the cubic inch size of the box, the more it can hold. It's safer to use a larger box than the code requires, and it's practical as well since you'll have room for later additions. To use a smaller box than required is not only unsafe, it's hard work to squeeze excess wires and devices into a tiny working space.

To use this chart: (1) Count the number of hot and neutral wires entering or leaving the box. (2) Add 1 for the grounding wire. (3) Add 1 if you prefer cable clamps built into the box you will work with. External clamps do not have to be added in. (4) Add 1 if you are going to connect a lamp or other device directly to the box. (5) For lamp installations, if a threaded rod or similar support takes up space inside the box, add 1 (unless you already added 1 for built-in clamps in #3 above; if so, disregard this step).

BOX TYPE AND DIMENSIONS (in approx. inches)	APPROX. CUBIC INCH CAPACITY	MAXIMUM NUMBER OF CONDUCTORS (plus counted hardware)	
		No. 14 wire	No. 12 wire
Octagon			
3¼ (1½ deep)	11	5	4
3½ (1½ deep)	12	5	5
4 (1½ deep)	17	8	7
4 (2 deep)	24	11	10
Square			
4 (1½ deep)	23	11	10
4 (2 deep)	32	15	14
4¹¹/₁₆ (1½ deep)	32	16	14
4¹¹/₁₆ (2 deep)	46	23	20
Switch box			
3 × 2 × 1½	8	3	3
3 × 2 × 2	11	5	4
3 × 2 × 2¼	11	5	5
3 × 2 × 2½	13	6	5
3 × 2 × 2¾	15	7	6
3 × 2 × 3½	18	9	8
4 × 2⅛ × 1½	11	5	4
4 × 2⅛ × 1⅞	14	6	6
4 × 2⅛ × 2⅛	16	7	6

box-with-built-in-bracket. If you're working on existing walls, you have to fit the box to existing conditions. To meet that challenge, many manufacturers have finally come out with a selection of boxes that have built-in anchor screws that securely grab the sides of plaster or plasterboard.

FIGURE 8-8 In remodeling, you rarely have access to studs or other concealed wooden supports. This type of box is ideal. The manufacturer's template guides you in cutting a hole to precisely match the box's size and shape; fish your cable into place, slip it into the box, place the box into the wall cavity, and tighten down the two mounting screws which force brackets against the inside of the gypsum board to make a solid installation job.

There's one utility-box feature you should be familiar with. You may want to mount two (or more) outlets or two (or more) switches side by side; or perhaps you simply need a much-bigger-than-normal box to accomodate all the connections that have to be made. Many utility boxes are gangable: they have removable sides that permit you to interlock two or more boxes. We grouped five separate boxes into one unit to permit us to control several living room spotlights, a dimmer, and a three-way light switch all from one location. When you interlock boxes, the electrical-code limitation remains on the number of connections you can make in a box. If you are permitted to run five conductors into or out of a box of a particular size, and you gang two of them together, you can still run only five into or out of each box (for a total of ten in this example).

Often, people installing paneling and other improvements that add depth to their walls don't know how to preserve existing switches and outlets without ripping loose the old utility boxes and remounting them flush with the new surfaces. Some do-it-yourselfers simply leave gaps between the old boxes and the new switches or outlets. That's an invitation to a fire. For under a dollar, you can buy utility box extenders. Determine the width and height of each old utility box and then measure how much extension you need to bring it flush with the wall. Extenders are available

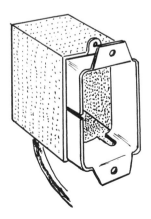

FIGURE 8-9 To extend the capacity of a utility box, or simply to keep its outer edge in line with the raised surface of a paneled wall, you can easily slip in or screw in a box extender such as this one.

in thicknesses from ½ inch to beyond 2 inches. A few extenders are adjustable in depth.

WIRE CONNECTORS

Wire connectors have been on hardware store shelves for so long, it's shocking how many do-it-yourselfers still use electrical tape to cover and hold the wires they've twisted together. Taped connections are neither as secure nor as durable as wire connectors.

Inside the plastic case of every good wire connector is a cone-shaped steel spring that threads tightly onto your twisted stripped wires. The connectors come in various sizes to accommodate as many wires as you're working with of whatever size you're joining. Buy the kind that has a wide, flexible apron around its open end, to maximize protection against leaving uncovered a bit of exposed wire.

GROUND FAULT INTERRUPTERS

If you're wiring a new outdoor or bathroom circuit, your local electrical code may require you to install a combination circuit breaker and ground fault interrupter (GFI) instead of a traditional breaker or fuse. The GFI provides maximum protection against the greater potential for electrical shock that exists in a kitchen, workshop, basement, or similar area. Even if the code doesn't require a GFI for these places, you might want to invest in one or more of them. Have it installed by an electrician or—if you feel comfortable working inside your home's main load distribution center ("circuit breaker box")—install it yourself.

You can also buy GFIs that replace ordinary wall outlets in hazardous areas. Self-contained GFIs, complete with test and reset buttons, now come packaged with complete instructions for do-it-yourselfers, and sell for upwards of $30. For a good bit more, you can buy a portable GFI unit that doesn't need to be wired in; it simply plugs into any adequately wired outlet.

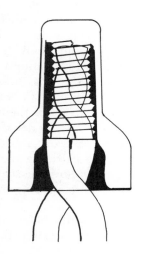

FIGURE 8-10 This x-ray view of wire connectors shows why they are preferable to common splicing. As you twist this type of connector over the lightly twisted ends of your wires, its metal spring locks the wires together. To use one, first grab with a pliers the loose ends of all the wires you plan to join, twist your wrist (which will twist the wires too), grab the ends once more and twist again. Then turn on a wire connector as firmly as you can.

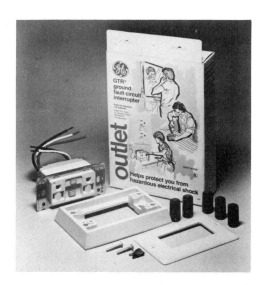

FIGURE 8-11 You can replace an electrical outlet, using a ground fault interrupter (GFI) kit such as this, with a safety device that shuts off electricity in a split second after someone in your family has created a situation in which he or she might get a serious shock. Be sure your house wiring is adequately grounded before you install a GFI, or the device will not work. (Courtesy General Electric.)

WALL OUTLETS

The new wall outlets that are polarized and grounded are so inexpensive, no home improver should overlook replacing oldstyle outlets with them. Grounding is essential for the safe operation of appliances and large electrical gadgets. (The old pigtail grounding adapters—those plugs with the attached wires that screw onto your outlet box covers—have been considered inadequate since the last rewrite of the National Electrical Code.) Polarization helps many radios and TVs get better reception. The newer sets come equipped with plugs that have unequal-sized prongs. The bigger prong connects to the negative pole of your electrical line.

While you're shopping for wall outlets, look at the elegant flush outlets that are being used in high-priced new homes; they're also available for do-it-yourself home improvers. Many hardware stores and most electrical wholesalers stock these "Decora" style outlets. Be prepared to pay a premium for them even though, except for their streamlined look, they're no different from the old-fashioned models.

Elegant or simple, outlets that are *backwired* are very handy if you're doing a lengthy job. With back wiring, instead of having to bend and screw down every wire connection, you simply shove the stripped wire directly into a hole in the rear of the outlet where a spring mechanism grabs it securely.

Power strips, those prefabricated strips of grounded outlets, save time when you want to update a kitchen, workshop, or other small space where lots of outlets are needed. A typical power strip comes in increments of 3-foot lengths with a pre-installed outlet every 6 inches. One end of the strip is finished off. The other end fits into a junction box which you wire permanently into a new or existing house circuit. (There are many "power strips" on the market that include a flexible cord so you can nail the strip onto a wall and quickly plug it into an existing outlet. Be forewarned: the National Electrical Code has *not* approved them except for *temporary* use, and then only under *very limited* circumstances. Any other use risks short-circuiting, fire, or possible electrocution. In fact, even approved power strips may short-circuit or catch fire if you use more than a few of their plugged-in appliances at once.)

SWITCHES

Switches with illuminated handles, as well as luxurious flush switches that match Decora-type outlets, are available if you're updating old switches or installing new ones. Look for a UL listing on any you buy and be prepared to pay a premium.

Dimmer light switches are becoming ever more popular. Manufacturers now offer not just wall switch dimmers, but tabletop lamp dimmers and dimmers for flourescent lights. You can even find a dimmer that'll work in place of a three-way switch (the kind in which two switches in different places control one light or group of lights, with either switch able to turn it on or off).

A four-way switch is a new wrinkle to many do-it-yourselfers, but the gadget has been around for generations. Wire up a pair of three-way switches at each end of the system, plus one or more four-way switches along the way, and you'll be able to hook up a light that your family can turn on or off at any number of locations.

FIGURE 8-12 Luxury on the wall with Decora style outlets, switches, and coverplates. (Courtesy Leviton Manufacturing Company.)

MOTOR SPEED CONTROLS

There are a number of appliances that work by sucking air out of your home: bathroom and attic fans, kitchen exhausts, and the like. To conserve that heated air they remove from your home, you can install a motor speed control. Electrically, it's very similar to a light dimmer, although you should never interchange them.

These controls are not the old-fashioned rheostats that simply redirected some of the current away from the motor and through a resistor—thus burning up the same amount of electrical energy no matter whether the motor ran at full tilt or at slow speed. The sophisticated modern control actually electronically interrupts the flow of current to a motor many times every second, saving electrical energy as well as slowing down your blower motor. It also incorporates feedback circuits to automatically restore full power if the motor is in danger of stalling. Models that control motors up to 0.4 hp fit into standard switch boxes and generally cost under $25.

Like most of the gadgets we've mentioned in this section, these handy helpers come with simple installation diagrams. To help you get some practice so that you can read any diagram you come across, we're going to ask you to follow along with us now as we demonstrate how to install a four-way switch easily, inexpensively, and with little mess or bother.

A PLAN OF ATTACK FOR WIRING JOBS

If you are building a new house—or an addition—the wiring is so straightforward that you probably won't need much guidance. The procedure is:

1. Design the job.
2. Purchase the appropriate electrical cables, boxes, and components.
3. Turn off the fuse or circuit breaker.
4. Fasten together all the electrical parts you've assembled in step 2.
5. Turn the fuse or breaker back on and see if it all works. If nothing works, some wire is probably not well connected. If you blow the fuse or breaker, some wire is tightly enough connected—but probably in an improper place. Recheck all your attachments and try your outlets and switches again.

Let's look at the job in a little more detail. For an entire new circuit, which is what you'll probably need in an addition, you'll have to add an extra circuit breaker to your existing main box. This is a simple task, but it does require a building permit in practically every part of the country. In some localities, it also requires supervision—if not actual installation—by a licensed electrician. In places where do-it-yourselfers may legally tackle the job, we've found that electrical inspectors are perfectly able and willing to tell you how to go about it and even where to buy the best materials at the best prices, and then to come around and make sure you're doing the job properly.

If you have only a fuse box instead of a circuit breaker network, chances are high that you may not be able to add a new circuit. Again, your building department or a licensed electrician can advise you.

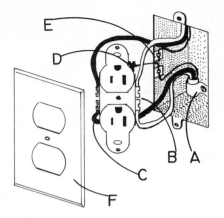

FIGURE 8-13 Here's the most complicated utility box installation you're likely to encounter. The power runs to this outlet in one cable (A) and from it to another outlet via the other cable. Notice how at (B) the white neutral wires connect to the white colored screws. At (C), both black hot wires connect to brass screws. Since there is only one green grounding screw (D), the bare ground wire from (A) runs first through a small *grounding clip* (E) slipped onto one edge of the metal utility box and then to the grounding screw. The second cable's grounding wire runs to a second grounding clip, thereby assuring that the metal box, the outlet itself, and the new cable being run from power already brought to this box are all securely grounded. Even the cover (F) has two purposes besides decoration: to keep careless fingers from sticking *into* the hot insides of this wiring job, and to keep flames from getting *out* if any electrical problem starts inside this box.

If this is an isolated outlet, or the last one of a run, or the only new one you're adding, then there'll be only one cable running into this box and you'll need only one pair of wires hooked to the outlet.

If you want to control the two halves of this outlet separately—let's say, one from a switch and one to be powered all the time—you can snap off the removable copper strip that joins the two brass screws and the one that joins the two white screws. In that case, this illustration would show the top cable powering the top half of this duplex outlet, and the bottom cable (A) powering the bottom half.

Count the number of conductors shown here (and add numbers for hardware and such) to determine how large a box is required to meet code specifications: 2 for the bottom hot and neutral wires; 2 for the top cable's hot and neutrals; 1 for the grounding wires; 1 for built-in cable clamps (the line from *A* ends on one of the clamps shown in this sketch); 1 for the device (the duplex outlet) being mounted on this box.

Adding the above, we get 7. Figure 8-15 shows that for seven wires of #14 size, we use a box at least 3 x 2 x 2¾"; for 7 of #12 size, a 3 x 2 x 3½" box is required.

Our publisher's legal department won't let us give you instructions which might encourage you to violate local building codes. So we'll start our directions from a point just after you've made the legal and approved connection to your circuit breaker, but before you've turned it on.

First, in designing where you'll run your new circuit's cable, keep in mind that most codes permit you to run no more than 35 feet of #12 size wire from a 20-amp circuit breaker to your most distant outlet. If you can come within that limitation and still run your main cable by way of an unused attic or basement, your work will be all the easier. Otherwise you'll have to drill ½-inch holes for the cable through every stud in your way. Whichever way you choose, be sure to protect the Romex with either 2 inches of wood or a steel plate whenever it passes through a stud. At least every 4½ feet, unless your cable is supported via holes in studs, use a cable support designed for Romex cable. When you get to where you want to go, fasten a box onto your chosen 2 × 4, cut the cable—allowing plenty of slack—strip 6 inches off the Romex's covering, then strip about 1 inch off each wire. If your boxes have built-in cable clamps, use one of them to fasten your cable securely into place just beyond where you've stripped away the Romex's outer covering.

Now install the outlet or other electrical equipment that goes into the box. Then, if you're going to install other items in the same room from the same circuit, take one end from your coil of unused cable, repeat the above directions for stripping cable covering and wire insulation, shove the end in your box, clamp it into place, and install those wires into an

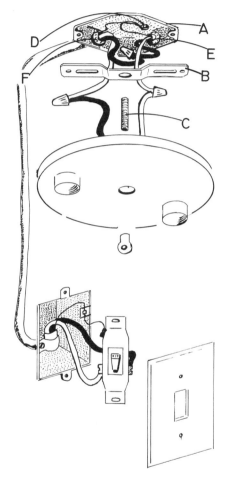

FIGURE 8-14 This is a typical wiring layout for an overhead (or wall) light controlled by a switch at another location. Power from the circuit breaker box usually comes to the installation at the overhead box, so the box (A) must be large enough to handle the appropriate number of conductors, six in this case. (The number is one fewer than calculated in Figure 8-14 because the cable clamps shown here are outside the box.) The offset crossbar (B) has standardized holes so you can screw it to the box; the fixture itself may screw to the crossbar, or slip over a hicky (C) (which is little more than a small threaded pipe) and be held in place by the ornamental knob that threads onto the hicky.

Power comes to this installation via cable (E); the white neutral from that line connects directly to the lamp's white wire. But the black, hot line runs to the switch. The switch here connects to the light via cable (F). Notice that switches violate the sacred rule about always hooking black to black, white to white. Since only the hot (black) side of a lamp is switched, it would call for a cable with two black wires, and no cables are made like that. Electricians know that, and expect to find a black-and-white pair connecting a switch to a lamp, exactly as shown here. (It is not necessary to tape or paint the white wire black inside your outlet box.) Do be sure to hook up the ground leads, shown here screwed under a screw (D) into the box itself; or, alternatively, slip them into grounding clips as shown both in Figure 8-14 and in the installation of the switch part of this sketch.

In designing a hookup such as this, you could have first run power to the switch instead of the lamp's utility box. However, this is more convenient since switches generally have only one set of terminal screws, whereas duplex outlets have two. To run power first to a switch, fasten short lengths of wire to your main cable connections; the short lengths hook up to the switch.

appropriate set of screws or backwiring openings. Most outlets and switches have space for two complete sets of wires—one for servicing the item, one for the convenience of running power to a neighboring item.

Now you can drill additional holes in your floors, ceilings, or walls to enable you to run the next leg of your circuit to the next spot you've chosen for a utility box. Here are some design factors to keep in mind when laying out new work:

- The National Electrical Code says you *must* have electrical outlets spaced so that no spot along the walls is further than 6 feet from an outlet.
- Outlets normally are spaced about 12 inches above the floor.
- Light switches normally are spaced about 48 inches above the floor.
- Outlets and switches are normally spaced about 8 to 12 inches above a cabinet top.
- A light switch should be available near every entrance to a room, so that people do not have to walk part of the way in the dark before being able to turn on a light. Therefore, if a particular room has one light and two entrances, you should plan to install a three-way or four-way switch system. (Electrical inspectors may accept alternate light switch arrangements, but if you're counting on that, be sure you get your inspector's okay *before* you tackle the actual wiring.)

That's how easy wiring can be when you're working on a new building or a new addition whose walls haven't yet been enclosed in plasterboard. Now let's show how to wire a four-way switch system into an existing, already finished home that you are in the process of modernizing, as an example of how you proceed when all your walls, floors, and ceilings are finished. You can learn how to install almost anything electrical from following our description.

Three-way and four-way lighting systems can be laid out in several ways. Notice how simple they all look on paper. They'll stay that way if you don't forget that they are simple. What throws a lot of people off-track is the fact that light switches only switch on—or off—the hot (black-colored) wire. The neutral (white-colored) line never touches the switch in any normal household situation—and that includes three-way and four-way switch systems.

The circuits shown in Figure 8-15 are different in one basic way: the place where the source of power comes from. If an existing electrical connection is close to where you want to locate a switch, then you'll run power to the switch first. If the existing power source is closer to the light the switch will operate, then you'll want to run power there first.

The first thing to do is to pick a source of existing power; you need not choose the one physically closest to the new installation. Select the one that makes it easiest to run wires to the new site while destroying the least amount of plaster wall and ceiling. Watch for paths that take your wire through closets, attics, and basements. Romex cable is stiff enough that if you measure carefully, you can snake it through the cavities between wall supports and ceiling supports and right to the spot where you want it.

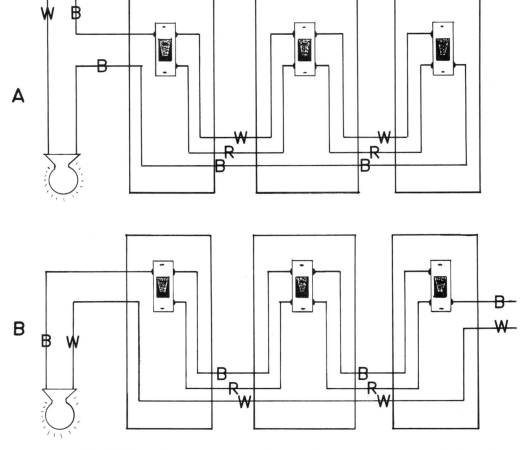

FIGURE 8-15 Even three-way and four-way lighting systems are simple, if you don't forget your fundamentals: switches switch only the black (hot) side of a wiring network. The sketch here shows how a light can be controlled from many locations. At each end is a three-way switch, between them any practical number of four-way switches. If you want to use only two switches, disregard the middle box.

In sketch (A), the power is brought in at the light's utility box. The white neutral connects to the lamp's white wire. The black wire runs to the three-way switch. Notice that you will need a length of three-conductor cable to make the installation: **B** here stands for the black lead, **R** the red, and **W** the white. Once you've bought the right switches and wire (such as #14/3 Romex), simply hook the color-coded wires to the appropriate terminals on your switches. Except for the extra one or two terminals, the switch installations will look exactly like the one in Figure 8-14.

Since lighting systems such as this often span great distances, it may be convenient to bring power not to the lamp but to the first switch. Illustration (B) here shows that alternative. Then simply match colored wires to carefully placed switch terminal screws.

If you can work out a system that keeps you within easy reach of your home's existing baseboards, you may be able to solve lots of wiring problems with a bit of careful carpentry. First you'll have to carefully rip away the baseboards between the starting and stopping points of your new wiring. Then snake your Romex cable down from an existing switch or outlet, through the cavity between the 2 × 4s that are behind your plasterboard, and to a hole at the bottom that you've cut into the plasterboard. Be sure that the hole is low enough to be covered up by the baseboard when you nail it back into place. Now you'll have to chisel a ½-inch groove into the plasterboard, going from your hole to the wall cavity below where you want the new wire to end up. Make a second hole there.

Measure the amount of Romex cable you'll need—allowing an extra foot or two for good measure—and cut the cable. Next measure the distance between the two holes and cut a piece of ½-inch electrical conduit (metal or PVC plastic) that length. Snake the Romex through the conduit—silicone spray on the Romex will help it slide along. Then slip the conduit full of cable into the long groove, snake the remaining Romex up into the wall cavity, and proceed with your wiring job. (The conduit is required to protect the Romex cable from a nail driven by an eager carpenter—you perhaps—years after you've forgotten exactly where the hot wires run behind your home's baseboards.)

SHORTCUTS TO ADDING ELECTRICAL CIRCUITS

If your needs fit what's available, we can offer several shortcuts to a lot of snaking of wires over attics and under basements and through wall cavities. If you shop creatively through the shelves of your home improvement center or the pages of your favorite mail order supplier, you may be able to find other new products that provide shortcuts too.

Let's say you could use an extra electrical outlet on a wall where there's an existing switch to some remote light fixture. You can (after turning off the power) pull out the old common switch and replace it with an appliance of the same size that combines both a smaller light switch *plus* an outlet. If you need a switch where you now have just an outlet, you can replace the old outlet with the same combination switch-outlet.

Maybe you want to install an extra light in a location where there's already one with a wall-mounted switch. Assuming you can snake the necessary wires to wherever you want to mount the light, it's a snap to replace the single switch with one appliance that has two separate switches.

We're happy to see that at least one company now makes available to consumers the kind of baseboard electrical raceway system that has been used for years in a great many commercial buildings. In a baseboard raceway system, you buy what amounts to a hollow vinyl baseboard plus a wiring network that fits behind it. The complete system you buy includes not only the hardware for mounting the wires and the baseboard covering, but facilities for connecting the network to your house wiring, electri-

FIGURE 8-16 This Carlon Baseway system eliminates the job of snaking wires through existing walls, by substituting almost a simple cut-and-paste procedure. The system utilizes wires contained inside an approved plastic baseboard cavity as shown in (A). Clamps hold outlets into place, and they're wired in the usual fashion (B). Easy-to-cut covers go next (C) over the wires and (D) over the outlets. Corners and other finishing elements are part of the system, too (E). (Photos courtesy Carlon.)

cal outlets that are an integral part of the system, finishing hardware, and do-it-yourself instructions. Moreover, you can paint or in other ways decorate the baseboard cover so that it fits into your decorating scheme. In the figure, we've shown such a system in operation.

Some day we'll be lighting our houses and powering our TVs with electrical power that's beamed through the air from some sort of high-powered but safe radio. Then we won't have to worry about wires and conduits and snaking through walls and such. But for the moment, the electrical industry has evolved reasonably priced, relatively safe components for us to work with. Try your own wiring and see how easy it is.

9
You Don't Have to Sink a Bundle into Plumbing Improvements

Let's once and for all put to rest any fears you have about plunging into major tasks in your home plumbing (or your gas lines, which involve the same procedures). For incentive consider this: The cost of a new faucet is less than half the additional cost of having a plumber install it. The installation cost of a new water heater is nearly half the cost of the heater itself. Labor costs to have a new bathtub installed can be more than double the price of even the fanciest tub.

On top of the financial incentives are the incentives supplied nowadays by the plumbing supplies industry. Most large home improvement centers stock a cornucopia of easy-to-use materials and tools that help you make a success of plumbing and gas line improvements. Faucets, hot water heaters, sinks, and such now come packed with installation manuals written (and illustrated) with novices in mind. There has been an industrial revolution in plumbing supplies that has made doing-it-yourself an attainable goal for most of us.

PIPES AND TOOLS

There are now three basic materials used for pipes in home plumbing and gas line systems: copper, iron, and plastic. You should never mix copper and iron pipes in the same water system, or you may set up an insidious corrosion problem. But you can mix plastic with either metal. (You may want to avoid that, too, unless you have a very long run of pipe to install, because you'll also have to add an adapter. Pipes made of each of the three materials have their own individual systems of locking together.)

Iron pipes come in two varieties, galvanized (grey in color) and black iron (black, of course). The latter is more expensive, so most people work with galvanized. For installing gas appliances (such as water heaters), most codes require the use of black iron. Except for use with gas, you can safely mix galvanized with black.

There are several different types of plastic pipe. Most are rigid thick-walled PVC, generally light tan in color. A few are flexible polyethylene: the latter have not yet met code requirements in some parts of the country.

Copper pipe comes in several types, but you're likely to find only two of them at local supply outlets. *Type L* is rigid like iron pipe, but of course it's copper colored. This is the material required for plumbing by most codes. *Type S* is thin enough to be flexible, which means you have to handle it carefully so it won't kink as you bend it. Most codes do not allow it for plumbing (a few permit it for gas line installations) so check carefully with local building authorities before buying and installing this product.

Where codes don't permit flexible copper tubing for main piping systems, they do allow you to use a foot or two of it between your pipes and new faucets or sinks. A great many faucets and similar appliances that are sold with do-it-yourselfers in mind include flexible copper connections inside their packages. The flexibility helps you line up watertight joints.

Iron pipes are threaded to screw into matching iron fittings. Copper pipes are soldered together in what are known to the trade as *sweat fittings*. And plastic pipes generally are glued together.

One problem that puzzles a lot of home improvement buffs is figuring the size pipe they need. If you're adding pipes onto an existing system, of course you'll use pipes of the same size. With a ruler to measure the inside diameter, outside diameter, or circumference, you can figure out the *trade name* size of those pipes, which is equal to their approximate inside diameter. What is called a 1-inch iron pipe actually measures 1.049 inches in inside diameter and about 1.315 inches in outside diameter (see Figure 9-1). There is no real need to understand the long history that led to this apparently irrational numbering system. You'll simply have to live with it if you buy pipe or fittings. Figure 9-1 will help you identify the size of a particular pipe you want to replace or the fitting that goes with it, in case you prefer to uncouple it only after a replacement is at hand. (Fittings are identified by the size of pipe on which they fit.)

Figure 9-2 shows the names of the various fittings that are used to join, bend, split, or change the size of pipes throughout plumbing systems.

124

FIGURE 9-1 Buying plumbing pipe: actual size of pipe compared to trade name.

TRADE NAME	INSIDE DIAMETER	OUTSIDE DIAMETER	CIRCUMFERENCE
Iron Pipe			
¼ inch	⅜	$^9/_{16}$	$1^{11}/_{16}$
⅜ inch	½	$^{11}/_{16}$	2⅛
½ inch	⅝	$^{13}/_{16}$	2⅝
¾ inch	$^{13}/_{16}$	$1^1/_{16}$	$3^5/_{16}$
1 inch	$1^1/_{16}$	$1^5/_{16}$	4⅛
1¼ inch	1⅜	$1^{11}/_{16}$	$5^3/_{16}$
1½ inch	1⅝	1⅞	6
2 inch	$2^1/_{16}$	2⅜	$7^7/_{16}$
Copper Pipe			
⅜ inch	$^7/_{16}$	½	$1^9{16}$
½ inch	$^9/_{16}$	⅝	$1^{15}/_{16}$
¾ inch	$^{13}/_{16}$	⅞	2¾
1 inch	1	1⅛	$3^9/_{16}$
1¼ inch	1¼	1⅜	$4^5/_{16}$
1½ inch	1½	1⅝	5⅛

MEASURING

To work with any pipe, you'll need a good measuring device such as a roll-up steel rule. In measuring plastic or copper pipes, be sure that you figure the amount of pipe that has to slip into each fitting along the way. It can be as small as ½ inch, but if you forget to allow for the several fittings in a hookup, you may come a frustrating inch or more short of where you want to end up.

The exact amount of pipe required inside each fitting varies according to pipe size and material used, so check this calculation for each job. Iron pipes are tricky to figure because the fittings screw together. However—something that few people realize—their threads are tapered. The first thread screwed into a coupling fits less snugly into its fitting than the final thread. The pipe and its matching fitting have to be threaded together far enough to result in a tight fit, but you can count on some leeway, about ¼ to ½ inch, by tightening anywhere from barely tight to extra tight. As an estimate, you can figure that ½ inch of each ½-inch or ¾-inch-sized iron pipe length will be lost to each set of threads when you've assembled them.

FIGURE 9-2 Pipe fittings are easiesr to buy if you know their names. Here they are: (A) tee; (B) reducing tee; (C) elbow; (D) reducing elbow; (E) 45° elbow; (F) street tee; (G) coupling; (H) union (for joining two pipes, but having facility to uncouple them easily); (J) reducing coupling; (K) bushing (for reducing size of pipe).

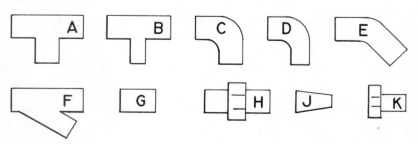

126

*You Don't Have to
Sink a Bundle into
Plumbing
Improvements*

In measuring pipe lengths that come to a bend at the end, or end in any kind of fitting, you're going to wonder, "Where do I measure from?" As Figure 9-3 shows, measure from the center of one fitting to the center of the next.

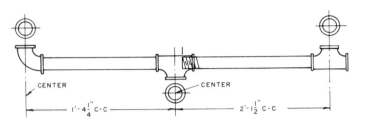

FIGURE 9-3 When measuring pipe lengths, measure from the center of one coupling to the center of the last one ("C–C", in plumber's jargon). (Courtesy Water Quality Association.)

CUTTING

To cut plastic pipes you'll need a hacksaw and also something to clean away the rough edges left by sawing: sandpaper, SurForm tool, file, or such. Be certain not to cut at an angle. To make your glued joints as tough as possible, you'll want a nice perpendicular cut that will fit snugly into the plastic fittings.

Cut copper pipes with either a hacksaw or a tube cutter. The latter is an inexpensive tool that resembles a C-clamp with a small built-in cutting wheel. You tighten the tube cutter around the pipe that must be cut, and rotate it as the wheel makes a tiny slice into the copper pipe. Then you tighten the cutting wheel a bit, revolve it once more, and continue this procedure until the pipe has been sliced neatly in two. With either a tube cutter or a hacksaw, you must ream away the rough-cut edges and then steel-wool the portions of the pipes that are to be soldered into sweat fittings.

Avoid cutting iron pipes unless you have facilities for threading them. The threading equipment is more expensive than most do-it-yourselfers want to invest in. Fortunately, do-it-yourself centers and hardware stores stock threaded pipe sections in a great many lengths.

Before installing pipes permanently, always slip them together loosely to make sure that (1) you've made all your measurements properly, (2) the pipes clear the many obstructions that may be in the way, and (3) they're not blocking easy access to anything important. Most do-it-yourself centers let you exchange undamaged pipes and fittings for equipment that's better suited to your job.

JOINING

Plastic home plumbing pipes and fittings are joined with solvents. The solvent melts part of both the pipe and the fitting, leaving a solid connection when the solvent evaporates. *Chemical welding* is the trade jargon for this procedure.

First try on the fitting to make sure that a good fit exists. Then dab the proper solvent onto the outside of the pipe and the inside of the fitting. Shove together the pipe and fitting, quickly and firmly, and then

127

*You Don't Have to
Sink a Bundle into
Plumbing
Improvements*

twist to ensure that the solvent is uniformly spread. The weld dries in minutes. Each chemical variety of pipe requires its own solvent; if you're unsure what to use, ask for information where you buy your pipes.

Once a chemical weld is set, the fitting can never be removed from the plastic pipe—unlike plumbing procedures for brass or iron pipe. To take it apart again, the pipe will have to be sawed. But that's a very easy thing to accomplish.

Rigid plastic pipe is relatively flexible, so *minor* corrections in direction and layout are quite feasible over the length of a long stretch of pipe. But it is not flexible enough to bend around corners. For that, elbows must be used.

To join copper pipes, use sweat fittings or compression fittings. Sweat fittings frighten a lot of people, who feel that soldering is a mystical art left over from the dark ages. But if you already own one of those

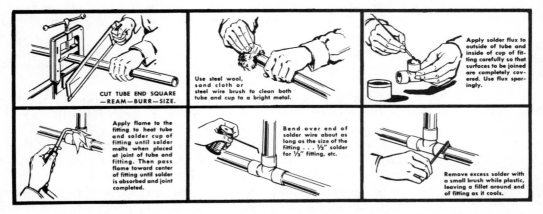

FIGURE 9-4 Here's the step-by-step procedure to achieve perfect soldering joints in copper pipe. (Courtesy Water Quality Association)

FIGURE 9-5 If you follow the directions shown in previous illustrations, this is how your sweat fittings will look during the soldering job. (Photo courtesy Spitfire Division of Wingaersheek, Inc.)

128

*You Don't Have to
Sink a Bundle into
Plumbing
Improvements*

popular propane torches you can buy half a dollar's worth of solder and half a dollar's worth of soldering paste, and with a bit of practice, you're in business. (Buy solid solder, not solid core or acid core.)

First be sure the fittings do fit together snugly. Then steel-wool the last inch of each pipe until it gleams. Then protect those clean ends from your hands, dirty gloves, and anything else that will redeposit grease or dirt on the parts to be soldered. Dab a generous amount of soldering paste onto all the parts to be joined, and slip the pipes and fittings into place.

Make sure that you're not working near flammables, and then light your torch. Go to work on one joint at a time, heating up evenly and on all sides the coupling and the last ½ inch of pipe. The pipes themselves should be made hot enough to melt the solder. Your torch can assist the melting process a bit, but only if the pipes are first hot enough.

When the pipes are hot enough, keep your torch in position and run the end of your roll of solder along the entire joint between the pipe and the fitting. Solder should flow smoothly *into* the almost invisible gap between the two. Assuming the pipes were hot enough, the solder will end up looking like a smooth grey patina on the edges of the copper fitting and pipe. You don't need—and don't want—gobs of solder hanging on anywhere.

When your first joint is finished, move on to the next. When they're all assembled, you can turn on the water to run a test. Turn off the water if you have to touch up any small leaks.

The compression fitting offers copper-pipe installers a nonsoldered alternative to sweat fittings. In recent years, several manufacturers have started to supply hardware stores and do-it-yourself centers with dozens of varieties of this handy device. In fact, you can now find compression fittings that substitute for practically any of the pipe fittings displayed in our earlier sketch.

With a compression fitting, you must still be sure that the copper pipes fit together well and you must still clean their ends thoroughly with steel wool. Then, however, you just slip a compression nut onto the pipe, followed by a compression sleeve. A matching compression fitting accomodates the other pipe. When you tighten the compression nut with a small wrench, internal pressure compacts the sleeve and effectively seals the pipe.

We've found that occasionally a tiny leak pops up at a compression fitting immediately after the water is turned back on. Don't worry. Let it drip for a few hours. During that time the sleeve may finish its compacting and stop the leak entirely. Only if that fails should you attempt to twist the

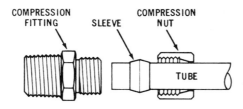

COMPRESSION FITTING SLEEVE COMPRESSION NUT TUBE

FIGURE 9-6 Compression fittings offer a fast alternative to soldered joints. Be sure your pipes are clean, free of burrs, and perfectly straight when you use them (or any other plumbing device). (Courtesy Brass Craft Corporation.)

129

*You Don't Have to
Sink a Bundle into
Plumbing
Improvements*

compression nut tighter. Too much tightening can be as bad as too little—but after you've installed one or two of them, we're sure you'll get the knack.

Iron pipes, of course, screw together with fittings that are threaded to match the pipes' threads. For plumbing jobs involving iron pipes, you'll need two wrenches—one to twist the pipe or fitting you're working on and the other to hold in place the fitting or pipe it's being threaded into. The preferred tools for this job are pipe wrenches.

The pipe wrench is a much misunderstood tool. It is wonderfully designed to tighten or loosen lengths of *round* pipe. The surface of its jaws is machined with teeth that grab firmly into the somewhat soft pipe metal. And the jaws are subtly angled to provide maximum grabbing power on round surfaces, at the same time allowing for limited use on squared-off fittings too. The jaws are also hinged so that the pipe wrench can be moved backward without pulling it loose from the pipe, twisted hard, then backed off again and twisted some more. The net effect is very similar to the ratchet action on a socket wrench. Some oldtimers still refer to the pipe wrench as the Stillson wrench.

Pipe wrenches come in sizes so small they fit into your pocket, up to sizes so large they scarcely fit into the family station wagon. Size is determined by the length of the handle. Two pipe wrenches of about 14 inches or 16 inches are best to buy for most home applications. Since it's not a minor investment, a vice grip pliers or channel lock pliers generally can take the place of the second pipe wrench.

Pipes and pipe fittings are not designed to create leakproof unions all by themselves. It is necessary to apply a substance that plumbers call *pipe dope*. The dope not only helps to form a watertight seal, but optimally keeps the joined threads from freezing together so they can be loosened years later if necessary. Dope comes in tubes or cans of varying sizes. Don't scrimp on this important, inexpensive substance.

HOW TO PLAN YOUR PLUMBING JOBS

By now, assuming you've been reading and not just flipping pages, you've absorbed the basics of working with the various materials you're likely to encounter in a plumbing job. Now we'll try to save you some money and some headaches as you get ready to apply what you've learned.

First of all, we have to advise: *do* plan ahead. We've watched so many people stand in hardware or home improvement stores and pick out one of these, two of those, and a big one of those over there. Having done enough plumbing in our lifetimes, we know that the stuff they pile into the shopping cart won't work together. When they get home, they'll find out that they've picked up the wrong materials. But why not save yourself those extra trips, extra dollars, and extra aggravation?

Look at the area you're about to improve with something new in plumbing. Will new plumbing alone do what you want?

Next *make a drawing*. If you're going to have to do some carpentry or tile work too, be sure your plans for that match your plumbing plans. If

130

*You Don't Have to
Sink a Bundle into
Plumbing
Improvements*

you're tackling anything major, *measure* the bathroom or kitchen or what-ever area you're changing, and make a sketch of those measurements.

Shop around for the big purchases. For instance, find out how big is the new sink you'd like and see if it fits into your drawing. If you're adding a water softener, have you got room to put it in? What extra attachments—drains, salt storage facilities—should you allow for? Put them *all* in your sketches.

Then *locate* your existing pipes. Are they copper, iron, or plastic? How big are they? Are there fittings near the start of your planned pipes that you can get easy access to, or will you have to take out some of the old pipe and add new fittings? Write down all of these figures because you'd be surprised how fast you can forget if you have ½-inch or ¾-inch pipe; in the store, they all look like the ones you have in the walls back home.

Next pick the brains of experienced clerks at your favorite stores. Most of them have helped someone through your job a hundred times and may have some advice that will save you time, money, headaches, and more.

Plan ahead. Watch for sales. Ask clerks if they know of sales coming up that can save you money on major appliances.

Finally, buy your materials and schedule the job. If you have to work weekends, try to plan the trickiest parts for when the hardware stores are open. You can count on needing something extra once the pipes are torn apart, and you're going to have to contend with unhappy family members if they need to wait a day for hot water. (If you're repairing instead of improving, consult our companion book *How to Fix Damn Near Everything* for to-the-point tips.)

NEW FAUCETS

Installing an entirely new faucet assembly represents a significant invest-ment. There are so many fancy replacement handles available, including some in 24 carat gold and platinum, that you might want to keep your old spigot and just change the handles. But faucet installation is not a difficult job. If you've successfully followed this far, it should come easy. Even the fanciest single-lever and double-faucet sets for bathroom and kitchen sinks seldom require more than two nuts to hold them in place. New faucets and handles usually are sold as integral parts of these sets.

Before rushing to the store to select a shiny new superfaucet, there are several items to check in advance. Measure the distance between the centers of your faucets. They commonly come in what trade users call 4-inch centers, 6-inch centers, 8-inch centers, and so on. Some standardization has taken place, and bathrooms now use 4-inch center faucet sets on sinks and 8-inch center layouts for showers. Kitchen sinks most often have 8-inch centers.

Before buying a new set of faucets, count the number of holes in the kitchen sink. This is not as obvious as it seems. Kitchen sinks can be two-hole, three-hole, or four-hole, and the number determines what kind of faucet set you must buy. If a deck covers the top of the sink, you may not

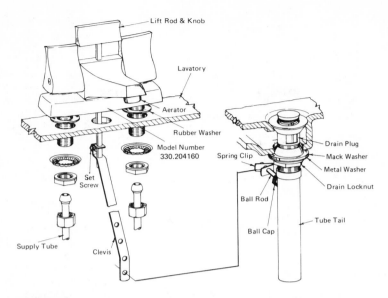

Lift Rod & Knob

Lavatory

Aerator

Rubber Washer

Model Number
330.204160

Set
Screw

Supply Tube

Clevis

Spring Clip

Ball Rod

Ball Cap

Drain Plug

Mack Washer

Metal Washer

Drain Locknut

Tube Tail

FIGURE 9-7 Here's how easy it is to install a new faucet. Generally two nuts secure the faucet to the sink, and two compression fittings link the hot and cold faucets to the hot and cold water pipes. The pop-up slips into place and gets tightened down; then simply make the mechanical connection to the lift knob. (Courtesy Sears, Roebuck and Company.)

be able to see at a glance that there is one hole for the hot water, one for the cold water, and a third for the spout that mixes hot and cold. In that case, peer under the sink with a flashlight.

Two-hole sinks require what is called an exposed deck faucet. Hot water runs through one hole, cold through the other, and the two streams are mixed within the deck itself before moving into the spout. With three holes, you have the option of buying either a concealed deck faucet set (which means that the porcelain of the sink will be seen between handles and spout) or an exposed deck. Four-hole sinks are designed for use with spray attachments. If your predecessor decided to do without a spray, a snap-in cover may partially conceal the fourth hole. Some single-handle kitchen faucet sets are made to accomodate spray attachments on the decks, thus using three-hole sinks for four holes' worth of convenience.

Bathroom sinks have traditionally been two-hole designs, although a small hole in the center accomodates the pop-up handle. A few very fancy models have widespread handles—up to 16 inches—with a third hole in the center for a mixer spout.

Plan in advance for the installation of new faucets. Study each old connection before you dismantle it. If you're extremely lucky, it will have a flexible tube linking the faucet itself with the solid plumbing farther down the line. If not, plan to add the flexible connector. Determine where the next closest coupling in the pipe has been placed; it may be at the shutoff valve if there's one under the sink. If there aren't any shutoffs on the hot

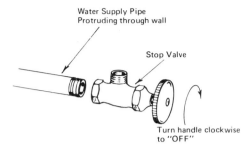

FIGURE 9-8 What you call a shut-off valve, plumbers (and stores) call a *stop*. Here's an angle stop being installed. They fit copper pipe (if you use a sweat-fitted or compression-fitted stop) or iron pipe (if you use a threaded stop, as shown here) or plastic pipe (if you use an adapter). (Courtesy Sears, Roebuck and Co.)

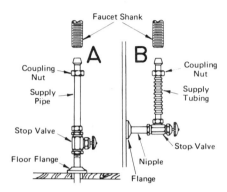

FIGURE 9-9 The floor stop plus flexible copper tubing make for easy installation of new faucets when the existing water supply pipe comes through the floor (A). But if hot and cold water pipes are in the wall under the sink (B) then an angle stop plus flexible supply tube provide a quick hookup. (Courtesy Sears, Roebuck and Co.)

and cold water lines, you might want to install them. In the plumbing trade, the small shutoffs are known as *stops*.

If your pipes run out of the floor to the sink, you'll want *straight stops*. If they come out of the wall, *angle stops* will not only give you the convenience of shutoff valves, but at the same time make the right-angle bends needed to link the horizontal pipes of the faucets with the vertical pipes coming in. Flexible supply tubes conveniently connect directly to these stops.

One faucet company in Indiana has built a business supplying do-it-yourself faucet installers. Its ad says, "Install this washerless two-handle faucet over the weekend." You should be able to do it in an afternoon even if you stop to do other things.

NEW SINKS

New sinks are about as easy to install as new faucets. Many even come with do-it-yourself instructions. Many people these days buy new vanities into which they recess their new bathroom sinks, and if you do likewise you won't even have to worry about supporting your sink's substantial weight.

Replacing an old tub with a new one is well within the skills of motivated do-it-yourselfers, but overall it may take more work than many novices realize. Typically you first have to rip away floor tile and then wall tile along the tub. Next you must disconnect the drain and water supply lines. Finally you can yank out the old tub, which may weigh 100 pounds or so, and set in place the new one. And then you have to hook it up, patch the floor, patch the walls. It's enough to make many people first try to

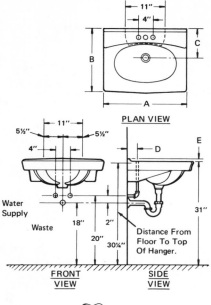

PLAN VIEW

FRONT VIEW   SIDE VIEW

Water Supply

Waste

FIGURE 9-10 This sketch for a do-it-yourself sink shows how to plan for faucets and water hookup. (Courtesy Sears, Roebuck and Co.)

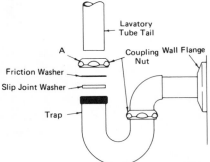

Lavatory Tube Tail

Coupling Nut   Wall Flange

Friction Washer

Slip Joint Washer

Trap

FIGURE 9-11 Here's a typical installation for hooking up the drain in a new sink. If, instead, the drain runs through the floor, another curve in the trap directs the flow toward the floor. (Courtesy Sears, Roebuck and Co.)

refinish the old tub where it sits. New epoxy kits designed to do just that finally work well (old ones never did), assuming you follow *all* of the directions meticulously.

Installing a shower in a new location is not a big chore, especially if you invest in one of the pre-fabs made from molded fiberglass or plastic. They weigh close to 100 pounds, but you simply set one into place, secure it, and hook it up to a drain and to a water supply. The job can be handled in a leisurely weekend.

HOT WATER HEATERS AND WATER SOFTENERS

Putting in water heaters and water softeners where none have ever existed can be a major undertaking. On the other hand, most people install them in basements or utility rooms where pipes are already running in plain sight, and there the job is easy. You simply have to pick out likely spots in those pipes to make your plumbing hookups. For an electric heater, you also need to make a wiring connection; for a gas heater, you need a gas hookup (using black iron pipe unless your local code accepts copper).

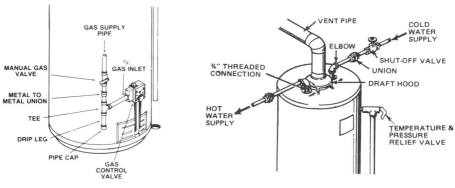

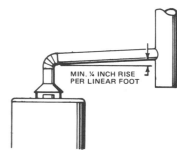

FIGURE 9-12 From Sears, Roebuck and Company, these easy-to-follow guidelines will lead the novice through installing a new gas hot water heater. The job is easiest if you install the new one close to the spot where your old one sat.

Most people simply want to replace their ancient heaters and softeners. If that's your goal, you'll probably need to do little more than uncouple the old hookup and substitute a few pipes to compensate for differences between the old arrangement and the new. The job can be done in an afternoon. Nearby we've reproduced a few illustrations from installation manuals, to show how simple the job is.

FIGURE 9-13 It's amazing what a little ingenuity, some new fixtures, and some puttering can do to change a dreary bathroom into a haven from the cares of the world. (Courtesy Kohler Company.)

NEW TOILETS   If you want to install a toilet where none has existed, you'll have to pipe water to the toilet—probably with ½-inch pipe—and run a drain from it—probably with 4-inch pipe. Almost all codes require, in addition, a vent pipe to the outside, probably through your roof unless an existing one is nearby. Code requirements for toilets are stringent because of the sanitation hazards inherent in improper installation.

Replacing an old toilet with a new one is simply a matter of pulling out the old, replacing the wax gasket between toilet and drain pipe, and bolting in the new. Making the water connection consumes only half as much time as putting in a new faucet, since you need only a cold-water hookup. Carefully measure your old installation and consult with your supplier to make sure the new one fits where the old one sits. Then go to it.

10
How to See Through Window and Door Design Problems

A few years ago we would have been reluctant to include this chapter. Frankly, the doors and windows then available required a lot of skills, tools, time, and persistence to install properly. Vast amounts of energy can sneak by inadequate windows and exterior doors, and homeowners eager to conserve that energy try to make sure that they are put in airtight. Until recently, smart people called in pros to do the installing.

But now, no doubt, your local building supply dealer stocks a number of pre-hung doors, pre-cut door frames, and windows that you can install in about the time it takes you to assemble a child's Christmas toy. In fact, for the last door-and-frame we bought, we gave our 16-year-old the set of instructions and he puzzled them out himself.

People don't install or replace windows and doors for energy conservation alone. Most often, the primary goal is to improve the appearance and serviceability of their homes. In many instances, nothing does that faster than knocking through a wall to put in a new door, or replacing a beat-up or too-small old window in the room that gets the most use. To help you, we'll explain the rudiments of window and door construction, as well as basic installation information. Then, for the rest of the chapter, we'll share design considerations to keep in mind as you study ways to improve your windows and doors or to use them as tools in improving your home's layout and appearance.

HOW TO FRAME A DOOR OR WINDOW

We're going to start right at the very first possible step you'll need if you're putting a door or window into a newly built home or addition. If you're simply replacing or modernizing, you can pick up the step-by-step account at the appropriate point.

In most homes, the walls are supported by vertical boards called studs, generally 2 × 4s or 2 × 6s. They are spaced 16 inches apart in most twentieth century homes, especially those using 2 × 4s; but builders are starting to use 2 × 6s spaced 24 inches apart. The walls are designed to hold up their share of weight only if the appropriate number of studs is used. However, since doors only 16 inches or even 24 inches wide would be tough for most people to squeeze through, builders (or do-it-yourselfers) have to *leave out* at least one or two studs to fit even an ordinary standardized door into a wall.

Actually, "leave out" is not 100 percent correct; "displace" is more like it. You must still put up the full number of studs but, in essence, you slide a few off to the sides to make room for the doorway or window. In addition, to provide support for the area above the window or door, a *header* is necessary at the top of your opening. The header is a small horizontal beam made from two boards. Small doors and windows can employ 2 × 6s for headers, but larger ones require larger boards. (Figure 10-1 tells you what size header to use in what size opening.)

Notice in Figure 10-2 how the "shoved-aside" studs get chopped off so they fit *under* the header. We've known many do-it-yourselfers who were afraid of ripping out old windows or doors, or building in new ones, for fear their walls would collapse while they were trying to frame in the opening. Rest assured that you can safely knock out three or four consecutive studs from any wall built reasonably well, without worrying about the house collapsing before you've replaced those studs. Replace them with a properly sized header plus at least one "cripple" stud for every displaced stud, and you won't have to worry about the ceiling sagging or nearby plaster or wallboard cracking. (Use 16d nails for fastening your framing boards.)

How big should you make your frame for the door or window? That depends on the window or door frame you intend to install. These vary from about 6 inches to 12 inches bigger than the actual door or glass area

FIGURE 10-1 Size of headers to use in framing doors and windows.

MAXIMUM SPAN (ft.)	HEADER (in.)
3½	Two 2 by 6s
5	Two 2 by 8s
6½	Two 2 by 10s
8	Two 2 by 12s

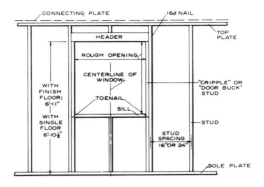

FIGURE 10-2 Terminology and design of typical door or window frame, and guidelines for where to nail in the headers. (Courtesy U.S. Forest Products Laboratory.)

involved. So first buy the door or window; then do your rough framing to meet the manufacturer's recommendations. After that your chosen window or door will slip neatly into its rough opening.

PRE-FAB DOORS

Figure 10-3 shows the cross-section of a finished, well-installed door frame from several different aspects. Fortunately you don't have to design, cut, and assemble all of the minor and major pieces. We've reproduced this drawing for two reasons. First of all, it shows what lies beneath many of your existing exterior doors, in case you ever have to work on them. Second, it shows you how lucky you are to be able to run downtown and buy a pre-fab door frame.

We bought one of the standard pre-fab units recently when we built a garage. We didn't even unpack it before we handed it over to our 16-year-old, Jeffrey, with no advice beyond, "Put it in by Saturday." We didn't even add, ". . . or else." He put it in. It works fine. The weatherstripping that came built into the threshold and packed in the kit for adding onto the sides, keeps those subzero Wisconsin winds out of the garage.

For interior doors, the finished frames are less complicated, and therefore less expensive, than those for exterior use. But we still recommend that you buy kits. The time and headaches they save are well worth the extra cost. In fact, if you want you can even buy an interior door already hung in its pre-assembled frame. You simply have to do the rough framing, slip the pre-fab unit into place, and nail it.

Often, your chosen door doesn't fit perfectly into even your well-installed frame. You'll probably have to use an electric sander, SurForm tool, or plane to trim the door's edges to size. Figure 10-5 gives the clearances you should shoot for as well as other important dimensions. And the next drawing shows how to set hinges into the door if you don't

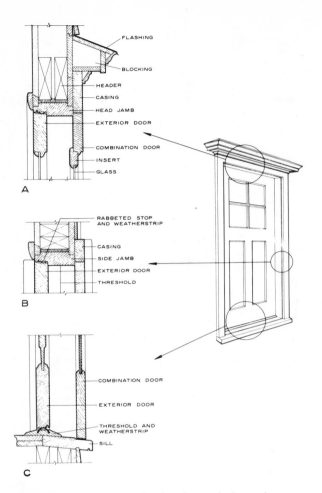

FLASHING

BLOCKING

HEADER

CASING

HEAD JAMB

EXTERIOR DOOR

COMBINATION DOOR

INSERT

GLASS

A

RABBETED STOP
AND WEATHERSTRIP

CASING

SIDE JAMB

EXTERIOR DOOR

THRESHOLD

B

COMBINATION DOOR

EXTERIOR DOOR

THRESHOLD AND
WEATHERSTRIP

SILL

C

FIGURE 10-3 Here's what lies beneath that calm surface of a well-made outside door. Fortunately you can buy it in a pre-fab kit these days; years ago, carpenters like Frank's grandfather actually built up this web of molding and supports from scratch. (Courtesy U.S. Forest Products Laboratory.)

buy a pre-hung unit. Use a chisel to gently carve away enough wood so the surface of the hinge is flush with the surface of the edge of your door.

Locks and knob sets come with almost universally adequate instructions for do-it-yourself installers. For the most part, to attach one easily you need an electric drill with a hole-cutter attachment. If your chosen lock set calls for a squared-out opening, you can sometimes simply drill small holes along the perimeter of the sketched-in opening, then chisel the opening into its appropriate size and shape.

When you're shopping for knobs and locks, don't overlook the fancier models available at less than fancy prices. You can get massive

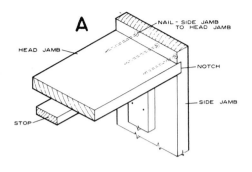

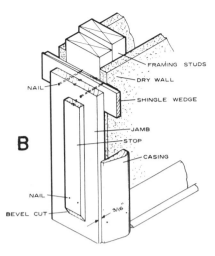

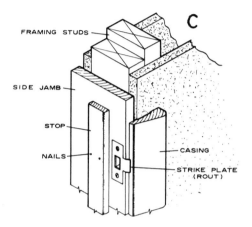

FIGURE 10-4 Interior doors are built about like this, whether a kit or made from scratch: (A) The top of the jamb comes notched if in a kit; you can skip the notching for a door you design and install yourself. (B) All that looks like trim is not necessarily trim in a door; some is functional. (C) Here's how the door strike goes in.

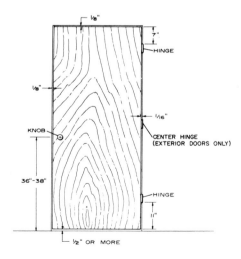

FIGURE 10-5 Clearances recommended for interior and exterior doors. (Courtesy U.S. Forest Products Laboratory.)

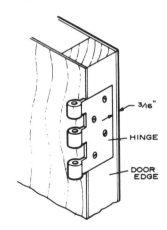

FIGURE 10-6 Space the hinges in your door according to this plan. With a router or chisel, pare away enough wood from the door edge to make the surface of your hinge flush with the edge of your door. Do likewise at the door frame. (Courtesy U.S. Forest Products Laboratory.)

bronze handles plus matching door-knocker-and-lock sets for less than you might think. It's a quick way of turning a utilitarian item into a decorative asset.

NEW WAYS OF LOOKING AT DOORS

A door doesn't have to look like a door. It can be made of fabric, for instance, and resemble a drape for a 1920s look. Or it can be a bamboo curtain that raises whenever you need access to the sleeping alcove or storage space or desk that it conceals.

When a long opening has to be closed off, the alternatives just mentioned will prove to be useful. You can also choose from among the dozens of styles of bi-fold, accordion, folding, and sliding door available. All the ones we've seen come with adequate installation instructions. But measure your opening carefully and for folding doors or bi-folds decide whether you want the edges to fasten inside or outside the doorway. Study the dimensions of possible choices before you buy them. If you're filling a standard-size doorway, you'll probably find bi-folds or shutter-type doors that fit. Otherwise you may have to buy the next larger size and trim.

Approach the installation of track doors with confidence. We learned that lesson the hard way. We assumed that those complicated looking bi-fold assemblies had to involve complicated hardware, and that

FIGURE 10-7   Of course, window treatments are for windows. But used creatively, they're excellent for other places, too. Here are some suggestions: (A) Slim-slat venetian blinds wall off a fold-down desk in this work and storage area. It's a particularly useful idea for one-room living spaces and can be used effectively in kitchens. Match the blind to the wall if you'd like it to disappear when closed. If you'd prefer an extra "window" in the room, select blinds of the same color as you use at the real windows. (B) Slim-slat blinds can also serve as room dividers—as can shades or vertical panels of woven woods. Blinds give you the option of a solid wall appearance or a super-graphic look. Woods create a warmer, decorative feeling. (C) The "closet" bed has come to life again because of energy—just as testered beds have been revived. Here, ceiling-mounted draperies can be closed for cozy twin-bed sleeping. They stack back over extra storage shelves. This treatment also screens out light for those daytime sleepers. (D) and (E) The drapery-door idea was sent to Kirsch by Ms. Sally van Schaick of Schenectady, N.Y. The door's between her hall and living room, and she put a drapery on both sides. She's also covered a seldom-used-in-winter outside door with draperies and finds her home stays warmer. You could do the same with woven woods. (Courtesy Kirsch Company.)

every panel in the four-door bi-fold had to be attached to the upper track. When we saw no such hardware or attachment devices in the manufacturer's package, we bought our own. Then we assumed that there had to be a lower track as well as an upper, when in fact most bi-folds operate perfectly well just hanging from their own hardware, and only their hinged end panels require bottom connections. The job took us an extra two hours as we tried to circumvent the manufacturer's easy instructions.

**INVITATION
TO A
(WINDOW)
HANGING**

Assuming you're willing to do the proper rough framing shown earlier in this chapter, you can simply slip into place almost any kind of window on the market today. Even professional carpenters don't enjoy fitting window parts in one at a time, so practically every window sold today is pre-assembled. Many even come with exterior molding pieces cut to size.

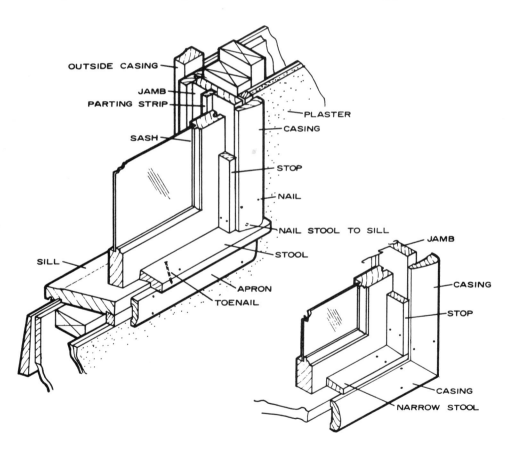

FIGURE 10-8 Two ways of installing a window from scratch (to help you to understand what lies behind your finished windows). Fortunately most windows installed today come pre-assembled, with kits for the molding included or available as an extra item. (Courtesy U.S. Forest Products Laboratory.)

FIGURE 10-9 Insulating abilities of typical windows. A measure of the ability of *all* the material in a window (glass, metal or wood frame, and sash) to *transfer* heat is known as its *U-value.* Its opposite, the *R-value,* shows the window's ability to *resist* the transfer of heat. Therefore, look for the highest R-values or lowest U-values. Many companies provide U-value or R-value figures for only their smallest units; their windows with large panes, of course, transmit a great deal more heat. When you're comparing windows, be sure that the figures are for same-sized units. Shown are values for one brand of well-made wood-framed windows. They were tested with room temperature at 70°F, outdoor temperature at 0°F, and a wind at 15 mph.

TYPE OF GLAZING	INSULATING VALUE "U"	"R"	INSIDE GLASS SURFACE TEMPERATURE
Single-pane window	1.04	0.96	14° F
Double-pane window	0.52	1.92	42° F
Double-pane patio door	0.58	1.72	41° F
Triple-pane window	0.33	3.03	52° F

Given all these considerations, your installation of a window where there was none, or a new one where there used to be an outmoded one, goes about like this:

1. Buy the window unit.
2. Rough-frame according to dimensions included with your window unit.
3. Test-fit the window in its rough frame and make any needed corrections.
4. Slip the window into place and nail it there.
5. Install the exterior molding, generally supplied with your window.
6. Install the interior molding, generally your responsibility to buy.
7. Promptly paint or varnish the window if it comes unfinished.
8. Enjoy.

Your lumber yards and home improvement centers are full of attractive improvements over the common chicken-coop window. Go shopping with stars in your eyes. Even architectural beauties like bay

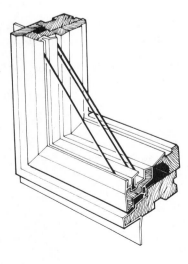

FIGURE 10-10 A cross-section of a very well-constructed, insulated window shows how the three layers of glass are separated by air to build up insulating power. (Courtesy Andersen Corporation.)

windows can be installed by motivated do-it-yourselfers. But do keep in mind that even the best designed triple-glazed wooden windows lose more heat in winter than the most haphazardly insulated walls. Don't plunk down your money without long thought as to (1) whether you really need that window (practically or aesthetically), (2) how big it has to be to provide the view you want, (3) whether you can put it on the sunny south to let in solar heat during daylight, and (4) how well insulated it is. A nearby chart shows comparative insulating values for the windows offered by one major manufacturer.

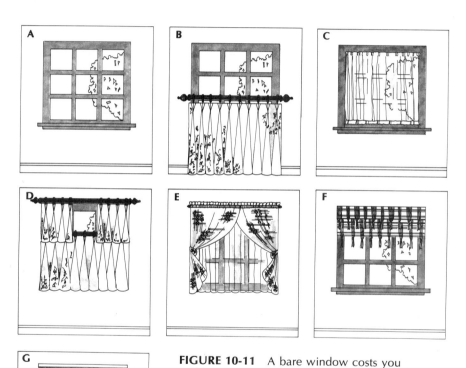

FIGURE 10-11 A bare window costs you nothing—except energy expense and possible sun damage to your furnishings. Both heat and cold can penetrate inside. (B) Although it's economical and easy to make, a single tier cafe curtain provides minimal protection from the outside temperatures. (C) A sheer curtain, shirred on spring tension rods inside the window frame, helps insulate a little bit. It also screens your view full time. (D) Adding a top tier to a cafe treatment helps to insulate. It can be closed against cold winds or red hot sun. The cost is minimal. (E) If curtains fit your budget or you really like their looks, do them in two layers—one opaque, one sheer. Close them when the day is very hot or cold. (F) Energy conservation is a super-sound reason to invest in woven woods. An outside mount is better than an inside. A solid weave is better than an open one. (G) Double treatments save, and double treatments of a woven wood save most. These are vertical panels hung on Archifold, as flexible as draperies. (Courtesy Kirsch Company.)

The economics of windows are such that it seldom pays to replace older units purely for the sake of upgrading their insulation value. (Fortunately some manufacturers offer extra insulating panes for do-it-yourself installation in older windows.) But if you're remodeling anyway, and want to install updated windows, then by all means buy the best insulated ones your money can buy.

**PRETTY
WINDOWS**

Energy savings can be had, also, from well-designed drapes and shades inside your windows. In Chapter 5 we introduced some information on that subject. The illustrations here add some more food for thought.

If energy saving is not your primary concern, there's plenty of new hardware and new fabric to help doll up windows. Even the simple tieback can be used creatively, as Figure 10-12 shows. Hanging plants turn windows into greenhouses. Even the old venetian blind has been streamlined in appearance and ease of installation. Now you can even find multi-colored blinds to accentuate your color scheme.

FIGURE 10-12   Same room, same basic furnishings, but in a summer-winter version. When it's cold outside (left), the window wears mini-blinds and yards and yards of fabric—sheer and lined draperies, topped with a box pleated valance. In the summer version (right), flat panels, made with pocket headings, hang from the valance portion of the triple rod set. (Open traverse rods completely so empty carriers won't show.)

Since sparseness helps you keep your cool, roll up the rug in summer and put things away. If you need extra seating, move outdoor furniture inside.

Accessories alone can do a lot. Use table skirts and pillows in the winter. On the wall, interchange a rya rug and mirror as fits the current season. Glass, chrome, any shiny surfaced objects, are for summer months. Books, candles, dried flowers are better in the winter. (Courtesy Kirsch Company.)

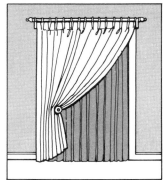

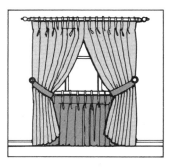

FIGURE 10-13 Even the simple tieback can be used creatively. (Courtesy Kirsch Company.)

FIGURE 10-14 Using drapery hardware or pickups from other counters of your favorite stores, you can turn ordinary windows into mini-greenhouses. (Courtesy Kirsch Company.)

FIGURE 10-15 To hang venetian blinds, carefully measure the window, order the blind, hang the 1-2-3 type hardware, and slip the blind into the brackets. (Courtesy The Siesel Company, Inc.)

11
How to Paint Damn Near Anything Inside Your Home

The subject of household painting is like the subject of sex. It isn't taught well in school, you can't learn about it at your hardware store, and there's so much misinformation going around that it's hard for people to enjoy it. But the fastest—and often the cheapest—way to vastly improve your home is to put on a coat of cheery paint. So to remedy the lack of knowledge about paints, we're including all the basic information you'll ever have to know.

WHAT'S THE BEST PAINT?

Reduced to simplicity, paint is a mixture of (1) pigments, (2) a mineral that makes the pigments opaque, (3) a natural or synthetic plastic that dries into a hard thin film to hold the pigments and opaquing medium to the wall, (4) a solvent that holds it all together until your paint dries, and (5) additives that make it easy to apply.

As with any other commercially prepared mixture today, the makers can use expensive ingredients or cheap ones. If a manufacturer chooses cheap pigments or opaquing minerals, the paint won't look good. If cheap

FIGURE 11-1 Your painting job doesn't have to be a nightmare. This chapter tells how to do it and still smile. (Courtesy Padco, Inc.)

plastics are dumped in, the paint won't wash well or last long. Should the maker scrimp on additives, the paint may look good and last well, but you'll have a tough time applying it.

So how do you pick out which paints have quality ingredients? The same way you pick out a cake mix or a car; you select a brand name you know to be good or a dealer you know you can trust. As with cake mixes and cars, you can also gain some insight into the various qualities of brand-name paints by checking *Consumer Reports*. Periodically, it rates paints, but since few brands are nationwide, you may not be able to find the brands it selects as best buys.

We've done a lot of painting in our days—walls, ceilings, siding, garages, furniture, metal, concrete—and we've bought major national brands as well as local private labels. We're not going to buy any more private labels without a trial on something small. In New York there was one local factory that made really good paint that the pros loved; we found a local factory in Wisconsin, but there the pros loved the paint only because of its price. Being old hands at slapping paint on walls, they knew how to make it behave even though the factory had scrimped on additives. Even Frank could make the paints behave if he worked at it, but Judi couldn't make that cheap paint stay, and she was trying to cover an entire home exterior with it. It almost caused a civil war.

One trick we did learn, over the years, was to choose custom-blended paints. For a few dollars extra, you can get exactly the shade you want. In addition, folks really do notice that the color's a little special.

Years ago there used to be a big difference in quality between the oil-based paints that require turpentine clean-ups, and the water-based paints that wash off brushes and hands in soapy warm water. Today, the differences are negligible. The oil bases with their natural and alkyd resin plastics are no better for almost any application but one (primers) than the water-based synthetic latex and acrylic plastics.

There are differences in paint formulations, however. Some are specially designed for use on metal, others for washability, others for brilliant color. Let *those* criteria guide your choice in paints. To help you, Figure 11-2 offers guidelines on which popular type of paint works best for which application.

The chart assumes that you are painting over already-painted surfaces. Few paints work well when applied to bare plasterboard or metal surfaces. When you're painting something for the first time, it's almost mandatory to use what's known as a primer. (Generally it's bad to use an oil-base over a water-base without a primer in between, though the other way round is fine.) The best primers are still generally oil-based, although some companies offer good water-base primers. The primer is designed to seal and stick firmly to a bare surface and to provide a good surface for applying your finishing coats. Pick a primer that's intended for the surface you want to prime.

BRUSH, PAD, OR ROLLER?

There's a great marketing war going on between the makers of brushes, pads, and rollers. Don't get caught in it. Good quality brushes, pads, and rollers all do a fine job. Poor quality ones don't do any kind of job. Beyond that, personal preference is the most important criterion. Our preferences influence this section, which is designed to help guide just your initial choices.

These days, most people are better off rejecting brushes for painting

FIGURE 11-2 There's a beautiful, durable, easy-to-apply paint product for every paintable surface . . . and in any color your heart desires. This table will help you select the best finishing material for your interior surfaces. A—First choice for ease of application or best results. B—Harder to apply, or poorer results. X—Not recommended.

SURFACES	FLAT PAINT	SATIN ENAMEL	SEMI-GLOSS	PORCH & FLOOR ENAMEL	QUICK-DRY ENAMEL	VARNISH (Especially urethane)	WOOD STAINS
WALL							
Plaster	A	A	B	X	X	X	X
Wallboard	A	A	B	X	X	X	X
Masonry	B	A	A	B	X	X	X
CEILINGS							
Plaster	A	B	B	X	X	X	X
Masonry	A	B	B	X	X	X	X
Acoustical	A	A	B	X	B	X	X
TRIM							
Wood	B	B	A	X	A	A	A
Metal or plastic	B	B	A	X	A	B	A
FLOORS							
Wood (painted)	X	X	X	A	X	X	X
Concrete	X	X	X	A	X	B	X
Hardwood	X	X	X	X	X	A	B
MISCELLANEOUS							
Wood paneling	X	X	X	X	X	A	B
Furniture	X	B	B	X	A	A	A

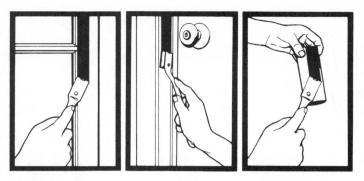

FIGURE 11-3   If you hate the care that a high-quality small brush demands, then your best bet is probably a trim-sized pad. Use it, toss away the pad; save the handle for your next painting job—if you can only remember which drawer you toss it into.

large walls. The good-quality wide brushes needed to do the fastest, neatest jobs are very expensive compared to good rollers and pads. Using ordinary, quality-built rollers requires a bit more practice, we've found, than learning to use good pads. Many people are particularly bothered by the fact that some rollers splatter a bit when used quickly. Even that aspect has been conquered by rollers with built-in spatter shields.

For trim and other small surfaces, we still prefer good brushes. But then we seem to do a lot of painting, and we carefully clean our brushes after every use so they're in good shape the next time we need them. (We avoid natural-bristle brushes for latex paint, choosing nylon instead.) If you're not so fastidious, you might prefer a trim-sized pad; you can toss out the used pad and save the handle for future use.

You can dip brushes directly into a paint can, if you want. But if you're working from a gallon-sized can of paint, you might be asking for trouble if you approach it that way. First of all, the full gallon is a bit heavy for small people to tote around and up and down ladders. Second, what happens if you tip the full gallon? That's an awful lot of mess. We often pour part of a gallon into another can and work from that. (We save coffee cans and washed-out old latex paint cans. If you're using a washable paint you can even use a metal or plastic household pail. Wash after using and it's as good as new.)

In using paint cans with brushes, a lot of people are annoyed at the amount of paint that accumulates around the rim as they wipe off the excess from the brush. That rim-full always seems to spill off. If you poke several nail holes in the rim before you get started, the paint will drain back into your can and save a lot of mess. When you hammer the cover back on, the holes will be covered up. An alternative trick, learned from the pros, is to tie a temporary string or wire across the top from one side of the handle to the other, and use it to wipe the brush.

Larger pads and rollers require some sort of tray. Don't skimp on price here either. Buy one that can attach securely to a ladder so you can

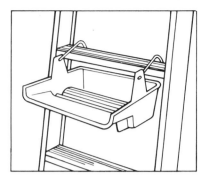

FIGURE 11-4 Invest in a tray that's made for pads and rollers so you can do your best work. Be sure to get one that clamps securely onto a ladder for painting ceilings and upper portions of walls. (Courtesy Padco, Inc.)

do the tops of walls and the ceilings without having to climb down every time the pad or roller needs refilling. Fill the tray no deeper than to cover the lower flat section, so you can remove the excess paint before lifting the roller. You can also tackle high areas by screwing a threaded broom or mop handle into the threaded handle of your roller or pad.

PAINT YOUR ROOM IN A WEEKEND

Painting an entire room shouldn't take more than one weekend. Friday night you can move out all the easy-to-carry furniture, the lamps, the clothes if you're painting the closet, the curtains and drapes. Move the really big furniture to the room's center and spread a large drop-cloth over it and the entire floor. (Buy the largest and heaviest dropcloth you can find. We've used the same one over a dozen times, and it's well repaid the investment.) If you're tempted to save a dollar or two by using old sheets, don't. Paint soaks through most fabrics very quickly. And if you choose a plastic dropcloth, be careful where you step once it begins to be spattered. Drips dry slowly on plastic and you could end up walking paint all over the house.

Spend about an hour, that Friday night, taking out all your picture hooks and other wall hardware and then preparing the walls and woodwork. Eliminate cracks, chips, holes, and similar blemishes. Scrape away all the loose plaster, wood, and paint that cling to the holes and cracks in the wall, and fill all but pinholes with patching plaster (spackle) or plastic wood. When it's dry, sand until each patch is flush with the wall.

If a hole is deep—about ¼ inch or more—fill only half of it at a time, waiting half an hour for the first dose to dry before you plaster again. Or—another painter's trick—stuff a tight wad of paper into the hole and then adhere your plaster patch to it. Nobody'll know the difference.

With a big indentation that isn't very deep, you needn't try to make its entire surface flush with the wall. Just sand to eliminate the obvious edges of the blemish. Nobody will notice that tiny depression if its edges are smooth.

Plastic wood comes ready-to-use in a can or tube, but for large coverup jobs patching plaster or spackle is a great deal cheaper. It comes ready-mixed or dry, and both are easy to apply. If you buy the dry, add the least liquid required to make it into a moist paste. The thicker it is, the easier it is to work. For patching, use whatever tool feels right—screwdriver, putty knife, old silverware, your finger, just so long as it smooths out the crack.

Woodwork that has suffered through layer after layer of paint often cracks like the skin of an alligator. Unless you really go for alligator-skinned woodwork, buy a can of quick-drying putty. With fingers or putty knife, smooth the putty over the cracks until they vanish. Once you've acquired the knack of alligator-taming, the procedure goes quickly. And if filling cracked woodwork becomes tedious, remember the alternative—scraping off all the paint and sanding down to the bare wood.

Once your walls and woodwork are smooth, vacuum all the places where dust or dirt has accumulated, including the tops of above-eye-level moldings. If some of that dust gets on your roller or brush, it can cause streaking and bumps; if you paint over it, the paint may start peeling months later. If you suspect that there's grime, grease, or other oil on walls or woodwork, get out a scrub brush and pail. This is one step even some pros overlook, but saving an hour now may result in peeling paint months from now, when you haven't even got any good paint left to match it with.

When you wash, tackle the ceiling first. Then wash the walls from baseboards upward, to prevent hard-to-remove wall-washing streaks. Regardless of the detergent manufacturer's instructions, rinse the walls really clean, or the paint will flake. Remove collars from light fixtures and, if you like masking tape, use the one-inch kind on all the edges of your windows where glass will meet paint. If you wait until just before you paint window-frames, you'll probably find an excuse to leave it off. (If you prefer, you can scrape the paint from the window glass with a scraping tool after the job's all done. Scrapers work best if (1) the windows are grimy, (2) you scrape within a few days after painting—though not the next day, and (3) you're patient and careful and change dull blades frequently.)

Painting is a daytime project. Trying to spread that silken new skin is well-nigh impossible by artificial light. When the sun dawns on a new day and light starts hitting your room, you'll see all the spots you missed while painting in the dark. So start your job early on Saturday. With your paint pan laid carefully away from careless feet, pour enough rich clean paint to fill the reservoir. If you're working with latex paint, the can may direct you to wet the roller or pad before painting. By wet they mean dampened slightly. Any wetter and you'll spatter.

First give all your patches a fast once-over. Then begin with the ceiling. With your eye, section it off into workable areas (about 2 feet by 3 feet each is ideal) and tackle them one at a time. If all your furniture is piled in the center, you may find it easiest to work from the center out to the four corners of the room. If so, do a small test strip, let that dry a half hour, and then paint next to it; if both areas are the same color, you can work from the center out; otherwise, you'd better begin at a corner.

After you start, you'll soon develop your own rhythm and technique.

A roller usually works best if you roll off some paint on the incline before you lift it; a pad should be wiped lightly along an edge of the pan. Lightly; take off just the drippy excess. Each dip should last for your 2′ × 3′ area. Be generous; resist the temptation to spread the paint really thin, or a one-coat job will become a two-coat procedure. Unload your roller or pad with a large M or V and then spread the paint out in one-way strokes. Don't be disappointed if you need a second coat; most light paints are slightly transparent and, unless you're closely matching the color, a second coat is often needed to cover even a lighter paint job.

Before you've finished painting your ceiling, the paint near the starting-point will have begun to dry. It will probably look splotchy with missed spots that pros call holidays. Resist the temptation to dab at those places until your entire ceiling is dry; paint lightens or darkens as it dries, and becomes more opaque too.

Now for the walls. If there are sharp moldings between the ceiling and wall, just pick up the roller and roll side to side and top to bottom. If wall and ceiling meet in a neat right angle, you'll only mess up the ceiling if you try to roll all the way so, as a preliminary, use a brush or trimmer on those edges, doing one wall at a time and following close behind with the roller. Hold the brush or trimmer as nearly parallel to the wall as possible, to avoid spattering the ceiling. If you're all thumbs, an old aluminum blind slat, a piece of stiff cardboard, or a painter's edger (available at many paint stores) will help. Don't consider your day done until you've cleaned out your painting materials.

Take Sunday morning off, have a good Sunday dinner, and then go at the trim and the closet. Keep the dropcloth down, to play it safe. Fill your brush or pad with as much paint as it'll hold without dripping; dip in only halfway and then turn the handle down as you carry it to the trim. Start in an unpainted spot and paint *into* already-painted areas for best coverage. Don't apply masking tape to any areas you painted yesterday, or when you peel off the tape the thin-skinned paint will come with it. It takes several weeks for paint to dry completely through. Don't glop your paint on; its strength doesn't depend very much on its thickness, and too heavy a coat will simply drip and form teardrops. (If your paint is water-base, an *immediate* rub with a warm soapy rag often erases unwanted spatters— even from a rug's edge.)

For very narrow wood trim, paint with the brush or pad's edge. It may be a two-inch tool, but it's only ½-inch across its point.

When you've finished the job, lift your dropcloth carefully. Some of those spatters may still be alive, ready to spill onto the carpet or a chair. Fold the edges into the center and then wrap it all up for next painting. (If the paint is oil-based, make extra sure it's all dry before you store the cloth or plastic away, or you may end up with a fire.) If you've got water-base paint, a prompt clean-up of all your brushes, pads, trays, rollers, metal edges, and other tools makes them good as new next time round. (Be sure to get into all the moving parts of your roller frames.) With oil-base paints, use turpentine or its equivalent, remove *all* the solvent when you're done, and opt for paper toweling that you can throw away instead of rags that, kept around, become fire hazards.

Leave the closet door open so it dries as quickly as the rest of the room, and Monday your room will be ready to use again.

DESIGN WITH PAINT

One paint dealer in our neck of the woods boasts that he can mix over 5,000 different colors of paint. Almost any store you go into has rack upon rack of custom-blends to choose from. With choice that difficult, it's no wonder most people opt for standard off-white. You've got to admit it's safe.

But just the color of your paint can lend drama to a room, or cheeriness, or warmth or coolness. You can take advantage of these effects once you know just a few basics about color.

First, remember that certain factors affect color. One is the type of light in the room. A shade that appears green in daylight might look blue under flourescent lighting and yellow under incandescent lighting. When choosing colors, try to see them in the kind of light your room will have.

Color is also affected by room or wall size. The larger the area covered by one color, the stronger the color appears. A color that seems soft on a small paint store sample card may turn out to be garish on your walls. (One trick we play on those paint chips is to project a mental picture of a large wall onto *them* instead of the other way around. It takes concentration, but it works.)

Surface texture, too, affects color. The same paint applied to different textures often seems to be a separate color on each surface. The identical color in flat, gloss, and semi-gloss may look like three separate colors, too. (Often, that subtle shade difference looks extremely attractive.)

Once your colors are on your walls, living conditions may affect them. Even the most fastidious housekeeper can't avoid cooking-fume yellowing on the kitchen walls and ceiling without at least a monthly scrubdown. If you start with a yellowish color, it will remain truer longer than if you begin with a shade in the blue family. (Soot, on the other hand, is bluish.)

Color, in turn, affects its surroundings. You can visually widen a long narrow room by painting its side walls a deeper or contrasting color. You can visually lengthen a square, squat room by painting its fourth wall in another color or shade. Light blue, violet, and turquoise make small rooms seem larger just as surely as shades of yellow make the dreariest room seem sun-bathed. Large rooms become intimate with warm colors—beige, persimmon, orange—on the walls. The home decorating magazines often run instructive articles on color, with photographic examples that show these effects.

Because they get little wear, ceilings are painted by professional contractors with the cheapest white flat around. White reflects the most light down—but if that's your goal, experiment with a semi-gloss, which reflects even more light. To make your ceiling appear higher, try a light pastel. We once painted our son's room sky-blue and stenciled on some tiny stars for a really high-up effect. If you want a lowered ceiling, do it with a deep color. Light trim with dark walls, or vice versa, both create drama.

Color affects different people differently. Before you select any color, discuss it with the other people who have to live with it. A blue that's merely restful to one person may seem lifeless to another; a yellow that cheers up your partner may make you nervous and edgy. Children, especially, react strongly to colors. In their rooms, consider their favorites. And if you do have children, select paints that withstand frequent washing; there's no law against painting their walls with durable semi-gloss. With kids around—even with kids not around—semi-gloss or gloss is often preferred for all the woodwork, and semi-gloss is often chosen for the entire kitchen and bathroom.

Which *are* the light colors, and which are dark? Which are warm and which are cool? The best way to understand the relationship of colors to each other is with a color wheel. We suggest that you buy a cheap set of crayons and color the wheel in Figure 11-5, so that you can actually see this relationship. It begins with the three primary colors—red, yellow, and blue. When one of these is added to another, we get a secondary color. Red and blue give us violet, blue and yellow give green, yellow and red give orange. Tertiary colors are made by adding a secondary color (violet, green, or orange) to a primary color. Tertiaries have hyphenated generic names: red-violet, blue-green, yellow-orange, etc.

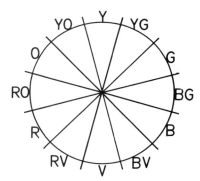

FIGURE 11-5 The color wheel, so familiar to art students, can help you select stylish decorating colors. For best results, why not color in this black and white wheel?

These twelve families comprise the basic color wheel. The addition of white to any color produces a lighter tint; black, a darker shade. Black, white, and their intermediate color, grey, are called *neutral;* they harmonize with any color.

A direct complement of colors is a combination of any two that are directly opposite on our color wheel. That's the simplest color combination you can choose. But there are others:

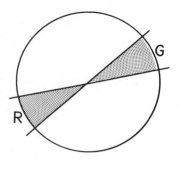 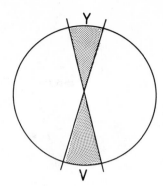

FIGURE 11-6 Direct complement: Colors opposite each other on the color wheel provide a pleasant contrast. The red-green complement (A) is kind of Christmasy for adult use, but it's great for kids. More subtle, the yellow-violet (B) is a decorator's favorite.

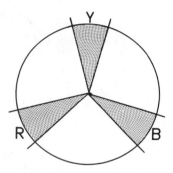 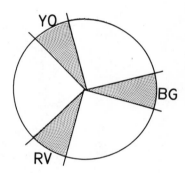

FIGURE 11-7 Triad: Any three colors equidistant from one another on the color wheel provide cheeriness and variety. The primary triad of red, yellow, and blue (A) is great for kitchens, kids' rooms, and such, while a triad of other hues, such as yellow-orange, red-violet, and blue-green (B), lends more subtlety.

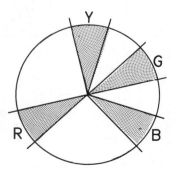

FIGURE 11-8 Alternate complement: Simply stated, a triad plus the complement of any one of the three. Used together, these four tones can be restful, but never dull.

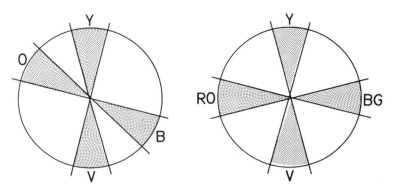

FIGURE 11-9 Double complement: Two sets of complements, as long as they do not touch each other on the color wheel, lend drama, such as (A), or romance, such as (B), to any setting.

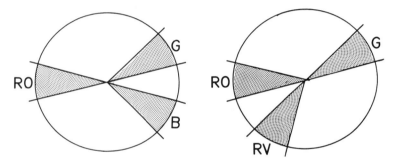

FIGURE 11-10 Split complement: Hospitality with a touch of intrigue, that's what comes of using three colors, two of which are alongside the first's direct complement on the color wheel. Notice how distinct each of the two very similar color schemes is in real life: both have red-orange and green, but the blue (A) lends a regal touch whereas the red-violet (B) leans toward the orient.

FIGURE 11-11 *Analogous:* Use any three to six colors alongside each other on the color wheel, and enjoy the subtle shade-changes they add to your room. (A) For a touch of spring in bedroom, bath, kitchen or elsewhere, use yellow-orange, yellow, and yellow-green. (B) For more formality with many of the same hues, try yellow, yellow-green, green, and blue-green.

1. Triad—a triangle of any three colors equidistant from each other on the wheel
2. Alternate complement—a triad plus a direct complement of one of the three colors
3. Double complement—two sets of complementary colors from anywhere but right next to each other on the wheel
4. Split complement—three colors, two of which are adjacent to the first color's direct complement
5. Analogous match—any three to six colors that are adjacent to one another.

The standard colors in any paint store are the ones that are made by mixing just a few primary, secondary, or tertiary tints into a white or grey base. The custom blends may have as many as a dozen different colors intermixed in varying degrees. It's that complexity of color that makes custom blends so appealing to the eye.

HOW TO PAINT AND PRESERVE FURNITURE AND SHELVES

So often once you've tackled a major improvement, or even just painted a room, some of the built-ins and furnishings now look out of place. Other times, you've added new built-ins—shelves, sideboards, valances, and such—that require a coat of finish. Actually, as this section demonstrates, what's needed—to make them really look as finished as they should—is more than just a slapdash coat. So here's all you'll ever need to know about finishing anything made of wood.

Finishing wood furniture and decoration doesn't have to cost a great deal, nor consume hours and hours of time. But it does require some thought. The finish should match the furniture's use. Softer finishes, in general, bring out the beauty of natural fine woods. If you don't have a fine hardwood to begin with, forget the soft finish. Likewise, putting soft shellac or oil in the path of tough kids is a waste. Figure 11-12 describes the respective merits and demerits of most furniture finishes so you can compare them and choose the one most suited to your needs.

For most hardwood projects you have to use wood filler. That includes hardwood veneer, too. The grain on woods such as maple, mahogany, walnut, oak, and other hardwoods is so coarse that you will never get it down to a smooth satiny finish that holds out dirt unless you smear on what's called *paste wood filler*. The product comes with its own directions, which you may want to alter a bit.

After you've sanded the wood with your finest sandpaper, apply wood filler. If your particular brand recommends various dilutions for different types of hardwoods, follow them.

Make sure you don't wait too long before you wipe off the excess filler. If it dries thoroughly, you'll have to start sandpapering the project over again. Dried paste wood filler is about as tough as lizard skin.

After you wipe away excess filler, give the filler left behind time to dry thoroughly. Then sandpaper the wood once again with extra-fine sandpaper. Each time you add something to wood, you have to sandpaper it again to bring it back to a satiny, smooth surface.

FIGURE 11-12 Pick the best finish for your home improvement projects.

FINISH	GOOD POINTS	WEAK POINTS	RELATIVE COST	PRELIMINARIES FOR FINISHING
LIGHT-WEIGHT VINYL	Easy to apply. Resists dirt. Easy to clean. Wood and nonwood (marble, burlap, prints, etc.) easy to obtain.	Cuts easily. Won't resist many common solvents. Heat spoils it. Moisture and temperature extremes loosen adhesive. Won't fit on three-dimensional design surfaces.	Moderate	Smooth, clean surfaces with no large blemishes.
HEAVY-WEIGHT VINYL	Very rugged. Wood "grain" is embossed into surface for added realism. Easy to clean. Available in prints, marble, etc.	Heat spoils it. Sensitive to a few volatile solvents.	Expensive	Smooth, clean surfaces with no large blemishes.
FORMICA-TYPE PLASTICS	Extremely rugged. Very easy to clean. Resists heat and solvents. Available in wood, marble, prints, etc.	Brittle during installation. Not recommended for covering small areas.	Expensive	Smooth, clean surfaces with no large blemishes.
PAINT				
Enamel	Rugged. Easy to clean. Resists many common solvents.	Looks childish or cheap in some uses. Brushes require cleaning in turpentine or benzine.	Inexpensive	Smooth surfaces, well sanded. Primer coat of paint is important. Sandpaper paint between successive layers.
Water-based	Resists many common solvents. Brushes clean in water.	Looks childish or cheap in some uses.	Inexpensive	Smooth surfaces, well sanded and well cleaned.
Colored lacquer	Rugged. Easy to clean. Resists many solvents. Looks elegant on modern furniture.	Brushes require solvents for cleaning. Flammable until dry.	Inexpensive	Smooth surfaces, well sanded. Sandpaper between successive layers.
Antique	Rugged. Easy to clean. Resists many common solvents. Looks elegant if well applied.	Takes time to apply. Brushes require solvents to clean in most applications.	Modest	Smooth surfaces, well sanded. Primer is important on bare wood. Can be used on already-painted wood and in some cases to conceal surface defects.
VARNISH	Protects natural appearance of real wood. Easy to clean. Relatively rugged.	Brushes require solvent to clean. Doesn't resist water or alcohol well. Dries relatively slowly. Won't stand up under heavy use.	Inexpensive	Smooth surfaces, well sanded. Hardwoods must be treated with filler. Fir plywood may require sealer. Sandpaper or steel wool between successive layers.
CLEAR LACQUER	Rugged. Easy to clean. Resists many common solvents. Looks elegant where clear, shiny look is appropriate. Dries quickly.	Requires solvents to clean brush. Flammable until dry.	Inexpensive	Smooth surfaces, well sanded. Hardwoods must be treated with filler. Fir plywood may require sealer. Sandpaper or steel wool between successive layers.
CLEAR WOOD SEALER	Very rugged. Easy to clean. Protects wood very deeply. Resists most household hazards except cigarettes. Brings out grain well.	Requires turpentine to clean brush.	Inexpensive	Smooth surfaces, well sanded. Hardwoods must be treated with filler. Sandpaper or steel wool between successive layers. (Often used for several first coats, and then another type of finish such as urethane or varnish is applied.)

FINISH	GOOD POINTS	WEAK POINTS	RELATIVE COST	PRELIMINARIES FOR FINISHING
URETHANE	Very rugged. Protects against almost all household hazards. Easy to clean.	Requires solvent to clean brush.	Modest	Smooth surfaces, well sanded. Hardwoods must be treated with filler. Sandpaper or steel wool between successive layers.
DÉCOUPAGE FINISH	Each coat is very, very thick and smooth. Provides a smooth covering over rough or uneven areas.	Requires solvent to clean brush. Not as rugged or easy to keep clean as more conventional finishes.	Moderate	Surface does not have to be smooth, but natural woods should be well sanded to show off their grain. A clear wood sealer should be used for one or more preliminary coats to bring out wood grain.
FURNITURE OIL	Brings out grain of wood. Luxurious "unvarnished" appearance.	Gives wood very little protection against wear or solvents.	Inexpensive	Smooth surfaces, well sanded. Several coats of oil are usually rubbed in with a lot of buffing.
WAX	Easy to apply. Natural, "unvarnished" appearance.	Gives wood very little protection against wear or solvents.	Inexpensive	Smooth surfaces, well sanded. Several coats of oil are usually rubbed in with a lot of buffing.
SHELLAC	Preserves natural look of wood. Easy to apply.	Requires alcohol to dilute shellac and clean brush. Minimum resistance to wear, abuse, and solvents or water.	Inexpensive	Smooth surfaces, well sanded. Hardwoods must be treated with filler. Fir plywood must be treated with sealer. Sandpaper or steel wool between coats.
ORANGE SHELLAC	Often used to provide an instant old-pine look. This effect works best on pine and on fir plywood.	Requires alcohol to dilute shellac and clean brush. Minimum resistance to wear, abuse, and solvents or water.	Inexpensive	Smooth surfaces, well sanded. Hardwoods must be treated with filler. Fir plywood must be treated with sealer. Sandpaper or steel wool between coats.

Stain comes next in our book. You'll find that most cans of wood filler recommend staining first, filling later. If you do that, you'll also have to color the filler. Matching colors gets to be pretty touchy. Good penetrating oil stains can penetrate the filler as well as the wood, so save yourself some headaches—fill first, stain second.

Softwoods such as pine or fir plywood don't require paste wood filler; their grain is more compact. But fir plywood does require some special treatment to tame its otherwise wild grain structure. The grain will show right through many, many layers of paint or clean finishes. Unless you want an embossed look on plywood, tame its grain.

Buy yourself a can of Firzite or a competing brand. The product is sold especially for keeping fir plywood grain in check. Stain the plywood first, if you plan to go that route, and then apply Firzite. If you feel the Firzite has dulled the effect of your stain, you can always apply a second coat of stain after the Firzite dries.

Stain is good for softwoods and hardwoods alike, although you may be wondering why people would invest a pretty piece of change in natural walnut or oak boards if they plan to stain the wood later. Why not use cheap pine or plywood first, and then apply expensive-looking stain?

Because of the grain, for one thing. You might be able to stain pine to match the color of dark oak, but you'll never match the distinctive grain patterns of oak. And you'll never get a hard oak surface by staining pine or plywood.

Many people have the idea that hardwood just naturally comes out looking dark and daring. Most of it doesn't. If the wood you've chosen is lighter and drabber than you hoped for, don't despair just yet. Oil or stain may be called for. But let's run a test first, the sort of test you should use before slapping a lot of wood finish onto any project you hope to cherish.

Take a wooden scrap typical of the whole item you're building. Sandpaper the scrap as finely as you will sandpaper the finished wood, or surface roughness on your test piece will hang onto more of those deeper-colored solid particles in stain than will smooth wood, and your test won't be accurate.

Apply something oily to your test wood. A good rich furniture polish might do it. Any of the paint oils in a set of artist's colors will do fine, linseed oil in particular. For test purposes you can even squirt some household lubricating oil or cooking oil onto the wood and wipe it around. If oil gives your wood the richness you're looking for, then oil is your answer and not stain. Varnish and wood sealers contain enough oil that when you apply them, your wood will pick up the oil you want to have.

If your test colors are not what you wanted, switch to stains next. Use them only on your test pieces first. Wood and wood stains are so divergent in their qualities, there's only one way to find out how they will react with each other—try the chosen stains on your chosen wood.

Your first choice in a stain should be one with the same name as the wood you're working with or trying to duplicate. If you have oak wood but

FIGURE 11-13 Stain carefully. Prepare a sample piece of wood by sanding it as carefully as you do the real thing. Then test the sample with stain to be sure you're going to like the color. Finally, apply your choice of wood finish, such as varnish, to see how the stained wood will look when nearly completed. (Courtesy United Gilsonite Corporation.)

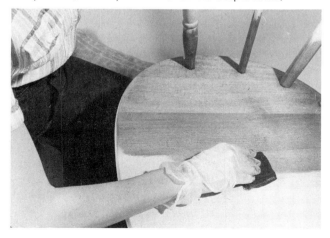

want it darker, try a dark oak stain. About the only kind of stain amateurs should try is *penetrating oil stain.* Follow the directions when you apply it to your test wood. Let it dry, cover it with an oily substance to duplicate the contribution the varnish or other finish will make, and then evaluate your test wood.

If your test piece has about the hue you're after but is too light, give it another treatment or two with the same stain. That should match your requirements.

If the hue is right but the test came out too dark, dilute your chosen stain with turpentine. Then run another test. You can also make a stain come out lighter by giving it less time to dry before wiping away the excess with a soft cloth.

If your early choice of stain is not the right hue, you have two options. You can go out to buy an entirely new stain, this time choosing one with more red, more yellow, or perhaps more purple. Or you can simply add other stains to the can you already have.

A stain such as yellow maple will add yellowness to most stains. Red oak or medium-red mahogany stains will add redness. For more purple coloration, choose a dark mahogany stain.

For many people the most distressing wood stain is mahogany. Part of the problem has to do with the wood itself. Many people remember the deep, dark, purply—almost black—Duncan Phyfe table that Grandma cherished. The wood for that table probably came up from Honduras or Brazil. Today a great deal of mahogany comes from the Philippines. The grain of Philippine—Luan—mahogany is similar to the Honduras species, but the color is not. You have to apply mahogany stain to Luan mahogany before it looks like that old, dark, Honduras kind.

When applied to plywood or pine, mahogany stains often look terrible. You're stuck with wood that looks like it has been painted with cheap purple paint. So proceed carefully with mahogany. Good results are well worth the trouble.

Some stains are easier to use and more pleasing than others. From experience in our own projects, as well as looking over the shoulders of others, walnut stain works well on most hardwoods, pine, or plywood. Maple and yellow maple stains soak into plywood with excellent results, although they may be too light on pine. Light oak and dark oak work well too. All light-colored stains such as ash generally prove disappointing.

Non-woodsy colored stains show off wood grain and add distinctive color to furniture. Red, yellow, orange—any color works if it matches your color scheme. This idea is more useful on large areas. On small areas, the color variation looks more accidental than intentional. On fir plywood, colors come out exceptionally dramatic. Buy some flat or semigloss enamel in your chosen color, some linseed oil too, and make sure you have turpentine around the house. Dilute the colored enamel half and half with linseed oil. Brush it onto your test strip sparingly and give it a chance to dry. Soft grain should soak up the color and turn quite bright. On hard grain, there'll be a soft tint of color.

If you have trouble getting more color into one kind of grain, dilute the enamel with turpentine. Turpentine soaks in better than linseed oil, especially on pine that isn't thoroughly dry.

Apply sealer after the wood is colored, filled, and sanded to perfection. Don't skip this step unless your home is off-limits to children of all ages who spill, drop, and scratch things. Head for your hardware or paint store and look for a can of *penetrating wood sealer.* The product will be very thin and watery looking. It soaks deep into the surface of your wooden furniture to seal up the grain against dirt, pollution, and damage.

Apply sealer evenly with a brush. It soaks in and dries quickly. One coat may not change the appearance of the wood. Apply two or three more coats. The sealer should then become apparent on the surface. As soon as the sealer produces a uniform, dry sheen, you have applied enough. Never use more than six coats of the sealer, however, no matter how much it soaks in unless you plan to use sealer as your final finishing material.

Penetrating sealer can make a fine finish. It resembles what many people call a Danish oil finish, but it's tougher. Sealer shows off the grain and color of natural wood very well. Ironically, it doesn't look finished enough for some people who want furniture to have an obvious and glossy top coat.

Finishing can never be completed with a single coat. Varnish, shellac, penetrating wood sealer, and even urethane finishes need thickness to provide glistening beauty and protection to wood. Between applications you should sandpaper away any surface irregularities. Sand, varnish, sand, varnish, sand, varnish . . . the procedure can *and should* go on for days. Each coat has to dry thoroughly before you sand it or add another

FIGURE 11-14 When you apply varnish, such as the polyurethane shown here, it often helps to buy the quick-drying variety. As you carefully apply five or six coats—often more—a certain amount of dust gets trapped along the way. You can sand out some of it as you go along. You'll have to sand *less* if the finish you work with dries in one hour instead of four. (Courtesy United Gilsonite Corporation.)

coat. In the meantime, you can show off your new piece of furniture and even use it carefully.

Instead of sealer first and then another finish on top, we have started using nothing but polyurethane on most of our projects. We apply first a 50/50 mixture of polyurethane plus mineral spirits or turpentine. If that soaks into the wood so it can scarcely be seen, we apply another coat or two. Then we switch to 25 percent solvent and 75 percent polyurethane for one or two coats. Finally we apply as many coats of undiluted polyurethane as we desire—sanding in between.

Here's a surprise for you. If you don't sand the final coat of varnish, lacquer, shellac, or other woodfinishing product when it dries, the finish may look like it came out of a can. If you want your handmade furniture to look like it belongs in an expensive showroom, wet-sanding with a super-fine grade of sandpaper adds the final touch to a well-executed wood-finishing job.

When you reach this stage in your project, make sure you have super-fine sandpaper that is approved for wet-sanding. Even glossy furniture finishes deserve a touch-up with sandpaper, except for those modern pieces you feel must have a "wet look."

Wet-sanding is like polishing. Use the best furniture oil or oily furniture polish around. Linseed oil works well too. In a pinch, you can even use cooking oil; it's better than no oil at all. Pour a generous amount of oil on the important surfaces of your new furniture. Wet your super-fine sandpaper in the oil and very gently rub over the finish. After you've given the furniture a thorough once-over, wipe away some of the oil to see what's left behind. If you have sanded the top or sides evenly, the finish should now have a luxurious gloss, but it won't have that "out-of-the-can" look.

The more you wet-sand, the more gloss you remove. Going beyond the once-over-lightly stage, you soon approach what's known as a *satin-gloss* finish. In order to get down to a *dull satin* look, you may have to trade in your superfine sandpaper for some wet-grade extra fine. The difference between these two grades of sandpaper is pretty subtle, and so is the difference in the finishes they produce.

Dull satin, by the way, isn't an accurate description, but who are we to change a phrase that has been used for so long? There should be so much varnish, shellac, or lacquer between the wood and the top layer of satiny finish that you get a "through the looking glass" effect. It really doesn't look dull at all.

We've known people who worry that they're going to sand away all the varnish from their first few furniture projects. With oil on the wood, you'd have to sandpaper a long time before wiping away any noticeable amount of varnish. So relax.

PAINT

Paint is little more than varnish with pigments added. In fact, enamel used to be exactly that—a can of varnish into which some creative soul squirted pigment and an opaque medium.

There's no need for a lengthy discussion about how to paint furniture. All you have to do is reread the section on how to varnish. The same rules apply, and that includes the advice on sandpapering the final coat.

Applying a coat or two to woodwork and walls may be a good idea. But to create a professional-looking piece of painted furniture, be prepared to treat it to at least half a dozen coats and to sandpaper the paint between most coats. Even then there's more to painting than meets the untrained eye. Aside from the final sanding, which takes off the cheap surface gloss and imperfections, there's another reason why a lot of professionally painted furniture looks unpainted. *It's been painted with more than one color.*

Say you want an ivory-colored piece of furniture. That's easy—buy some ivory paint. But also invest in a small can of tan, light brown, or gold glaze.

After you apply enough ivory paint to last a lifetime, sandpaper it lightly. Then uncap your second color and dig out a soft rag or paper towel.

Dip your rag into the second paint and wipe it all over your lovely ivory paint job. With a second rag, wipe away most of the wet tan or gold. Wipe hardest near the middle of every large area. Wipe somewhat less vigorously near the edges and corners. In effect, you'll be leaving the most tan or gold color around the outsides of doors or tops. That creates what pros call a framing effect.

It's hard to wipe away the color that sneaks into grooves and carvings on the decoration and legs. That's fine. The extra color there adds an accent.

By the time you finish wiping the second color, nobody will know it's there except you and others privy to this furniture-finishing secret. The furniture will look ivory-colored. But it will look elegant, instead of like somebody just opened a cheap can of paint and sloshed it into place.

Don't worry about wiping away too much of the top color. You can always apply it again. If perchance you leave on more of the overcoat than looks good to you the next day, just apply another coat or two of the base color. Let it dry, sand it, and tackle the overcoat again.

With a pure white base you can use ivory, tan, or beige for a wiping color. For light brown, try dark brown wipe. Dark brown paint can stand a black wipe. Light green should get a dark green overcoating. Gold is widely used, especially over the ivory, olive, and powder-blue shades popular in French Provincial, Italian, and other Mediterranean furniture. With a dark green base, a black wipe would look rather conventional, while a wipe of light green could prove to be unique. Likewise for red, blues, oranges, and similar shades.

Stains also work well. A maple stain can be used on lighter colors, a walnut stain on darker ones.

Thus far we've concentrated on wiping off all but a mere trace of the second color. If you wipe less vigorously all over the piece of furniture, the second color becomes an integral part of the overall coloration. The texture of your wiping strokes also becomes part of the overall appearance. Finishes like that are popularly called antique effects. You can buy kits which preselect the base and glaze colors for your antique effect, or you can save money by assembling your own from the paint shelves.

When you paint furniture, forget about rollers. Even small rollers are harder to clean than brushes, which can get into the little nooks and crannies and corners common to almost all furniture.

Much has been written about the pros and cons of enamel, latex, and acrylic-based paints and the flat, semigloss, and gloss varieties for furniture painting. Most of what's written is true, but also impractical. A high-gloss, oil-based enamel *will* give you the most rugged service of the popular paint varieties, assuming it's of good quality and well applied. But many people don't like high-gloss furniture except for children or in very modern styles. Many are also put off by the thought of digging out a jug of turpentine to clean brushes and hands every time they paint.

You can get fine furniture finishes with good grades of waterbased paint. It's hard to recommend specific brand names or specific types because so many paints are manufactured locally. The best way to find a good paint is to choose a good local dealer.

Semi-gloss paint is the most versatile for furniture unless you want to end up with a very high gloss. Even if you want a very flat finish, avoid the flat paints. The formula that makes paint end up flat also makes it end up weaker than a good semi-gloss. With proper wet-sanding after the final coat, you can reduce even gloss paint to a lustrous flat finish which is finer to look at than any flat paint.

Colored lacquer is ideal when you want bright, sparkling, glossy color as well as a tough surface. It has the added advantage of drying so fast you can apply several coats in one day. Use lacquer the same way you'd use paint. Generally, however, you won't use a wipe of some second color over a bright, glossy finish. Make sure you buy *brushing* lacquer. A well-stocked paint or hardware store may have some professional-grade lacquers designed for use in spray guns. They don't brush on well at all.

If bright colors and a glossy appearance really turn you on, one place to go shopping for lacquer is your local hobby store. What they call model airplane dope is actually a fine grade of lacquer. Make sure you buy the variety designed for use on wood, not for use on plastic. There's only a limited selection of colors but they're bright!

Don't try to brush dope too much. The stuff dries so fast that if you keep brushing it back and forth, you'll be creating more brush strokes than you hope to eliminate. Dope is self-leveling. Left alone, it tends to spread evenly over your work.

12
Walls and Ceilings
Into Works of Art

Don't ask us to explain *why* people think of walls and ceilings as things apart from floors, windows, doors, and such. They even separate wall coverings from ceiling coverings—as well as from floor coverings and window coverings—even though most wall coverings do well on ceilings, and many floor coverings—tiles, parquet squares, even carpeting—can be used on walls as well as countertops. We won't buck convention much; this chapter will just lump together wall and ceiling coverings. But keep in mind, when you read following chapters, that the versatility of many of these materials is limited solely by your imagination.

Our previous chapter dealt with the most fundamental wall and ceiling covering of all—paint. But since tastes are individual, and so are problems with existing walls and ceilings, in this chapter we'll look at yours from start to finish, from how to erect a gypsum-board wall or ceiling to how to fasten mirrors onto them. We'll talk about patching up damaged walls, paneling your rooms, and decorating with wallpaper and other coverings. If you haven't looked carefully lately at other people's newly decorated surroundings, you may be due for some eye openers. Keep your options open until you read this entire chapter; better still, keep them open until you've finished the book.

Our first section may not be of immediate application unless you're planning to build an addition or move some of your walls, but glance through it anyway. Before you start to paint or cut a hole in your walls, it helps to know the fascinating hardware and materials that are hidden barely ½-inch beneath the surface.

DO-IT-YOUR-SELF GYPSUM WALLBOARD APPLICATION

Gypsum wallboard is the construction industry's name for what the ordinary homeowner calls a plasterboard wall or ceiling. Once upon a time, walls and ceilings were plastered individually by workers who mixed the mud at the site and troweled it onto wooden lath or mesh screening that had been nailed to a wall's 2 × 4 studs or a ceiling's joists. If you live in a very old house whose walls and ceilings are somewhat uneven, chances are you've got a real plaster wall. Most likely, yours are gypsum wallboard, which comes from the manufacturer to your local building supplies dealer in 4′ × 8′ or 4′ × 12′ sheets and consists of gypsum (plaster) coated and held together on both sides by paper.

Whether you're installing a new wall or ceiling or repairing a large hole in one, the following instructions apply.

PLANNING THE JOB

A little thought and planning before you start your project can result in better appearance and a saving in materials and time. Make a sketch of the area to be surfaced, laying out the wallboard panels so that you'll install them crosswise or perpendicular to the joists or studs. Use as long a board as you can handle, to reduce or eliminate end joints. For example, in a 1′ × 13′ ceiling where the joists run parallel to the 13-foot dimension, it's best to select 12-foot-long boards. If they're 8 feet long, an end joint will be needed in each course.

Where you can't avoid end joints, stagger them.

When wallboarding a complete room, it is usually better to apply the board on the ceiling first, then the walls.

ESTIMATING MATERIALS

Using your sketch, determine the lengths and number of boards required. In addition to ordinary wallboard, there are several kinds that are made for specific uses. Georgia-Pacific, for example, in addition to its regular wallboard, makes a water-resistant wallboard to back ceramic tiles in bath or shower areas, and a fire-resistant board that's rated to fulfill some special building-code requirements. If your ceiling joists are 16 inches on center, use ½-inch gypsum board; if they're 24 inches on center, use ⅝-inch wallboard.

To estimate nails, figure that for ½-inch-thick wallboard you'll need 5¼ lbs. of 1⅜-inch coated gypsum-board nails for each 1000 square feet of wallboard; for ⅝-inch-thick wallboard get 5¼ lbs. of 1⅞-inch coated gypsum-board nails for each 1000 square feet of wallboard.

You'll also need paper wallboard tape for flat joints and inside corners, metal cornerbead for outside corners, and joint compound for finishing. Figure 12-1 will show approximately how much ready-mixed joint compound and tape to buy for your wallboard.

Often, it's easiest to use both adhesive and nails for applying the wallboard; it's also most secure. You apply the adhesive to the respective joists or studs before each piece of wallboard is positioned and nailed to them, using a caulking gun and making a bead about ⅜-inch in diameter. For each 1000 square feet of wallboard, figure on 8 quart-sized tubes of adhesive.

FIGURE 12-1   Joint tape and joint compound (ready-mixed): how much to buy for gypsum board installation.

WALLBOARD (square feet)	READY-MIXED JOINT COMPOUND (gallons)	WALLBOARD TAPE
100–200	1	2 60-ft. rolls
300–400	2	3 60-ft. rolls
500–600	3	1 250-ft. roll
700–800	4	1 250-ft. roll and 1 60-ft. roll
800–1000	5	1 500-ft. roll

PREPARING
YOUR TOOLS

The basic tools you'll need are:

1. Wallboard cutting knife and heavy-duty knife blade
2. Wallboard hammer or regular crown head carpenter's claw hammer
3. 4-foot T-square or steel straight-edge
4. Steel tape measure
5. Utility saw or keyhole saw
6. Joint finishing knives, 4-inch and 10-inch blades
7. Plastic pan for joint compound (unless you're using ready-mixed)
8. Medium sandpaper for joint finishing
9. Caulking gun if you're using adhesive.

CUTTING
GYPSUM
WALLBOARD

Score the wallboard with your T-square or straight-edge and your wallboard knife. Holding the knife at right angles to the board, score completely through the face paper. Then apply firm, even pressure to snap the board. Fold back the partially separated portion of the board and use the knife again to cut the back paper. Rough edges should be smoothed. (Panels can be cut with a saw if desired, but the mess will be greater.)

To cut holes in the wallboard for electric outlets, light receptacles, and so forth, carefully measure the distance of the opening from the end and the edge of the board, and mark it right on the wallboard. Then outline the opening in pencil and cut with a keyhole saw. The cut-out must be accurate or the cover plate will not conceal your hole.

NAILING

In ceilings, nail along the joists at 7-inch intervals. With walls, if the studs are 16 inches on center, nail along the studs at 8-inch intervals. After

FIGURE 12-2 Cutting wallboard is easy if you use a sharp knife and hold your straight-edge tightly. (Courtesy Georgia Pacific.)

hammering the nails flush, "dimple" each one with a hammer blow firm enough to indent the board's face paper. But don't break the paper.

It's more difficult to install ceiling boards than wallboards because of the overhead positioning. T-braces can hold a board in place while it's being nailed. A satisfactory T-brace consists of a 2-foot piece of 1 × 4 nailed onto the end of a 2 × 4 whose length should be about an inch longer than the floor-to-ceiling height.

When you're using adhesive with nails, you need not nail along every

FIGURE 12-3 This is one of the hardest parts to visualize of the entire gypsum board application. You have to tap the nails hard enough to dimple the plasterboard, but not rip the paper covering. Here's what it looks like.

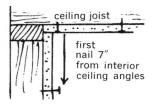

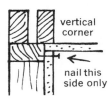

FIGURE 12-4 Don't nail close to the edge when you install gypsum to the ceiling. Nails there pop too easily, and you're better off with no nails than popped nails.

stud; just along each edge. Make sure each nail goes into a supporting joist or stud. Drive the nails to bring the wallboard tight to its supporting board, and then "dimple" each nail.

When you're applying wallboard horizontally to walls, install each top board before the bottom one. Push it up firmly against the ceiling and nail, placing nails 8 inches apart, and keeping all nails back 7 inches from interior ceiling angles. (Nails in the interior angles are apt to pop.) If you use adhesive with nails, you can eliminate all nailing except around the edges of the board. But if the wallboard bows out in the center, it may be advisable to secure it with a temporary nail, hammered in just partway, until the adhesive sets.

If the ceiling height of your wall is greater than 8′2″ or the wall is 4 feet wide or less, place the long edges of the wallboard parallel to its framing members, and nail just as you would if applying the board horizontally.

PROTECTING
OUTSIDE
CORNERS

To protect outside wall edges from damage, install metal cornerbead after you've put up the wallboard. Nail it every 5 inches through the gypsum board into the wood stud.

FINISHING
JOINTS

Although dry plaster (spackle) and joint compound mixes are cheaper, ready-mixed joint compound is easier for do-it-yourselfers to work with when finishing joints, corners, and nailheads. For taped joints, a

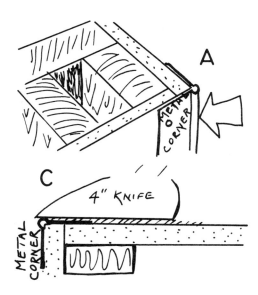
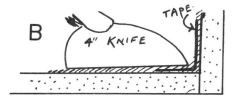
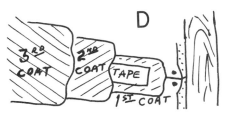

FIGURE 12-5 Here's how to finish off the job once the gypsum board is all in place. (A) Install cornerbead on outside corners which are most vulnerable to damage. (B) Spread ready-mixed joint compound with finishing knife over corners, both inside and (C) outside. (D) This final view shows what the build-up of a base coat, tape, and two covering coats of mix looks like peeled away.

FIGURE 12-6 After your first coat of joint compound, the tape goes up. *That's* when the room starts looking finished. (Courtesy Georgia Pacific.)

minimum of three coats of compound is recommended—an embedding coat under the tape to bond it and two coats over it.

The long edges of wallboard are tapered slightly to aid in finishing joints. With your 4-inch joint finishing knife, apply joint compound or its equivalent fully and evenly into the slight recess created by these adjoining tapered edges. Next, take your wallboard tape, center it over the joint, and press it firmly into the bedding compound with your wallboard knife held at a 45° angle. The pressure should squeeze some compound from under the tape, but enough must be left for a good bond. When it's thoroughly dry (at least 24 hours) apply a fill coat extending a few inches beyond the edge of the tape and feather the edges of the compound. To feather a surface, make a succession of small, light, overlapping x-like strokes across the area, working from top to bottom, and beginning or ending each stroke on the clean wall. The object is to spread the patching compound thinly out onto the untouched plasterboard so that it's difficult to see where its edges begin or end.

When the first finishing coat is thoroughly dry, sand. (Again, wait 24 hours.)

When sanding, wrap your sandpaper around a wood sanding block so you sand the surface evenly. Do not over-sand or sand the paper surface. This may outline the joint or nailhead through your paint.

Using your 10-inch joint finishing knife, apply a second coat and feather the edges about 1½ inches beyond the first coat. When this coat is dry, sand lightly to a smooth even surface. Total width of the compound-covered joint should be 12–14 inches. When you're finished, wipe off the dust in preparation for your paint, wallpaper, or other finish.

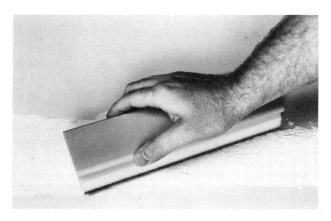

FIGURE 12-7 Wet-sanding the compound, a relatively new procedure, is more like playing with clay than sanding. (Courtesy Padco, Inc.)

FINISHING NAIL HEADS

Draw your 4-inch joint finishing knife across all nails to be sure they are below the surface of the board. Then apply the first coat of compound or spackle with even pressure to smooth it level with the surface of the board. Do not bow your knife blade with excess pressure as this tends to scoop compound from the dimpled area. When dry, apply a second coat; let that dry, sand lightly, and apply a third coat. An additional coat may be needed depending on temperature and humidity. Sand lightly before painting or wallpapering.

FINISHING END JOINTS

You perform basically the same steps with end or butt joints as you do with tapered edges, except that the two short or cut edges, being flush, require more feathering with a larger putty knife or trowel. Care must be taken not to build up the compound at the center of the joint, or you'll get ridging and shadowed areas. Feather the compound well out onto each side of the joint. Final application of compound should be 14–18 inches wide.

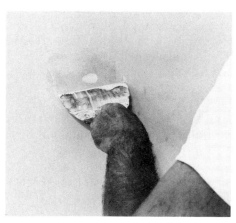

FIGURE 12-8 People just don't understand why you first have to knock the nail hard enough to make a dent in the plaster board, then laboriously cover the dent with wet, gooey plaster. Trust us—it's the time-tested way to keep the nails hidden beneath the surface. (Courtesy Georgia Pacific.)

FINISHING OUTSIDE CORNERS	Be sure, first, that the metal corner is firmly attached. Then take your 4-inch finishing knife and spread compound 3–4 inches wide from the nose of the cornerbead, covering its metal edges. When completely dry, sand lightly and apply a second coat, feathering edges 2–3 inches beyond the first coat. A third coat may be needed, depending on your coverage. Again, feather the edges 2 or 3 inches beyond the preceding coat.
FINISHING INSIDE CORNERS	Cut some tape the length of the corner angle you are going to finish. Apply compound with your 4-inch knife evenly about 1½ inches on each side of the angle. Use enough compound to embed the tape. Fold the tape along the center crease and firmly press it into the corner. Use enough pressure to squeeze some compound under the edges. Feather the compound 2 inches from the edges of the tape. When the first coat is dry, apply a second coat and feather its edges 1½ inches beyond the first coat. Apply a third coat if needed, let dry, and sand to a smooth surface. Use as little compound as possible right at the center of the corner, to prevent hairline cracking.
FINAL PREPARATION	After all joints are thoroughly dry, all surfaces should be sealed or primed with a vinyl or oil-base primer/sealer. You will then have uniform texture and suction over the entire surface you've wallboarded. When it's dry, decorate as you like. (Courtesy of Georgia-Pacific.)

HOW TO PATCH DAMAGED WALLS AND CEILINGS

To patch damaged walls and ceilings, you will need:

1. Patching compound
2. Perforated tape
3. Gypsum board scraps
4. Nails
5. A putty knife
6. A hammer
7. A can opener.

For your patching compound, you have three choices, all equally effective. You can use (1) a pre-mixed joint compound, which comes ready for application; or (2) a powdered joint compound, which has a longer storage life but must be mixed with water before applying; or (3) a patching plaster (spackle) which is cheapest and sets faster than joint compound and is therefore good for large holes.

PATCHING LARGE OPEN HOLES	To patch a large hole in gypsum board, first mark a neat rectangle around the damaged area and, using a knife or keyhole saw, cut out the marked area.

Next, on a scrap of gypsum board, lightly mark a "plug" the same size and shape as the rectangle, but don't cut it there. Instead, mark another boundary 2 inches bigger all around the "plug" and cut through

FIGURE 12-9 For large holes in wall board, cut a larger piece from a fresh board and pare it down to size according to directions given in the text.

the gypsum board on this line. This piece will be 4 inches wider and longer than the rectangular hole.

With a sharp knife, score lines for the plug through the first layer of your gypsum board scrap. Do *not* cut the bottom layer of paper. Peel off the 2-inch margin, leaving the bottom paper intact. That 2-inch margin around the bottom paper is what will hold your patch in place.

Spread patching compound around both the opening of the hole and its edges. Press the patch firmly into place and hold it a few minutes until the patching material has set.

Apply patching compound over the patch and out beyond the edges of the crack and the patch's margins. Feather the edges so the patch is level with the surface of the wall. Remove excess patching compound and let the area dry. If shrinkage occurs, reapply another coat of patching compound. If necessary, sand or add texture to match the existing wall or ceiling.

Before painting you must apply a primer since patching compounds and plaster are extremely porous. In some cases, a coat of paint can be used as a primer; the paint can's label will tell you if it's recommended as a primer. The primer, too, must dry thoroughly before paint is applied.

PATCHING SMALLER HOLES

A small hole can be filled with crumpled newspaper and then patched with joint compound or patching plaster. Small to medium sized holes can also be patched using a piece of string and a scrap of gypsum board slightly larger than the hole. Put the string through the scrap or around it, wedge it in the hole, and pull back on the string to hold it against the hole. Apply patching compound over it, holding the string taut until it's set. Then cut off the string and apply finishing coats of compound as with a larger hole, to level it with the surface.

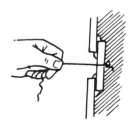

FIGURE 12-10 Small holes require less material but more ingenuity. This is one approach.

PATCHING
VERY LARGE
HOLES

For a really large hole, you may have to cut the gypsum board back to the studs and replace the entire damaged section. In that case, treat it as any wallboard (see previous section), applying tape and finishing off with patching plaster or joint compound.

REPAIRING
POPPING
NAILS

To repair popped nailheads in wallboard, reinforce weak areas with additional nails, driving them about 1½ inches above and below the popped ones. First bring the panel into close contact with the stud by pushing with your free hand; then drive the nail in and below the panel's surface until it dimples the paper.

Remove loose plaster from the dimpled areas, then sand lightly and fill each dimple with patching material. Dry overnight and, if shrinkage occurs, reapply patching material. When the patch is completely dry, sand lightly.

PATCHING
AND FILLING
CRACKS

When patching a crack, it's important that the patch's edges be even with the wall. To accomplish this, use light, feathering strokes when applying compound: a succession of small, overlapping x-like strokes from the top of the patch to the bottom. Make sure you start and end each stroke on clean wall outside the patch area.

Deep, wide cracks stay patched longer when reinforced with joint tape. Ordinary drywall perforated tape and patching compound may be used if you have them handy. First sand the area about 6 inches on each side of the crack. Then work the patching material down into the crack with a trowel, your finger, or some other flat tool.

Center your tape over the crack and press it down firmly with a wide spatula. Cover the tape with a coat of patching material. Smooth it, by feathering, well beyond the tape's edges. Dry overnight. Then apply another coat of patching material, extending 1½ inches beyond the edges of the last coat. Smooth the edges and let the patch dry. Sand lightly.

Narrow cracks may be filled with patching material, but first remove loose material from the crack with a stiff brush or screwdriver. You can bend the point of a can opener or similar object into a hook to enlarge and undercut behind the crack, providing a place for the patching material to grab onto for better holding power. If you're using patching compound that you've mixed with water yourself, dampen the edges of the crack before applying it.

For deep cracks, fill almost to the surface, let dry, and then add a thin coat. Smooth it out on each side of the crack about 2 inches, by feathering. Let it dry, then sand smooth. (Courtesy of Georgia-Pacific.)

LET'S TAKE
THE PUZZLE
OUT OF
PANELING

Used with care and thought, paneling brings the rich feel of wood to your walls. And there's no mystery to wall paneling installation. It's an easy do-it-yourself project that almost any homeowner can tackle. If your walls are 8 feet high and in good repair, simply follow the standard procedures we'll outline for installing wall paneling. If you have problems

FIGURE 12-11 Paneling has reached a new stage. No longer are the panels look-alikes. And the people who install panels no longer install 'em all alike either, as this tasteful family room shows. (Courtesy Georgia Pacific.)

like uneven walls, if your room has unusual architectural features, or if you're just looking for novel solutions to old decorating problems, keep in mind the few extra hints we've included.

Before making a paneling selection, it's wise to consider some basic decorating principles. Depending on your room's shape and size, paneling can highlight special architecture or diminish awkward dimensions. A review of Chapter 11's section on color is helpful; the same principles of using light color for making walls and ceilings recede, and dark color for the opposite effect, apply here.

Lines, such as V-grooves in wall paneling, create similar effects. Applied with grooves running vertically, paneling makes room walls appear taller but narrower. Horizontally, the grooves create a wider- and lower-looking wall. A bold, pronounced woodgrain pattern attracts the eye and accents the surface, while a more subtle woodgrain provides a muted backdrop for your furniture without calling attention to itself.

So carefully analyze your room's dimensions and take into consideration how color, line, and pattern interact when you choose your paneling.

TYPES OF PANELING

Prefinished interior paneling may be plywood or processed wood fiber products. Paneling faces come in real hardwood or softwood veneers—finished to enhance the natural texture, grain, and color—or in an overlay of paper or some other printed material that's given a woodgrain-simulating treatment. Both kinds are finished for durability and easy maintenance.

The most elegant plywood paneling is the kind with a real face veneer of walnut, birch, elm, oak, cherry, cedar, pine, or fir. They're normally ¼-inch thick, but range up to ⁷/₁₆-inch. Tropical hardwood plywoods, such as luan mahogany, may come in natural finishes, or with embossing, antiquing, or color-toning; or overlaid with patterned or woodgrained paper laminates. Most of these panelings are $5/32$-inch thick.

Processed wood fiber (particleboard or hardboard) paneling, prefinished with grain-printed paper overlays or printed surfaces, are less expensive. They can usually be found in thicknesses of $5/32$, $3/16$, or $1/4$ inch. They often require special installation techniques, so read the manufacturer's instructions printed on the back of each panel and follow the directions for cutting, spacing, placement, and application.

Most vertical wall paneling is called random-grooved (though its randomness is in many cases duplicated in every panel). Grooves are designed so that there are always several exactly 16 inches apart for nailing right over the wall studs. For this same reason uniformly spaced groove patterns come in 4-inch, 8-inch, 12-inch, or 16-inch arrangements. Some patterns have cross-scored grooves randomly spaced to give a plank effect. The grooves are generally striped darker than the panel surface. In more expensive paneling, they're cut in V-grooves or channel grooves; cheaper paneling just pictures the groove effect.

FIGURING YOUR NEEDS

Just as with painting and wallboard application, it's important to plan in advance. Measure your room width carefully, making note of window and door openings and other structural elements such as fireplaces as you go along. First total all four wall lengths; for example, in a 10' × 14' room, your total will be 48 feet. Divide this figure by 4 feet to get the number of panels. (In this case, it is 12 panels.)

Then, to allow for doors, windows, fireplaces, and such you can either measure the actual width or use these approximations: door, ½ panel; window, ¼ panel; fireplace, ½ panel. Always figure your needs a little long rather than a little short; a building supplies dealer will usually accept a returned panel, but if you try to match with a panel from a later factory run, you may find an obvious and disagreeable color variation.

If your walls are higher than 8 feet, you must calculate for the additional paneling.

STORING YOUR PANELS

Prefinished paneling is moisture resistant, but it's not waterproof and should not be stored—or installed—in areas subject to lots of moisture. Ideally, it should be stacked flat on the floor in a dry place with spaced sticks between sheets to allow air circulation, or propped on the 8-foot edge. It should remain in the room for 48 hours before installing, to permit acclimatization to surrounding temperature and humidity.

PREPARING YOUR TOOLS

You probably have most of the tools you'll need. For accurate measurement, a retractable tape 8 feet or longer, a large square, and a level will do the job. For trimming the paneling, you'll need a power or hand saw with a sharp, fine-toothed blade. To make cut-outs for electrical and wall switches, you'll need a sabre saw or a keyhole saw, and a drill to start the holes for these tools. You'll need a hammer and a nail set, plus a caulking gun and padded wooden block if you're gluing the panels into place. A miter box will help you make good-looking molding joints, and a pair of saw horses will elevate the panels to comfortable height for measuring and cutting.

Before you begin, take a minute to place the panels around the room on each wall. Especially with real wood paneling, there are subtle variations in color and pattern as well as groove sequence, and you'll want to find the arrangement that's most pleasing. When you've got your arrangement, number the panels on the back in sequence.

Make sure that freshly plastered walls are thoroughly dry. If your walls are straight, sound, and above ground, follow these instructions. If they're not, read further.

LOCATING YOUR STUDS

First you must locate your studs, the vertical solid wood members that make up the skeleton of most frame walls. Since you need to nail directly into this solid wood, locating each stud is important. In most homes, studs are usually spaced 16 inches on center, but 24-inch centers and other variations can be found.

If you plan to replace the present molding, remove it carefully; you may reveal the nailheads that are used to secure the plaster lath or drywall to the studs. These nails mark the stud locations. If you can't find the studs that way, start probing into the wall surface to be paneled with a nail or a small drill until you hit solid wood. With your first try, start 16 inches from one corner of the room, and make test holes at ¾-inch intervals on each side of the initial hole until you locate the stud.

Since studs aren't always straight, it's a good idea to probe at several heights. Once located, make a light pencil mark at the floor and ceiling to position all studs and then snap a chalk line at 4-foot intervals (the standard panel width).

MEASURING AND CUTTING

Start in one corner of the room and measure the floor-to-ceiling height for the first panel since walls are not uniformly 8 feet high. Molding can cover a small gap, but if you prefer a moldingless look, work precisely.

Transfer your measurements to the first panel and mark the dimensions in pencil using a straight-edge to provide a clean line. All cuttings should be done with a sharp saw that has a minimum set to the teeth, to reduce splintering. A cross-cut saw with 10 or more teeth to the inch is good, or use your plywood blade in your table saw. If you're using a portable circular saw or sabre saw, mark and cut panels from the back.

Cut-outs for door and window sections, electrical switches, outlets, and heat registers require careful measurements. Take your dimensions from the edge of the last applied panel for width, from the floor and ceiling line for height. Transfer the measurements to the panel, checking as you go. Unless you plan to add molding, door and window cut-outs should fit against the surrounding casing. If possible, cut-out panels should meet close to the middle over doors and windows.

For electrical boxes, shut off the power, then unscrew the protective plate to expose the box. Then paint or run chalk around the box edges and carefully position the panel. Press the paneling firmly over the box area, transferring the outline to the back of the panel. (See p. 112 for how to add an extender so the box will fit into your new, thicker walls.)

Drive small nails in each corner through the panel until they protrude through the face. Turn the panel over, drill two ¾-inch holes just inside the corners, and use a keyhole or sabre saw to make the cut-out. The hole can be up to ¼-inch oversize and still be covered when the protective switch plate is replaced.

APPLYING PANELS

The first panel is the important one. Put it in place and butt to the adjacent wall in the corner. Make sure it is completely plumb and both left and right panel edges fall on solid stud backing. Most corners are not perfectly true, so you will probably need to trim the panel to fit into the corner properly.

Fit the panel into the corner, checking with a level to be sure the panel is plumb vertically. Draw a mark along the panel edge, parallel to the corner. On rough walls like masonry, or adjoining a fireplace wall, scribe or mark the panel with a compass on the inner panel edge, then cut on the scribe line to fit. Scribing and cutting the inner panel edge may also be necessary if the outer edge of the panel does not fit directly on a stud. The outer edge must fall on the center of a stud to allow room for nailing your next panel. (If, before installing the paneling, you paint a strip of color to match the paneling groove color on the wall location where panels will meet, you'll mask the appearance of any slight gap between the panel edges.)

Many panels are random-grooved to create a solid lumber panel effect. But if you check carefully, you'll notice that there is usually a groove located every 16 inches. This allows most nails to be placed in the grooves, falling directly on the 16-inch stud spacing. Regular small-headed finish nails or colored paneling nails can be used.

For paneling directly to studs, 3d (1¼-inch) nails are recommended, but if you must penetrate backer board, plaster or drywall, 6d (2-inch) nails are needed to give a solid bite into the stud. Space nails 6 inches apart on the panel edges and 12 inches apart in the panel field. Nails should be countersunk slightly below the panel surface with a nail set, then hidden with a matching putty stick. (Colored nails eliminate the need to countersink and putty. Use 1-inch colored nails to apply paneling to studs, 1⅝-inch colored nails to apply paneling through gypsum board or plaster.)

ADHESIVE APPLICATION

Using adhesive to install paneling is a simple method which eliminates the chore of countersinking and hiding nail heads. Adhesive may be used to apply paneling directly to studs or over existing walls as long as the surface is sound and clean. But for this method to work, paneling must be properly cut and fitted prior to installation.

Make sure the panels and walls are clean and free from dirt and

FIGURE 12-12 Finding the location of a room's studs is important for sturdy installation of paneling. With an inexpensive stud finder, when the little needle bobs, you've found a stud.

FIGURE 12-13 Sawing panels is a painstaking job, since you want the neatest possible result. A handsaw works fine; power saws should be outfitted with a very fine blade to prevent chipping the panel. Do not let your power saw scratch the surface of the panel; when in doubt, saw from the underside. (Courtesy Georgia Pacific.)

FIGURE 12-14 Spray dark paint on the wall where the panels will meet; this conceals cracks in between.

FIGURE 12-15 Carefully drill and then saw out space for electrical switches, outlets, and similar obstructions. Their cover plates should conceal the holes when the job is finished. (Courtesy Georgia Pacific.)

FIGURE 12-16 For irregular edges, scribe a line onto the edge of your paneling with a compass, as shown here. (Courtesy Georgia Pacific.)

particles *before* you start. Once applied, the adhesive makes adjustments difficult. However, used properly, adhesive gives a more professional appearance.

A caulking gun with an adhesive tube is the simplest method of application. Trim the tube end so that a ⅛-inch wide adhesive bead can be squeezed out. Once the paneling is fitted, apply beads of adhesive in a continuous strip along the top, bottom, and both edges of the panel. On intermediate studs, apply beads of adhesive 3 inches long and 6 inches apart.

Set the panel carefully in place and press firmly along the stud lines, spreading the adhesive into the wall. Then, using a hammer with a padded wooden block or a rubber mallet, tap over the glue lines to assure a sound bond between the panel and backing.

Be sure to read the adhesive manufacturer's instructions carefully prior to installation. Some require the panel to be placed against the adhesive, then gently pulled from the wall and a few minutes allowed for the solvent to evaporate and the adhesive to set; then the panel is re-positioned and tapped home.

UNEVEN SURFACES

Not every wall is a perfect wall. In fact, some can be a downright disaster—chipped, broken and crumbly plaster; peeling wallpaper; gypsum board punctured by a swinging door knob or a runaway tricycle; rough poured concrete or cinderblock walls. These problems must be fixed before you attempt to install prefinished paneling.

Most problem walls fall into two categories. Either you're dealing with plaster or gypsum board applied to a conventional wood stud wall, or you're facing an uneven masonry wall—brick, stone, cement or cinderblock, for example. The solution is the same, but getting there calls for slightly different approaches.

On conventional walls, clean off the obviously damaged areas. Remove torn wallpaper, and scrape off flaking plaster and any broken gypsum board sections.

On masonry walls, chip off any protruding mortar. Don't bother making repairs. There is an easier solution. Construct a lightweight wood frame system—furring strips—to which you apply your paneling. Furring strips are either 1-inch × 2-inch lumber of ⅜-inch or ½-inch plywood strips cut 1½ inches wide. The furring strips shown in the diagram are applied horizontally 16 inches apart on center on the wall (based on 8-foot ceilings) with vertical members at 48-inch centers where the panels butt together.

Begin by locating the high spot on the wall, the area that protrudes farthest into the room. (To determine the high spot, drop a plumb line.) Fasten your first furring strip, making sure that the thickness of the furring strips compensates for the protrusion of the wall surface. Check with a level to make sure each furring strip is flush with the first strip, and use wood shingles or wedges between the wall and strips to assure a uniformly flat surface.

Your finished furring wall should have a ½-inch space at the floor and ceiling with the horizontal strips 16 inches apart on center and the vertical strips 48 inches apart on center. Remember to furr around doors, windows, and other openings.

On stud walls, the furring strips can be nailed directly through the shimming wedge and the gypsum board or plaster into the stud. Depending on the thickness of the furring strip and wall covering, you'll need 6d (2-inch) or 8d (2½-inch) common nails.

Masonry walls are a little tougher to handle. Specially hardened masonry nails can be used, or you can drill a hole with a carbide-tipped bit, insert wood plugs or expansion shields, and nail or bolt the shimmed frame into place.

Just as a fine painting requires the right frame, prefinished paneling may call for decorative moldings in order to look professional. Moldings can frame the windows and doors, cover the seams and joints at the ceiling and floor line, and finish off and protect corners.

Any good molding installation starts with accurate measurement. Don't assume floors and ceilings are the same length on the same wall. Measure each separately.

Moldings should be cut with a fine-toothed saw. Where they meet at right angles—at corners and around windows and doors—the meeting pieces should be trimmed at opposite 45° angles so that together they form tight right angles.

Some people use prefinished moldings that harmonize with their paneling's color. Others prefer to start with unfinished wood moldings and stain them to either harmonize or contrast in color. For instance, dark molding highlights the lighter colors of birch and elm paneling. (Courtesy of Georgia-Pacific.)

HOW TO GET THE HANG OF WALL COVERINGS

As with any other do-it-yourself improvement, the hanging of wall coverings is easy if you assemble the right tools. You'll need a stepladder or stepstool, a pencil, a scissors, a yardstick, a single-edged razor blade or razor blade knife, some string, and either an inexpensive wallpaper tool

FIGURE 12-17 Paneling that's installed to fit the room's needs is comfortable to live with for a long time. Don't install paneling that you're likely to tire of in a few years. The owners of this home thought carefully before choosing their paneling. (Courtesy Georgia Pacific.)

kit or the following ingredients of one: paste brush, smoothing brush, seam roller, and paste bucket. A wide-bladed putty knife or window squeegee is also helpful to have. For pre-pasted material, you'll also want a water tray.

PREPARING THE WALL

For starters, be sure the walls are smooth and clean. Remove old wallcovering or, if you can't get it off without damaging the wall, seal it with a coat of shellac. Scrape or sand off any rough paint or plaster. Fill cracks and holes with spackling compound and sand smooth. Wash painted walls with trisodium phosphate (beet salt) and rinse with clean water. (Water soluble paints and stains must be removed or they'll come right through.)

For best results, the walls should be sized. (Ask your dealer for wall size and he'll know what you mean.) Some people skip this step and survive, but why ask for trouble when sizing takes so little time? On unpainted plaster, wood, or plasterboard, sizing is especially important.

BUYING YOUR MATERIALS

Make sure you buy enough wall covering so that all the rolls are from the same dye lot. It's better to buy too much than too little; the extra may come in handy some day for repairs, and you may decide to repeat the effect by using the leftover covering to cover valances, windowshades, or even a flush door. (We covered 3 of the 4 doors in our tiny bedroom hallway to minimize the broken-up effect given by all those doors.)

Be sure, too, that you've selected a paste that's compatible with your wall covering. Your wallpaper dealer will assist you. Unless it's pre-mixed, follow the directions on the package, mixing until every lump is out and it's perfectly smooth. If you encounter lots of lumps, it's better to strain the paste than to get the lumps behind your wallpaper on the wall. If you have just a few lumps, you can break them up with your fingers.

PUTTING UP PAPER OR VINYL

Make a plumb bob by tying a long piece of string to your scissors. Choose the most inconspicuous corner of your room—preferably one close to a window or door—and measure from that corner to a point about an inch

FIGURE 12-18

or so less than the width of your wallcovering. (If the covering's 27 inches wide, measure about 26 inches.) Tack the string at your measured spot, and when your scissors stops moving back and forth at its end, draw a line along the edge of the string. The idea is to have a guide line that's precisely straight up and down so that your wallpaper hangs straight right from the first piece. (If you like, you can buy a professional plumb line, which is a weighted, chalked string. If you hold the tool firmly at the bottom and snap the string, it leaves a chalk line on the wall.)

Now, go to several places around the room and measure from ceiling to baseboard. More than likely, your wall is higher in some places than others. You want to find the maximum height. Add 3 or 4 inches to that maximum height and cut a strip of wallcovering that long; this will allow for slight shrinkage and for uneven ceiling and baseboard.

On a table or the floor, cover the back of the wallcovering with paste, smearing lots of it on the edges. (On the floor, gobs of spattered paste are a hazard. An ironing board works fairly well, but be sure to cover it with a plastic or an old sheet before you begin pasting on it.) If you're working alone, fold the strip wet side to wet, top to bottom, carefully so you don't get any creases in it. If you have a partner, ask him to hold one end. Carry it to the wall.

With pre-pasted brands, roll the strip in a water tray, very lightly, with pattern side in and back side up. Soak for the recommended time and draw the strip slowly out of the tray. Make sure both sides are wet.

Line up the right-hand edge of your first sheet of wallcovering with the chalk line on the wall. Don't be afraid to slide the wet material around,

FIGURE 12-19

and even lift it, until you've got it even. Smooth out the strip with a wet sponge or wallpaper brush, working down the center and out to the sides to remove wrinkles and large bubbles. (You can use the squeegee if you have one.) If you're working from the corner, allow the excess material on the left to wrap around onto the adjoining wall. Find your pattern match and cut the next strip accordingly. Soak or paste and hang with the seam butting against the first strip unless directions that come with the wallcovering specifically tell you otherwise. When you butt the edges, be sure not to stretch them. (If you overlap any seams but very thin wallpaper ones, the edges will come loose; if you stretch them, they'll come open.) But make sure they're good and tight—against each other and against the wall.

FIGURE 12-20

Roll the seams lightly with your seam roller unless you're hanging flocked or embossed wallcovering; in that case, skip this step, instead tapping the seams down with the tip of the smoothing brush's bristles. When you're matching your pattern, match a dry strip to a dry strip or a wet strip to a wet strip; wet wallcovering does shrink slightly as it dries.

Don't skip the areas around doorways and windows, intending to come back later. Work straight around the room. As you finish each strip, wash it off with plenty of clean water and a sponge to get rid of the extra paste. Wash paste off painted areas also.

After three strips are up, trim them at the ceiling and baseboard with a razor blade or razor blade knife, and then go on.

You'll have a neater, more professional looking room if you remove electric outlet and switch plates before hanging the wallcovering and trim the covering so that the plates cover the edges. Just be careful when cutting wet coverings around live electrical wires; turn off the current if you can.

When hanging plain colors or random matched textures, if you reverse every other strip top to bottom, the color comes out looking more uniform. And if you must overlap vinyl covering, such as in archways,

FIGURE 12-21

corners, or on ceiling-and-wall applications, use a paste that's especially made for adhering vinyl to vinyl, or the edges will eventually loosen.

Corners are seldom straight. When you come to one, extend your wallcovering 1 inch onto the adjoining wall by cutting it, lengthwise, parallel to the corner. The succeeding strip should be hung with its first edge flush up against the corner—or against the paper, if it's too heavy to overlap.

Don't try to cut your wallcovering to fit around windows and doors. Just paper right over the edges, making diagonal cuts up to the corners of these obstructions to get a neat fit. Then trim off the excess the same way you do at the top and bottom of each strip.

Here's a clean-up tip. As you trim, place scraps, glue sides together,

FIGURE 12-22 If you still think of wall covering as simply ''wallpaper,'' prepare to be surprised. They're a decorator's delight. (Courtesy Reed Wallcoverings.)

on one centrally placed newspaper. Then, when you've sponged down the last strip, all you have to do is fold up the newspaper and throw it away.

Put away the tools, move the furniture back in place, and you're ready for rave reviews. (Courtesy of Wall-Tex: Columbus Coated Fabrics Division of Borden, Inc., and of Style-Tex. All how-to-do-it illustrations courtesy of Style-Tex.)

HOW TO MAKE A MURAL SET YOUR MOOD

A photo mural can bring the outdoors inside by putting a mountain, meadow, forest, or beach on your wall; at the same time it'll move your walls optically outward. "The concept is centuries old," says David Nordahl, chief designer for Environmental Graphics, a photo mural maker. When French art patrons used to commission painters to adorn their walls with eye-befuddling fantasies, it was called *trompe l'oeil,* meaning "trick of the eye." Today camera techniques are combined with lithographic ones to produce finely detailed illusions that are affordable as well as scrubbable and strippable.

Photo murals that lead the eye furthest beyond the wall have the highest amount of space-expanding qualities. They act even more forcefully than do light-colored end walls in making a room look longer than it is.

Do-it-yourselfers often get stuck, in considering murals, because their walls aren't exactly the dimensions of the murals, or there are windows or other obstructions in the way. But there's nothing to keep you from leaving out part of a mural, or wrapping it around the corner of the room. And mural papers can be cut and pasted on window shades and even blinds. Flush doors are easily covered with part of a mural to match the rest of the wall.

FIGURE 12-23 Let your imagination play games with your walls—with wall coverings (Courtesy Environmental Graphics.)

Putting up a photo mural is much like putting up a wallcovering; drop a plumb line before you begin. If, due to high or uneven walls, your mural doesn't reach from ceiling to floor, you may be able to create an attractive border with paint or another wallpaper, or with an attractive molding.

HALLS (AND OTHER PLACES) OF MIRRORS

Mirrors can make magic. If you've got a room that's tiny, low-ceilinged, sparsely furnished, dark, or just uninteresting, a mirror or several can change all that. If you've got a room that's huge, high-ceilinged, cluttered, or glaringly bright, a mirror—or several—can pull it all together and subdue it.

Add a single strip of floor-to-ceiling mirror, for elegance and added depth and dimension. Place mirrored panels strategically around a room, and you can stretch boundaries and capture light. With space at a premium, the ability of mirrors to visually move walls back by double their depth is a real boon. (If you mirror both facing walls instead of one, you've quadrupled the length of a room!) To widen a narrow space, mirror one of the long walls. To heighten a room visually, put in floor-to-ceiling mirror strips—or, for real drama, mirror the ceiling. Add beams, latticing, or molding strips, and you've created instant architectural interest.

Here are some more ideas: Alternating mirror and wood, wallpaper, or stucco strips create fabulous textural contrasts and special architectural effects. You can run the strips horizontally, diagonally, or even in zigzag patterns—though such treatments are best for contemporary rooms.

You can even get beveled mirror strips that'll work as ceiling moldings.

FIGURE 12-24 (Courtesy Binswanger Mirror Products.)

If your aim is to brighten a dark room, place your mirrors where they'll catch and bounce back the most light. The wall that faces the most windows is a natural choice. A framed mirror placed at the right angle can double a table lamp's wattage, just as crystal sconces cast twice the light when placed on a mirrored backing or mounted on a mirrored wall.

You can select grey, bronze, or amber mirrors to cut down the glare in a room that's too bright—or combine these colors with traditional mirroring for an interesting wall. You can mirror a narrow hallway, a staircase, and of course bath and bedrooms. Sliding and bi-fold doors even come in mirrored models now. In mirroring, your imagination is the limit.

In short, the material you choose to cover your walls and ceilings is limited only by your goals and tastes. Paint, paper, vinyl, mural, mirror, or even cloth or carpeting—all have been used by adventurous do-it-yourselfers to improve their homes. So let yourself go, and go to it. (Courtesy of Binswanger Mirror Products.)

13
Step Onto a New Floor

The single most used part of your home is, of course, its floor. Grandpa and Grandma simply laid down the most rugged boards they could find, and that was that. If they could afford it, they put linoleum in the kitchen, expecting to replace it at least every five years, and tile in the bathroom, which they hoped would last forever. Maybe they'd have a rug in the living room and throw rugs on a few other spots about the house, such as where Grandpa hopped out of bed every morning to do the chores, or where Grandma landed when she got up to light the fire so he could dress for the chores in comfort.

Nowadays we demand as much beauty on our floors as we expect on the other surfaces of the house. What we lay down has to look good as well as wear well. Fortunately, modern science is up to our demand.

WHAT'S WHAT IN VINYL FLOORING

The old linoleum has been replaced by hardier vinyl, which looks pretty good too. The problem is that it's tough to sort out what's what. Manufacturers' terminology is confusing. Product information is often skimpy. There are almost as many grades of vinyl sheeting on the market as there

FIGURE 13-1 You could lay quarry tiles one by one, or roll out the vinyl. It was the latter treatment in this floor. (Courtesy Biscayne Decorative Products.)

are patterns and colors. And, contrary to common belief, not all vinyl floors are perfect for all rooms.

To choose wisely, analyze the function of the room you're improving before you even enter a floor covering shop. A foyer, for example, has to stand up to more footprints than the living room, and must take muddy boots and dripping umbrellas in stride. This means a vinyl floor with an *extra tough* wear layer and, if you're lazy like us, a carefree no-wax finish as well.

A dining room usually has to put up with heavy furniture and spills galore. So the flooring to pick is one with excellent indentation resistance and cleanability.

A floor that's as soundproof as possible is important for rooms where little kids play, or where dads use noisy tools, or where teenagers dance. A generously cushioned floor will spare your nerves.

Function means less than fashion in a fairly formal living room. You probably spend relatively little time there and, since it's such a public place, you may find it's the one most frequently redecorated. So there's really no need to spend a lot of money on technological sound-dampening or wear-improving features.

For a kitchen that functions as meeting place, playpen, crafts studio, party site, and family room, as well as cooking and eating spot, buy only a top-of-the-line vinyl flooring. Here you want it all: top wearability, resistance to household spills, quiet and comfort underfoot, and no-wax beauty.

Cushioned floors aren't just quieter and more comfortable underfoot. They're also warmer, an important aspect to consider with today's heating costs. And, in the hands of amateurs, the 6-foot, 9-foot, and 12-foot wide rolls install in half the time of inlaid vinyl tiles. The money saved in do-it-yourself installation may offset cushioned vinyl's higher cost.

Not all vinyls are the same. Some products feature fillers or a lot of air, rather than high-density vinyl foam that provides the impact resistance and tensile strength you may need. A product that's pure vinyl, from the backing to the printing inks, is generally the best choice.

There are three types of wearlayers put over most vinyl sheets and tiles: vinyl, urethane, and a combination of urethane, vinyl, and acrylic that's processed through an ultraviolet oven and is sometimes called "miracle acrythane." Vinyl is a tough, nonporous product, but it doesn't match the gloss-retention of the urethanes. Urethanes, however, rate fair-to-poor in stain and abrasion resistance. Acrythane claims a super-tough, nonporous finish combined with top stain and scratch resistance.

Almost all top-of-the-line and even middle-grade vinyls are billed as no-wax floorings. But there is no resilient floor that won't dull in heavy traffic areas over a long period of time. Damp-mopping with a light detergent is all the normal care any good no-wax floor needs. If a dulled area appears in the traffic path of flooring with a vinyl wearlayer, you can buff lightly with a nylon pad to restore the luster. Urethane wearlayers should not be buffed. Instead, apply a light coat of any acrylic finish; that will bring even a severely dulled area back to life.

Top-grade vinyl's lifespan can be up to 15 or 20 years, so your best choice is usually a quiet pattern that you won't grow tired of quickly.

If you choose rolled vinyl flooring, before you make your purchase analyze your room's use patterns in addition to determining its dimensions. Most rolls stocked by local distributors are 9 feet wide, but many are 6 or 12 feet. Assuming your room's smallest dimension is no bigger than the vinyl roll of your choice, simply have the clerk cut off the right length. If you have to splice two pieces together, buy a carpet tape recommended by your dealer and make the splice where traffic is minimal. If you match patterns, splices will be all but invisible.

Take your purchase home, move the furniture out of the way, roll out the vinyl, and move back the furniture. If you can move the furniture out completely, you'll probably save time in the long run because you won't have to jockey the vinyl around for a good fit. But if you can't, do as we've done: move it all to one side of the room, roll the vinyl over the vacant half, lift the furniture back over to the covered side—making sure not to pull your laid vinyl away from the wall—and then roll out the rest.

We like to have the entire rolled vinyl floor in place before we trim it to size around the edges with our utility knife. Even then, we generally trim in two stages: first, we cut it almost to size and then, after giving it a day or two to flatten or stretch to its final shape and size, we do the last little bit of trimming.

For a kid's room, try this idea. Buy enough to allow a foot or so extra all around the room, and run the excess up onto the wall for a small but rugged wainscot. Top it with a molding and you've got a durable yet attractive buffer that absorbs the tossed blocks and tricycle crashes that can devastate most ordinary walls. (In part, courtesy of Biscayne Decorative Products.)

SQUARING AWAY ON A TILE-LAYING JOB

Vinyl tile, asphalt tile, vinyl-asbestos, and similar 9- to 12-inch floor tiles drive a lot of beginners up the wall—needlessly. If you decide that tiles are for you—based on cost, patterns available, and versatility in covering odd-shaped areas—then you should be able to tile an entire room in a relaxing weekend or one long evening.

First measure your room and decide on how many tiles you need. If you choose 12-inch squares, simply multiply your room's length (rounded off to the next highest even foot) by width (again, to the next highest even foot). The answer equals the number of tiles you should buy—*unless* you have large areas, such as under cabinets, that you don't plan to tile. In that event, measure the width and length of the left-out portions (rounding off to the next *lowest* even foot) and multiply. Subtract the total of your left-out areas from the first figure you got, and that's how many tiles to invest in.

For 9-inch tiles, do all the calculations above and then multiply your final result by 1.9, or use the simple chart in Figure 13-2.

If you have an irregularly shaped room, divide it into rectangles and calculate the number of tiles for each; then add them all together.

At the same time you buy your tiles, also buy a good adhesive recommended for them. (Of course, if you've chosen a tile variety that has

FIGURE 13-2 How to estimate the number of 9-inch tiles to buy. (Courtesy Borden, Inc.)

Feet	1	2	3	4	5	6	7	8	9	10	11	12	13	14	15	16	17	18						
	1	2	3	4	5	6	7	8	9	10	11	12	13	14	15	16	17	18	19	20	21	22	23	24
1	2	4	6	8	10	12	14	16	18	20	22	24	26	28	30	32	34	36	38	40	42	44	46	48
2	3	6	9	12	15	18	21	24	27	30	33	36	39	42	45	48	51	54	57	60	63	66	69	72
3	4	8	12	16	20	24	28	32	36	40	44	48	52	56	60	64	68	72	76	80	84	88	92	96
	5	10	15	20	25	30	35	40	45	50	55	60	65	70	75	80	85	90	95	100	105	110	115	120
4	6	12	18	24	30	36	42	48	54	60	66	72	78	84	90	96	102	108	114	120	126	132	138	144
5	7	14	21	28	35	42	49	56	63	70	77	84	91	98	105	112	119	126	133	140	147	154	161	168
6	8	16	24	32	40	48	56	64	72	80	88	96	104	112	120	128	136	144	152	160	168	176	184	192
	9	18	27	36	45	54	63	72	81	90	99	108	117	126	135	144	153	162	171	180	189	198	207	216
7	10	20	30	40	50	60	70	80	90	100	110	120	130	140	150	160	170	180	190	200	210	220	230	240
8	11	22	33	44	55	66	77	88	99	110	121	132	143	154	165	176	187	198	209	220	231	242	253	264
9	12	24	36	48	60	72	84	96	108	120	132	144	156	168	180	192	204	216	228	240	252	264	276	288
	13	26	39	52	65	78	91	104	117	130	143	156	169	182	195	208	221	234	247	260	273	286	299	312
10	14	28	42	56	70	84	98	112	126	140	154	168	182	196	210	224	238	252	266	280	294	308	322	336
11	15	30	45	60	75	90	105	120	135	150	165	180	195	210	225	240	255	270	285	300	315	330	345	360
12	16	32	48	64	80	96	112	128	144	160	176	192	208	224	240	256	272	288	304	320	336	352	368	384
13	17	34	51	68	85	102	119	136	153	170	187	204	221	238	255	272	289	306	323	340	357	374	391	408
	18	36	54	72	90	108	126	144	162	180	198	216	234	252	270	288	306	324	342	360	378	396	414	432
14	19	38	57	76	95	114	133	152	171	190	209	228	247	266	285	304	323	342	361	380	399	418	437	456
15	20	40	60	80	100	120	140	160	180	200	220	240	260	280	300	320	340	360	380	400	420	440	460	480
16	21	42	63	84	105	126	147	168	189	210	231	252	273	294	315	336	357	378	399	420	441	462	483	504
17	22	44	66	88	110	132	154	176	198	220	242	264	286	308	330	352	374	396	418	440	462	484	506	528
18	23	46	69	92	115	138	161	184	207	230	253	276	299	322	345	368	391	414	437	460	483	506	529	552
	24	48	72	96	120	144	168	192	216	240	264	288	312	336	360	384	408	432	456	480	504	528	552	576

the adhesive already applied to its back, you can skip this step.) The makers of Elmer's Professional Floor Tile Adhesive recommend that, on ⅛-inch tiles, you use a gallon of adhesive for every 100 to 150 square feet of floor, and for thinner tiles a gallon for every 200 to 250 square feet. Ask your dealer for guidance, however, and be sure she gives or sells you a notched trowel that has the right size notches for applying your adhesive.

For best results, your floor must be smooth and flat. Vacuum it to remove loose particles. Scrub away all the grease, wax, oil, and such. Be sure any paint sticks solidly; scrape up loose portions. Nail down any loose boards and make sure nails elsewhere are tight and level with the boards.

If your old floor is a wreck, cover it with ¼-inch Masonite or ⅜-inch plywood. Ordinary adhesives do not adhere well in damp areas, so if dampness is a problem, discuss that in advance with your dealer.

For a neat-looking finished job, remove the quarter-round moldings from your baseboards. When your tile is all in place, you can reinstall the moldings or replace them with new ones.

To get started, measure to find the midpoint of each of your four walls. Mark each midpoint on the floor with a small nail. Stretch a chalk-line string or an ordinary string between the east and west wall midpoints and mark that line on the floor. Do the same between the north and south walls' midpoints. When that's done, you should have a string cross stretched across your floor. Using a large square, make sure that the lines intersect at a right angle. If they don't, adjust one line until they do.

Now, using either a ruler or some of your tiles (don't put adhesive down yet, or peel the backing from adhesive-backed tile), mark off consecutive tile lengths along one leg of your cross from the central point toward the side of your room that is most in the limelight. Do the same for the leg that's on the next most seen part of your floor adjacent to the first leg you've marked. Your aim is to be sure that the last tile on each leg will not be narower than 3 inches (for 9-inch tiles) or 4 inches (for 12-inch tiles). If the last tile on either leg will be too narrow, adjust your nails and cross lines accordingly. Then leave your adjusted strings in place to guide you in laying down your first tiles. (Some manufacturers' instructions suggest that you draw lines on the floor for guides. The trouble is, once your adhesive is down your lines may be obliterated.)

FIGURE 13-3 To lay tiles neatly, first set up your room's centerlines (A) according to directions given in the text. Spread out some tiles to make sure you'll be left with at least half a tile at the walls. Then lay down your adhesive (or pull the covering off self-stick backings) and lay a row along each of your guidelines in one quarter of the room (B). Finally, fill in that corner (C) and then move on to the next quarter.

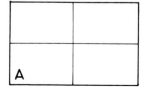
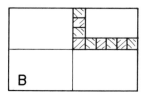
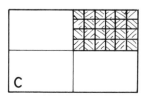

Starting at the center of your room, spread adhesive over one-quarter of your room (one-half if it's a small area). Then, also at the center, begin laying tiles. Put down a single row along one leg of your cross mark, and another single row along the leg that's at a right angle. Next, fill in the tiles between the two legs. (Figure 13-3 explains this process graphically.)

We've found that many people spread too much adhesive. It doesn't guarantee better results. It simply keeps tiles from lying flat on the floor. The excess adhesive often forces up between the tiles, making a mess days or even weeks later.

Butt each tile against adjacent tiles. Lower it—don't slide it—into place. If your tiles have a pattern to them, make sure you've got the pattern properly aligned *before* you press the tile into place. It's nearly impossible to correct without making a mess.

When you reach the edges of your floor, you'll have to cut tiles to fit. Cut one tile at a time since you can't assume that your walls are perfectly square. You'll be very disappointed if you cut a dozen tiles at once only to discover that some of them are too small. Don't forget to take your tile's pattern into account when you're cutting.

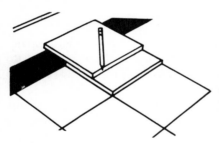

FIGURE 13-4   To cut a tile accurately for fitting against a wall, put down a dry tile atop the last tile you've laid; then on top of that one, lay another tile flush with the wall, and draw a pencil line on it as shown here. Cut on that line, and the tile will slip neatly into the void.

FIGURE 13-5   To cut accurate tile shapes for corners, follow the procedure outlined in Figure 13-4, and repeat using the same tile on the other side of the corner. You'll end up with two lines, as shown in this illustration.

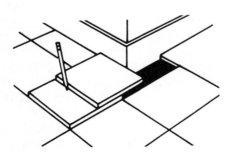

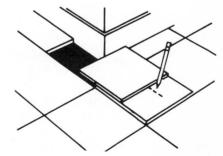

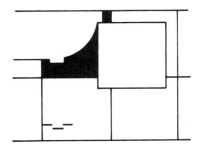

FIGURE 13-6 For irregularly shaped corners and edges, such as the one pictured here, move the top tile a few inches, mark your line, then move it a few more inches and mark again. Continue until you have a rough outline of the shape. Cut carefully; it's easier to trim off excess tile than to wish you'd left a bit more the first try. (This and previous two illustrations, Courtesy Borden, Inc.)

In a nearby illustration, we show a simple way to measure tiles at room edges. The next drawing demonstrates how to measure corners, and a third how to tackle odd-shaped areas.

When your job is completed, promptly scrape any excess adhesive off the tiles with a putty knife. If it's started to harden, gently rub with steel wool or scouring powder. Never use solvents unless they're specifically okayed by your adhesive can; they may damage your new tiles.

Before you move your furniture back into place, let your adhesive dry thoroughly. An hour and a half is recommended on Borden's adhesive, but follow the advice on your chosen product.

CERAMIC TILE FOR CENTURIES OF PERMANENCE

Your goal may not be to keep your flooring looking new for centuries, but if you do, ceramic's for you. Just a glance at an old Roman ceramic floor preserved in a museum will prove it to you. For the ultimate in permanence, with almost no maintenance, ceramic tile is the prime choice. We laid beautiful Italian ceramic tile on the floor of our living-and-dining room as well as the adjoining kitchen. Then we faced our fireplace, countertops, and the wall behind the stove with the same tile. It was a substantial investment in both money and time, but it really looks twice as luxurious as its cost. We vacuum the floors regularly and once in a while attack them with a damp mop, and that's that.

There are several considerations to take into account before settling on stone tile. For one, it's cold to walk on—an asset in warm climates, but a possible disadvantage in cold ones. For another, it has no resiliency, which means that anything dropped on it breaks. If you've still got children underfoot, that's a definite liability. A third point is that, because it's virtually indestructible, it'll last long after you get tired of it, if you've picked a poor pattern choice.

Before settling on our pattern, we shopped carefully. We wanted one that would go well with whatever we might do in the way of decorating and redecorating those rooms. It had to be something we'd enjoy for the rest of our lives in this home. (The same would have been true if it was quarry tile or slate we were shopping for. They're as durable and are laid just about the same way as ceramic tile.)

You can lay tile over almost any sound floor that you have now: wood, primed plywood, vinyl, old tile, and so forth. Just let your dealer

FIGURE 13-7 Looks like brick? It's vinyl tile available in 12-inch squares. Try to find the lines between squares! (Courtesy GAF Corporation.)

know what's on your floor now so he can supply you with the proper adhesive and grout. Grout comes in a wide variety of colors. You can match, accent, or contrast a color in the tile. In fact, if you have trouble visualizing abstractly, you may want to lay your tile before you pick the grout color since the tile will look different once it's all down from the way a few tiles looked on a salesroom floor.

Since tile is so tough, you'll also need some special cutting tools. Your dealer rents or sells them for modest prices. Make sure, before you start, that you have enough sharp cutting blades. A dull blade will wreck more tiles than it cuts cleanly, causing lots of frustration.

Preparing the floor is done the same way as for the tiles in the preceding section. After you've got your strings squared as in vinyl-tile laying, mark off your tiles from the center to the edges of your floor along the string lines—but, unlike vinyl, be sure to leave about ⅛ inch between tiles for the grout. (Some ceramic tiles, especially small ones, come in mesh-backed sets with the spacing between them pre-determined.) It's a good idea to play with your string-guides so that, in the most visible two edges of the room, your tiles meet the walls without any cutting needed. Cutting is time-consuming and often tricky, so the less you have to do the better you'll like the job.

Using the proper notched trowel to spread adhesive, work on small areas at a time instead of the large sections you spread in vinyl tile laying. An area 3′ × 4′ is plenty large enough. Otherwise the adhesive will start to dry out before you've laid down your tiles. If you're installing extra-thick tile with a deep back pattern, you may also have to spread some adhesive on the back of each tile. (To know if you're laying too little or too much adhesive, pick up your first tile after you've laid it and look at the back. If only its feet are adhesive-covered, and not its back, spread your adhesive thicker. If the adhesive has spread around the back and up the sides partway, you're already spreading it too thick.)

FIGURE 13-8 Set each tile with a slight twisting motion. Press firmly into place. Align tile so all joints are uniform and straight. Most tile today comes with built-in spacers, so getting uniform joints is no problem.

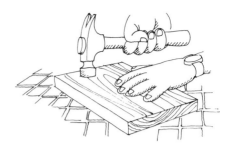

FIGURE 13-9 When you're tiling a floor, it's important that the tiles are flat and firmly embedded in the adhesive. So, before the tile sets, slide a flat board across the surface while tapping with a hammer.

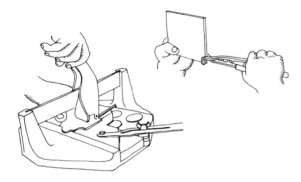

FIGURE 13-10 A tile-cutter can be rented for a few dollars and is easy to use. Ask the dealer to show you how and practice on a few tiles before you get into the tile installation itself. A tile nipper is what you need to shape cuts to fit around pipes, etc. Nip off little bits at a time, or the tile might break. Smooth the rough edges with carborundum stone.

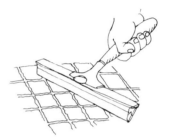

FIGURE 13-11 Wait 24 hours or so after tiling to begin grouting. Then use the grout according to the manufacturer's instructions. Apply the grout with a rubber float or squeegee, spreading it diagonally across the joints. Wash excess grout off the face of the tile with a wet sponge. (This series of illustrations, courtesy of Tile Council of America.)

Set ceramic tiles with a slight twisting motion. Then press firmly into place. Don't slide the tiles against each other. It's important to leave that gap of approximately ⅛-inch for 8-inch tiles (less, for small tiles) for expansion and contraction of the underlayment.

From time to time, stand back to examine your work. Don't panic if tiles are a bit out of line or the spacing between them is uneven. Until the adhesive sets, you can wiggle the tiles around to bring them into line. Even a wrong-way tile can be corrected if you notice it within about a half hour of laying your adhesive. Before moving on to your next area, slide a large flat board across the surface of your work and walk on it or tap it with a hammer. The goal is to get a level surface.

Cutting tiles is a slow process. Your best bet is to leave enough width around the edges to be able to trowel your adhesive on, and finish the rest of the room first. Then divide your work into even smaller areas than before—perhaps just two rows at a time. Measure separately for each tile you cut, and use a tile-cutter to make your cuts. After a bit of practice, you'll probably get the hang of how to operate this simple tool and, if you keep your confidence and a sharp cutting edge, you'll get perfectly cut tiles every time. (Judi never did develop the confidence and, though she laid every tile in the large floor, it was Frank who finally did the tile-cutting.)

For tiny irregular cut-outs, use a tile nipper. Patience is needed because you must nip off little bits at a time so you don't break the tile you're working on. With patience, even Judi could nip tiles. For large irregular areas, use a rod saw and, again, patience. Be careful not to bang the rod saw's frame against the tile as you saw or you may crack the tile. You'll develop the hang of this skill, too.

Before you grout, give the adhesive plenty of time to set. Grout is about like wet clay when you apply it. Your dealer can supply a rubber trowel that forces it between the tiles. We thought about using a cookie press, but never did get up the nerve to try one. For odd corners, we haven't found anything better suited for grouting than our fingers, and in those cases it helps to wear a thin plastic work-glove. Wipe away excess grout as you go along. Then, when it's had plenty of time to dry, use a damp sponge and a dry cloth to polish away the thin film of grout that

FIGURE 13-12 A two-story atrium in the heart of a Long Island, New York, solar home. The atrium presents a year-round "garden" view for every major room in the house. Designer Allen G. Scruggs chose to pave it with ceramic tile. (Courtesy Summitville Tile Company.)

inevitably remains behind. Seal with several coats of a silicone sealer, to keep the grout clean and colorful.

DON'T FORGET ABOUT WOOD FLOORS

Technology has come to our aid. Modern floor coatings make renewing wood floors easier than ever. The new finishes not only speed the job of refinishing, they also give you more durable, longer lasting results than were ever possible before now.

Once you decide that what you really want is a warm wood floor— warm both to the foot and to the eye—you can choose from two types of coating—a clear finish, or an enamel.

Clear finishes are intended for use on hardwood floors to highlight the natural wood-grain with a durable glossy or satiny sheen. They come in urethane and in ordinary varnish.

Urethane is one of the most durable clear floor coatings commercially available. You can choose from gloss or satin. It's extremely resistant to abrasion, scuffing, and general hard wear under normal use. It is non-yellowing and retains its appearance for years. Common household liquids such as water, alcohol, milk, and food acids don't affect the finish and are easily washed off with a damp, soapy rag. Urethane may be applied with a good quality brush or pad.

Varnish is similar to urethane in appearance. It, too, is designed to highlight natural woodgrain but only with a glossy finish. Water, alcohol, and other common household liquids are easily washed from varnished floors; however, varnish does not possess the extreme durability and abrasion resistance of urethane. To apply it, a brush is better than a pad.

Enamels are opaque coatings available in a wide range of colors. Although enamel paints are also made for use on walls and ceilings, for your floor you'll need a special floor enamel. You can put it on cement or metal as well as on wood, and it'll dry to a glossy finish. Urethane enamel is the most tough and durable of enamels; use it on inside or outside floors where you want long-lasting, wear-resistant, weather-resistant finishes. It resists heavy foot traffic, food acids, harsh cleaners, detergents, dirt and grease.

Less expensive floor enamels are recommended for general use on interior floors. Although they resist marring, abrasion, and common household liquids, they're not as durable as urethane enamel.

To achieve a natural wood finish with urethane or varnish, it's usually necessary to completely remove the old finish by sanding with a power sander. It's usually easy to rent one locally. To do the sanding, remove all quarter-round strips at the baseboard, taking care not to split them. Identify each piece with a mark so it can be replaced in the same position after you're done. Move out all rugs and furniture. In fact, if you take down the drapes, pictures, and everything else that's around, you'll eliminate a lot of time-consuming dusting and vacuuming later on.

Countersink all nailheads on the floor, taking special care to do so where you removed the baseboards. Clean the surface of all dirt, dust, wax, peeling paint or varnish, stains, and smudges. Follow sanding directions that come with your equipment. Vacuum and then damp-mop to get up every bit of sawdust.

Once your floor is sanded, you can change its color, if you like, by applying stain. Or you can leave it the natural color. (If there are watermarks or other dark spots your sander didn't take out, you may want to disguise them by darkening your floor.) Before staining an entire floor, test the color in an obscure spot to be sure that's what you want. Apply stain uniformly and sparingly with a clean brush or cloth. Wipe uneven areas with a clean cloth dampened with mineral spirits. Allow stain to dry at least 12 hours before applying a urethane or varnish. If there are cracks or holes to fill, with an open grain wood such as walnut, oak, or mahogany, do your filling with a paste wood filler *after* you've applied your stain.

Read and follow directions carefully when applying your urethane or varnish finish. Several thin coats are a great deal better than one thick one. Apply the finish uniformly, at a moderate speed so that you prevent foaming. To avoid missed areas, use your brush or pad in two directions—first across the grain and then with it. After the first coat dries, sand it lightly—and be sure *all* the sanding dust is removed with a wiping cloth or vacuum cleaner before you apply the second coat.

To enamel previously painted floors, scrape off all loose or chipped paint and sand rough paint edges smooth. Glossy areas should be dulled with a light sanding. Vacuum away every bit of sanding dust and check to ensure that the entire area to be enameled is completely free of dirt, grease, wax, and such. After that, you're ready to paint.

If your wood floor is beyond refinishing, or you want a different pattern of flooring, you can put down a new floor anywhere tile can be laid. Check out the wood parquet floor kits at your local home improvement center. Applying them is pretty much the same procedure as applying vinyl tiles.

Putting in a new wood floor is a substantial investment, but if you love wood your investment will be repaid. Shop carefully among the many patterns, and your choice will content you for the rest of your life in this home.

14
Bathrooms:
New and Renewed

There's nothing difficult about redoing an old bathroom or even adding a new one, once you've learned how to work with the new plumbing tools and techniques described in Chapter 9. Whether you're doing the whole job, or just making a few small improvements, there's little you won't be able to do yourself.

WHATEVER YOU DO, DO IT FIRST ON PAPER

If you're planning to put in a new bathroom where there never was one before, don't do a thing until you make a plan. If you're planning to change around the layout of your old bathroom, don't do that either before you make a plan. The best way to design the most efficient and attractive bathroom for your home is by trial and error. We don't mean a costly campaign of adding one of these, ripping out two of those, and trying something else until you get what you want. We want you to sit down at a comfortable table with the dimensions of the area you have to work with and the dimensions of the plumbing appliances you need to choose from, and shuffle the appliances around on your dimensions until

FIGURE 14-1 So help us, the "old" fixtures here are all new, lending whimsicality to this redone bathroom. (Courtesy Kohler Company.)

you find the layout that looks—on paper—like it does the most of what you want. After that you can start planning colors and other decorating aspects of the overall design.

Do your initial planning on graph paper. The method we recommended in Chapter 1, using ¼-inch squares for each inch of floor space, *will* work for bathrooms. But we (and most designers) prefer to choose a ½-inch scale since it permits more detailed layouts in these relatively small rooms. Sometimes just a gap of 3 or 4 inches between a door and a sink can spell success or diaster to a layout. We suggest you use that ½-inch scale too.

To assist you in designing your new bathroom, we've drawn the basic bathroom appliances for you, to the same scale of ½-inch-equals-one foot-of-floor-space. You can cut out the models or trace them. (If this is a library book, trace!) We've chosen common popular appliance dimensions that are standard in the plumbing industry for the tubs, toilets, sinks, and bidet, but before you settle on your actual purchases, check their measurements with your sketches in hand. If they don't fit, you may have to compromise in your drawing or in your appliance.

To make your trial-and-error layouts, keep the following considerations in mind.

1. Before you begin, whether you're remodeling an existing bathroom or adding one, locate the existing waterpipes. You'll have the least amount of work and expense if you can install new appliances close to pipes that are already installed.

2. If you can't hook up new appliances where old ones used to be connected,

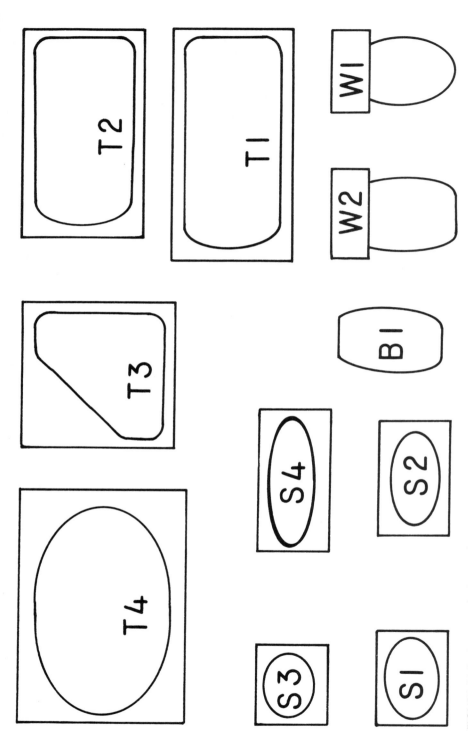

FIGURE 14-2 Here are bathroom fixture models drawn to standard industry dimensions. They will help you plot your own bathroom if you use them on graph paper (bought or home-made) on which ½ inch represents 1 foot. In all cases, items are numbered in descending popularity. For example, among sinks, the 24-inch model (S1) is most used, the 30-inch model (S2) next most, then the 20-inch (S3), and finally the long and lean 36-inch (S4). B1 is a bidet—slowly working its way into bathrooms on this continent.

your second least expensive alternative is to put them against a wall back of which pipes are presently located. (For instance, locate a new bathroom next to the present bathroom, kitchen, or utility room if you can use waterpipes there.)

3. Measure your existing space carefully. In bathrooms, every inch counts.
4. Carefully measure all doors and show on your plans how far they open into the bathroom you're designing. Don't put anything in the way of an opening door.
5. Shop around to get a feel for what's available, what colors are in vogue, prices, and approximate dimensions. (But beware of colors that will be *out* of vogue in a few years.)
6. Most major plumbing manufacturers supply helpful booklets that often have attractive, innovative ideas for space efficiency and beauty. Study their sketches and borrow the ideas you prefer. Decorating magazines and pamphlets from manufacturers of bathroom tile, wallboard, and other appurtenances are all worth a look, too.

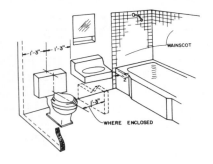

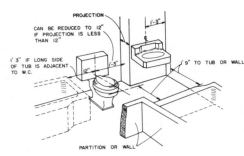

FIGURE 14-3 To guide your planning, here are government house planners' recommended dimensions above and around the major bathroom appliances. (Courtesy U.S. Forest Products Laboratory.)

RENEWING AN OLD BATHROOM

When most people tackle an outmoded or scarred-up old bathroom, they stick to the original dimensions of the room. They add some new features, but they rarely rip the whole room apart. Walls are almost universally redecorated and, being most vulnerable to fashion, the sink is sometimes replaced. (The sink-vanities of the 1970s, for example, yielded in many homes to the pedestal sinks of the early 1980s that were reminiscent of the old sinks that people had ripped out to put in their sink-vanities.) When it comes to replacement, the toilet lags a distant third, with floors right behind them. Tubs are about the last item pulled out. Unless they're so old or so discolored as to be an absolute disgrace, most do-it-yourself homeowners are intimidated by their size and complexity.

But we suggest that you don't limit your thinking, early in the planning, about what you can replace and what you can't. Think about the unused nooks and crannies and poorly designed cabinets and closets in your room. In fact, look around at the space abutting your bathroom. Are you using all of that closet that backs up on it? Do you need that last foot or two at the end of the hallway that leads to it? If there's a jag for the bathroom into one wall of your bedroom, would you like to move the jag further into the bedroom? Will it achieve better use of your space? Jotting down information like this early in your planning will insure that your time and money get you all the bathroom you need.

Now you're ready to start your planning. Make a list of all the things you'd like your new bathroom to include. Do let yourself dream. Try your first few designs on paper, to see how many of the features you'd like to include actually fit into the existing space. If you've got some that won't fit, expand the bathroom if you can by getting rid of some expendable space—on paper first, of course.

Finally, try a dream sketch. Lay out the absolute ultimate in tub, toilet, bidet, sink, vanity, settee, garden space, and whatever else you'd love to see in your rebuilt bathroom. See how much of the adjoining space it all juts into. You may find it's possible to achieve.

If you've got space limitations, then let your imagination make up for them. For instance, if you can't add a knickknack shelf *on* a wall, see if you can fit one *in* a wall by knocking out a rectangle of plasterboard. You've got a depth of about 4 inches—plenty of room to put bottles, jars,

FIGURE 14-4 Here's one way of adding a bath without adding a new room onto your house. If your bedroom—or some other convenient room—is large enough, chop off part of it for a completely equipped bathroom. (Courtesy U.S. Forest Products Laboratory.)

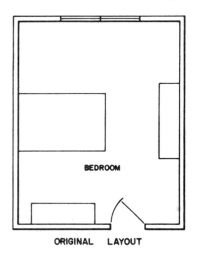

ORIGINAL   LAYOUT

BATH AND CLOSET ADDED

FIGURE 14-5   If you have room, a spacious bath is fun. You can include some less traditional uses. (Courtesy Monarch Tile Company.)

FIGURE 14-6   You can afford luxury in a small space if you use good design sense and attractive decor. (Courtesy H & R Johnson, Inc.)

boxes, even a plant. You don't need a mirrored medicine cabinet, either. Kitchen or utility room cabinets may give you more space at less expense. Even a fine wood cabinet can be installed for an elegant look, so long as its glue isn't water-soluble. A coat of polyurethane keeps it from swelling in high humidity. Think about back-of-the-door mirrors and picture-framed mirrors. Consider an unbathroomy light fixture.

Don't crowd your bathroom remodeling plan. A 30-inch sink may be fine in that new model home, but could you really tell it from a 24-inch model if you didn't see them side by side? When in doubt, you're safer sticking to smaller appliances. Space is the biggest luxury-producer of all in a bathroom.

ADDING A BATHROOM

Ah, the ultimate in luxury—another bathroom in the house. But don't just stick it anywhere. Stop and think a bit. Where you put it should depend on your primary need.

Are you adding to have one tidy bathroom when guests pop in unexpectedly? Then you'll want it near the living room if possible. Or is it because the kids have been tracking their mud and their playmates all over the house? Then you'll want it near the kitchen or the playroom or the back door. In neither case does the ordinary homeowner need a tub in this bath—though if you've got a pool, you may decide a shower's a good idea.

In a house with large bedrooms, you can turn part of one bedroom into a bathroom. But you'll need to figure on 6-foot short-wall space for a

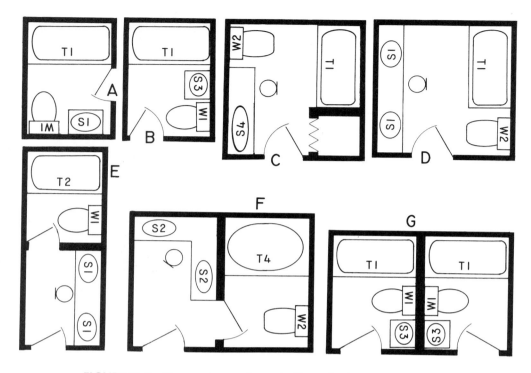

FIGURE 14-7 Here are layouts for typical home bathrooms, relatively modest in size but well equipped. With the right tiles, mirrors, fixtures, and care, they can be truly "magazine-page rooms." (A and B) Both fit in the minimum space, 5' x 7'. (C and D) Given just a bit more space, here's what you can add to a standard bathroom. These are 8' x 8'. (E) In a long and narrow 4'6" x 12' room, this bathroom has all you need. (F) For privacy plus spaciousness, this 8' x 10'6" bathroom makes good use of space. (G) Two totally equipped bathrooms, each 5' x 7', make use of pipes in only one wall, a very economical arrangement.

full bath, so pick a bedroom that's at least 16 feet in one dimension; if it ends up less than 10 feet long after you've made the renovation, you're going to be unhappy with that bedroom space.

If you have a little extra bedroom—or a large extra closet or dressing-alcove—you can make that into your bath. In fact, if you've got a bedroom that's tiny, consider changing that into a bathroom and then building an addition for extra bedroom space. If a small bedroom backs up against one wall containing pipes in your existing bathroom, kitchen, or utility room, converting this room may be your simplest solution.

If you're planning to finish an attic or to build extra living space into a basement, think about including a bathroom there. Putting a new bathroom above or below an existing one saves having to run many feet of extra water, drain, and vent pipes. (Chapter 22 discusses how to finish attics, Chapter 23 basements, and Chapter 21 how to build a dormer that expands ceiling height to house a new bathroom.)

The minimum size for a full bathroom is 5' × 7' but larger sizes are

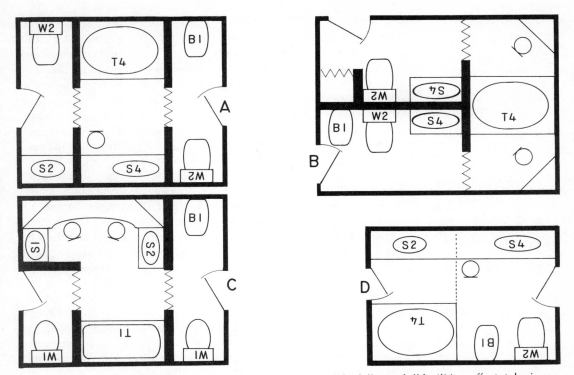

FIGURE 14-8 Bathrooms built for two make full use of all facilities, offer total privacy when properly designed, and give luxury and spaciousness without bringing along a big price tag. (A) This one takes up 10′ x 12′, yet offers two private bathrooms and a shared tub/sink/dressing area. (B) Two entrances to this 14′ x 11′ his/hers or ours/theirs heighten the feel of privacy even though the tub and dressing area are shared. (C) This one is 10′ x 12′, like (A) above, but has an entirely different emphasis. Here the major part of the bathroom is devoted to tub and dressing table. Toilets and bidet are put into small, utilitarian nooks to each side of the main area. (D) In only 8′ x 11′, this bathroom offers privacy, convenience, plus two entrances. In cramped quarters, keep only one entrance.

certainly recommended. Increasing one dimension even slightly allows for extra storage space and more luxurious sinks and tubs. Back-to-back bathrooms, however, don't have to have double the 5′ × 7′ minimum, because they can share some facilities. A tub is the most commonly shared item, but a pair of adjoining bathrooms can also share a large, luxurious washing-and-dressing area. Nearby blueprints offer inspiration for tackling your own design problems.

SMALL IMPROVEMENTS THAT MAKE A BIG DIFFERENCE

There's no need for you to feel overwhelmed by those super bathrooms displayed in designer magazines. (We'll let you in on a secret: many of them don't exist in reality. They're tacked together in a photo studio and disassembled as soon as the pictures come back from the lab!) But neither should you feel bound to make your own bathroom as utilitarian as Grandpa's red suspenders. You can use this checklist of tips to add convenience, to sprinkle a dash of glamor, or to do a little of both.

• *A colored appliance:* If you've got all white appurtenances, and you'd love to have them in color, your wish can come true even if you can't replace every one of your appliances now. Choose a colored toilet and order an extra tank-top (at nominal charge) in white; then add a white seat and it'll look custom-made. (Even white terry covers will have the same effect.) If it's the sink that needs replacing, investigate the two-tone sinks a few manufacturers are making. We got ours at Sears, and it has a white bowl and blue trim. The blue matches our tile floor and the new blue seat; we also picked up the blue in accents around the room, and our blue and white bathroom sure is perkier than the old utilitarian all-white.

• *New fixtures:* Toss out your scarred, outmoded faucets and spigots. You can buy fancy new ones at building suppliers, department stores, or through mail order houses—and they cost less than a dinner out. Nearly all of them come with readable installation instructions, and you should be able to have the old ones out and new ones in within an afternoon of light puttering. It's amazing what new faucets can do for a mature sink.

• *Improved fixtures:* For a few dollars, you can buy a watersaving showerhead that will nearly double the showering time you can get from the same amount of hot water. We've got one that's so well-designed, we don't notice the difference in water pressure—but there's a significant difference when it comes time to pay the bill for heating our water. And it takes ten minutes to install.

But for our favorite improvement we nominate the washerless faucet. It really can go for years and years without beginning to drip-drip-drip. If you keep putting off your plumbing repairs, it's well worth the hefty initial investment. Look for one on sale.

• *Updated walls:* Tile walls behind showers fall apart with distressing regularity. There are two common causes: moisture inside the wall, often due to leaky pipe fittings or faucets; and moisture on the wall, coming from improperly installed or maintained wall material. Once the gypsum board behind your tile or plastic wallboard starts to crumble, your only permanent solution is to replace the wall entirely. Simply knock it all out, since there'll be very little—if anything—worth saving. Correct any leakage problems. Then replace the gypsum board (see Chapter 12) and carefully install a new waterproof covering.

There's no law that says the wall around your shower has to be identical to the other walls in your bathroom, so there's no need to chase all over the state trying to find an exact match. If your other walls are tile, a complimentary tile pattern—picked up, perhaps, in a tile-framed wall mirror or other accessory—may add instant elegance. Shop around, and take home returnable samples of tile or wallboard to try out in your room. (Chapter 13 tells all you need to know to install tile on your walls; with our hints and the manufacturer's instructions, you won't go wrong. Chapter 12's instructions for wallboard installation will help you with that job—but do make sure to use the special materials that make bathroom wallboard waterproof.)

• *Blowers and heaters:* Mildew plagues bathrooms, especially the windowless bathrooms that are a feature of many newer houses and apartments. You can kill the mildew with cleaners that are available in supermarkets, or stronger chemicals that can be found at hardware and wallpaper stores. But then you'd better get after the moisture problem that led to the mildew in the first place.

In most cases the moisture collects during long hot showers. A blower can do a lot to rid your room of that moisture before it builds up. Installation is within most do-it-yourselfers' capabilities. Choose the blower with the largest yet quietest motor you can afford and be sure to vent it to the outside according to the instructions that should accompany the unit you invest in. Some local plumbing codes permit you to link your blower fan to the vent for a clothes dryer, and it's a simple procedure if you have easy access to that duct.

There are two ways to wire a blower. You can hook it up to a separate switch of its own, in which case you can leave the blower running as long as you like—but then you'll have to count on people who use the shower to remember to turn on the blower. Or you can hook it to the same line that controls your bathroom lights, and it'll go on and off whenever the lights are turned on and off. (See Chapter 8 for wiring tips.)

If you're a bath-taker, shower moisture isn't a problem—but keeping the room warm enough for a good long soak may be. A bathroom heater or heat lamp can solve that problem. It isn't hard to hook up, but be sure to follow meticulously all the manufacturer's warnings about keeping insulation and combustibles clear of the apparatus.

If your family takes both tub baths and showers—or if you just plain like the idea of bathroom luxury—take a look at the attractive units that combine heater and blower; that arrangement spares you from having to tackle two minor wiring jobs. But if you've got easy access to an outside vent on one wall, do put the blower there and, if someplace else makes more sense for your heater, opt for two separate units.

• *Tub spruce-ups:* Many bathroom remodeling jobs stop short of the tub. The problems encountered in ripping out the old and putting in the new sometimes seem like just too much of a hassle. But you can create the illusion of a new sunken tub or an elegant raised one. Simply build a step at the side of your tub, as wide as convenience dictates, and finish it off with the tile or other floor covering you're using. When finished, the tub will look as built-in as if you started from scratch. To give it even greater elegance, if you have the few extra inches, add a riser and small ledge at the height of the tub, and put the tile there, too. Just be sure that you caulk all joints so that splashing water doesn't seep through. (That small step is utilitarian, too. It makes bathing small children and cleaning a tub's inside area a lot easier.)

• *Whirlpools, hot-tubs, saunas, and such:* If you really want to go all out for luxury, you can buy one, two, or all three of these from manufacturers and plumbing outlets. There are even combination tub-sauna enclosures on the market. Whirlpool tubs and many hot-tubs need carefully grounded electrical connections; we suggest that only the most experienced do-it-yourselfers tackle such an installation, and only with the greatest care. With saunas, the biggest problem is the extreme moisture build-up. Be sure that your walls and ceiling can handle it. With all these products, ask to read the instructions—and read them from beginning to end—*before* you make your purchase.

If what you want is something new, these suggestions have been aimed at providing options to choose from. But don't invest in needless new items just because you're plagued by not knowing how to fix the plumbing and fixtures you own. A better investment might be to buy a copy of our companion book, *How to Fix Damn Near Eveything.* An entire large chapter gives detailed instructions for fixing major and minor plumbing complaints from stopped-up drains to drippy faucets.

15
Kitchens That'll Make You Caper

If you or your partner is one of those rare souls who just adores cooking, wouldn't it be grand to create your culinary masterpieces in the finest kitchen money and imagination can provide? And if you and your mate both hate to cook, wouldn't it be less tedious tackling that daily drudgery in a bright, modern kitchen that's designed for convenience and ease of cleanup?

Even if you fall into neither category, the kitchen is the focal point of enough at-home activity that an investment in improving it is one of the surest ways to enhance the resale value of almost any home. So why not invest now, while *you* can reap the rewards, instead of just before you put your home on the market? And, as this chapter will show, there are small but significant improvements even renters can make to increase their in-kitchen pleasure.

HOW TO MAKE SWEEPING CHANGES

First, let's assume that your present kitchen is old and inadequate and very little in it, if anything, deserves to be retained. You can design your new kitchen better than almost any professional contractor or architect, because you know your needs better than they do. As with all your other designing, start with a list of all the appliances, built-in gadgets, and timesavers you'd like in it and an estimate of how much more drawer- and closet-space you want or need. Shop around a bit—at least enough to amass the dimensions of the cabinets and appliances you require—and check the room dimensions you'll have to work with. Then begin making your sketches.

The trial-and-error moving around of cabinets and appliances—on paper—is one of the most effective ways to design a new kitchen. But let's see if we can help to direct your trials and eliminate possible errors. In Chapter 1 we showed how to use three different kinds of scale drawing to help lay out any room; we used a kitchen as the example, back then, because it's the most complicated to visualize of all your rooms. A simple floor plan is seldom enough because you have cabinets at two different levels—base cabinets and wall cabinets—and you have to take into account the sometimes unalterable location of major appliances such as ranges, refrigerators, dishwashers, sinks, and such.

You can start with a floor plan, drawing both levels of cabinet on it—the wall cabinets, which are generally 12 inches wide, and the base cabinets, which are approximately 24 inches wide. Once you've worked out a general layout on a floor plan, do test it out with a simple three-dimensional view. No doubt you'll find plenty of ways to improve on your blueprint once you visualize the height as well as the width of the elements you'd like in your new kitchen.

When professional designers develop kitchen layouts, they divide the kitchen into three centers:

1. The storage center, with the refrigerator and freezer as the main focus
2. The food preparation center, with the stove and food processing gadgets included here
3. The cleanup center, with the sink (and dishwasher and trash-disposer, if you like) as its central unit.

To show the route you're going to be walking many times a day between these three centers, they draw a triangle from points 1 and 2, 2 and 3, and 3 and 1 (where the cleaned utensils are stored). They suggest that the three legs of that triangle you draw between your sink, refrigerator, and stove—the three major components of your centers—should not be longer than a total of 25 feet, or you're going to be doing too much walking around in your kitchen. In fact, 20 feet is even better. Keep that *kitchen triangle* in mind as you figure out whether your appliances ought to—and can—be moved someplace where you'll get more efficiency.

In addition, kitchen designers have evolved four rather standardized layout schemes for kitchens. They take into account the kitchens' general shape, available space, and preferred layout. The four schemes have been graphically dubbed "U" layout, "L" layout, corridor layout, and sidewall layout. In general, the "U" and corridor schemes offer the shortest triangles. The sidewall layout is required in very narrow kitchens, and

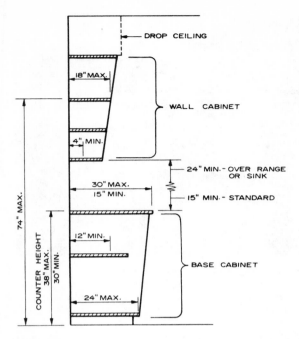

FIGURE 15-1 Dimensions of standard kitchen cabinets to guide your planning. (Courtesy U.S. Forest Products Laboratory.)

the "L" arrangement must often be used in small kitchens or square ones when they double as family eating rooms.

But these schemes, and the kitchen triangle, don't take into account the fact that, whether you eat in the kitchen or in a separate dining room, you must keep *that* location in mind, too, for most efficient kitchen planning. From point 2, the preparation center, food is taken to another point, the eating center, before it's brought to the cleanup center, point 3. And since the table is set with dishes and utensils for every meal, it's a good idea to have storage of *those* things nearby; the most efficient place is right at the cleanup center, not at the storage center.

So we suggest that, instead of the traditional triangle, you work with a quadrangle, the fourth position—somewhere between preparation and cleanup—being the eating center. Your layout will end up being even more efficient than those of the pros (who may never have had to serve the family a meal in their lives).

It's important not to confine your imagination with solid walls when you're preparing your two-dimensional blueprints. Often you can knock a hole in a wall, or take out the entire wall, to provide a pass-through between kitchen and dining room that will dramatically shorten the amount of walking required to get food onto the table and dirty dishes into the sink.

FIGURE 15-2 Don't let the confines of your kitchen's four walls confine your planning. You can often knock out large parts (or all) of the wall to your dining area, or build in a simple pass-through to save steps. (Courtesy Tile Council of America.)

The quadrangle concept is useful in helping you lay out not just appliance and cabinet placement, but countertop space as well. As you sketch your designs, keep in mind the following:

• Try to provide ample counterspace on both sides of your sink and range, plus on at least one side of the oven and refrigerator. Otherwise, you'll be walking a lot to put down the things you take off and out of these appliances.

• Plan to locate adequate storage cabinets so that all your food supplies are in or near the refrigerator—the food storage angle in your quadrangle. (Also plan, if you can, for a cabinet in an out-of-the-way place for long-term storage and infrequently needed items.)

• Try to keep pots and other cooking utensils stored close to the food preparation center of your quadrangle.

• Don't try overly hard to keep symmetry between the wall cabinets and base cabinets at the expense of sensible storage needs. (You don't need to put 24-inch-wide cabinets over 24-inch-wide cabinets despite the advice of most cabinet-makers.) What's most important in your design is the most efficiency most economically achieved. Besides, once you look at your real kitchen and not the simple two-dimensional blueprint, the fact that the top cabinets are only 12 inches deep and bottom ones are 24 inches deep destroys all semblance of symmetry anyway.

• Many artistic kitchen designs call for lots of open storage. But if you're fastidious about cleanliness, or lazy like us, try to get everything behind doors and into drawers. The best grease-trapping fan in the world won't keep grease completely out of the kitchen air, and once in the air it settles on everything that's exposed.

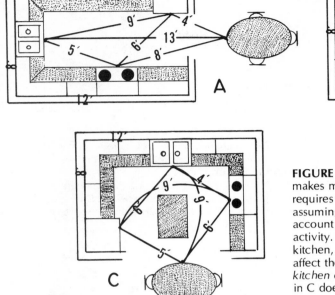

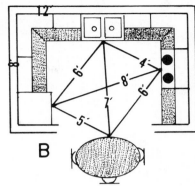

FIGURE 15-3 The U-shaped kitchen makes most efficient use of space and requires fewer steps than most other designs, assuming it's properly laid out to take into account the four centers of food preparation activity. In these three designs for an 8' x 12' kitchen, you can see how various layouts affect the length of the various legs of the *kitchen quadrangle*. Notice how the island in C does increase storage space, but also increases walking distances.

• If you're a two-cook family, be sure to allow plenty of elbow room for both chefs so they don't trip on one another.

After you try a few sketches, it will become obvious that even if you're starting from scratch on blueprints for a house that's yet to be built, you're not going to achieve everything:

• Minimum walking distance between the four legs of your quadrangle
• Maximum storage for every supply right where it's handiest
• Maximum beauty
• Maximum elbow room for every cook
• Maximum flexibility for later changes or additions
• Maximum durability
• Minimum maintenance work
• Minimum cost

As you work out your various compromises, no doubt your plans will keep changing. Don't call a halt on design changes, no matter how long it takes, until you're sure that you've arrived at a plan that (1) you'll be able to make into reality, and (2) you'll enjoy using in practice for many years to come.

At some point in the planning stage, begin to shop in earnest. There is a wide variety in price and design when it comes to kitchen components, so you'll have to make your choices before a final plan can be drawn.

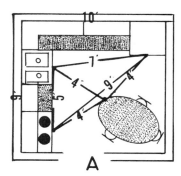
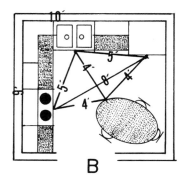

FIGURE 15-4 In this L-shaped kitchen, sized 9' x 10', merely locating the major appliances in their most efficient positions can noticeably decrease the number of steps taken by chief cooks and bottle washers—every day! You may decide that every leg of the kitchen quadrangle is not equally important: you may not move between the sink and refrigerator as often as you move between the stove and refrigerator.

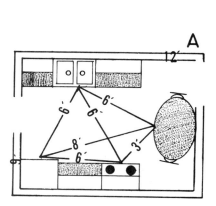
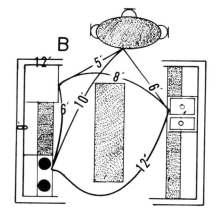

FIGURE 15-5 The corridor-type kitchen layout is often imposed on home owners and apartment dwellers, rather than being a design of choice. But it's a workable arrangement, particularly if you can put in an island. Both of these kitchens are 9' x 12', but (A) has 14 feet of wall cabinets and 14 feet of base cabinets. Because of its island and arranging, (B) has 16 feet of wall space and up to 23 feet of base cabinets.

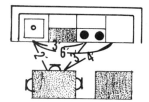

FIGURE 15-6 The one-wall layout *is* limited. But if you can find room for an "island," it's less limited. Along this 8-foot wall, you can count on 6 feet of base cabinet space, 8 feet of wall cabinets (with a short refrigerator), plus up to 3 feet additional storage at an island.

Although cabinets come in many standard sizes and shapes, not every manufacturer offers every possible size wall and base cabinet. Both top-of-the-heap and economy-priced makes vary from the standard, and you'll need to fit the options into your plan.

In nearby sketches, we've amalgamated basic designs from several kitchen designers and cabinet makers. They'll help you get started on your own plans.

REPLACING CABINETS IS EASY AS PIE

Most manufacturers of kitchen cabinets pay careful attention to the needs of do-it-yourselfers, since these days they represent a sizeable market. Nearby we've reproduced installation sketches from two cabinet suppliers. Glance over them to see how straightforward the job can be.

Just before tackling this book, the two of us ripped out every old cabinet in our kitchen, pushed away the wall between kitchen and dining room, mounted new cabinets, rewired and added lots of outlets, installed a new built-in oven and gas range top, tiled the floor and the countertops, and were able to start cooking and washing in the kitchen again only three hectic but rewarding days after we started. We finished the job at a more leisurely pace: lowered the ceiling, painted the few scarce feet of plaster

FIGURE 15-7 Manufacturers of cabinets are in love with do-it-yourselfers these days. They prepare comprehensive booklets aimed at explaining kitchens, and pack comprehensive guidelines for installation with every cabinet. Because of that, even the best cabinets are now affordable. (Courtesy Home-Crest Corporation.)

wall that still showed, put new molding around the window, finished off the wooden supports around the new pass-through, and so forth.

Planning is what makes possible a smooth do-it-yourself conversion such as ours.

- We sketched the new kitchen thoroughly, having first lived in the old one long enough to know its limitations and having read enough home decorating magazines to know what our dream kitchen looked like.

FIGURE 15-8 Here's a page from one company's brochure for do-it-yourself cabinet installers. These are sketches of Montgomery Ward's wall cabinets, with an explanation of how to read the codes which are universal among kitchen cabinets: the first two digits indicate the width in inches; the second two digits indicate height in inches. So a W-3017 cabinet is 30 inches wide and 17 inches high. (Courtesy Montgomery Ward.)

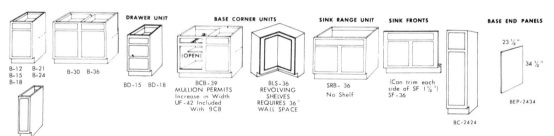

FIGURE 15-9 Base cabinets do not require the same coding as wall cabinets; they are all a standard height. The Montgomery Ward models shown here are all 34½" high and 24" deep (except for the depth of some corner cabinets). (Courtesy Montgomery Ward.)

FIGURE 15-10 Corner cabinets are challenging, but fun. This sketch shows dimensions for some of the more popular versions. Be sure to study the dimensions of your chosen cabinets before designing the details of other parts of your own kitchen. (Courtesy Montgomery Ward.)

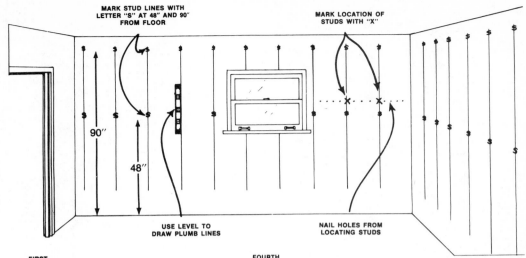

MARK STUD LINES WITH LETTER "S" AT 48" AND 90" FROM FLOOR

MARK LOCATION OF STUDS WITH "X"

90"

48"

USE LEVEL TO DRAW PLUMB LINES

NAIL HOLES FROM LOCATING STUDS

FIRST
Shut off water lines to sink.

SECOND
Disconnect stove and refrigerator. It is recommended that the refrigerator be moved into another room in the house to avoid damage and to allow more working space in the kitchen while remodeling is being done.

THIRD
Remove old cabinets, tops, baseboard and molding that will be in the way of new cabinets. Rough-in new plumbing and electrical lines as needed.

NOTE:
Locate studs by driving a trial nail through the wall at a height that will be covered by the wall cabinets after they are installed. Studs are usually 16" from center to center.

FOURTH
Patch walls as needed from damage due to tear out and rough-in.

FIFTH
Mark locations of studs (vertical 2 x 4s in wall) as shown in example above.

SIXTH
Check walls and floor to determine their plumb and level condition. See sketch below:

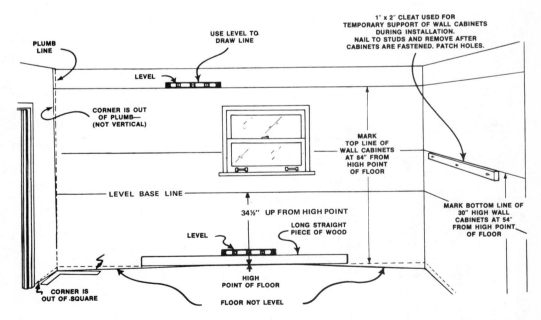

1" x 2" CLEAT USED FOR TEMPORARY SUPPORT OF WALL CABINETS DURING INSTALLATION. NAIL TO STUDS AND REMOVE AFTER CABINETS ARE FASTENED. PATCH HOLES.

PLUMB LINE

USE LEVEL TO DRAW LINE

LEVEL

CORNER IS OUT OF PLUMB— (NOT VERTICAL)

MARK TOP LINE OF WALL CABINETS AT 84" FROM HIGH POINT OF FLOOR

LEVEL BASE LINE

34½" UP FROM HIGH POINT

LONG STRAIGHT PIECE OF WOOD

LEVEL

MARK BOTTOM LINE OF 30" HIGH WALL CABINETS AT 54" FROM HIGH POINT OF FLOOR

HIGH POINT OF FLOOR

CORNER IS OUT OF SQUARE

FLOOR NOT LEVEL

FIGURE 15-11 From the brochure of one major cabinet maker, "How to Install Kitchen Cabinets," these scenes show how easy it can be. (Courtesy Home-Crest Corporation.)

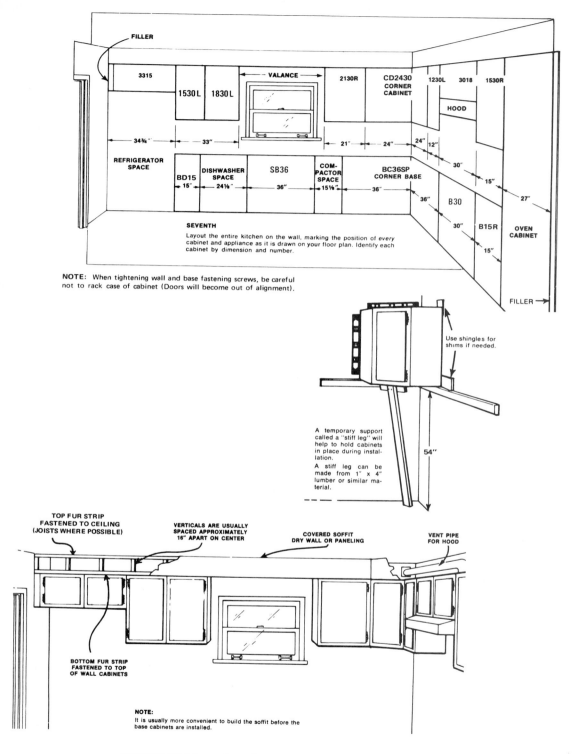

FILLER

3315

1530 L   1830 L

VALANCE

2130R

CD2430
CORNER
CABINET

1230L   3018   1530R

HOOD

34¾"   33"   21"   24"   24" 12"   30"   15"   27"

REFRIGERATOR
SPACE

BD15

DISHWASHER
SPACE

SB36

COM-
PACTOR
SPACE

BC36SP
CORNER BASE

15"   24⅛"   36"   15⅛"   36"   36"   30"   15"

B30

B15R

OVEN
CABINET

SEVENTH

Layout the entire kitchen on the wall, marking the position of *every* cabinet and appliance as it is drawn on your floor plan. Identify each cabinet by dimension and number.

NOTE: When tightening wall and base fastening screws, be careful not to rack case of cabinet (Doors will become out of alignment).

FILLER →

Use shingles for shims if needed.

A temporary support called a "stiff leg" will help to hold cabinets in place during installation.

A stiff leg can be made from 1" x 4" lumber or similar material.

54"

TOP FUR STRIP
FASTENED TO CEILING
(JOISTS WHERE POSSIBLE)

VERTICALS ARE USUALLY
SPACED APPROXIMATELY
16" APART ON CENTER

COVERED SOFFIT
DRY WALL OR PANELING

VENT PIPE
FOR HOOD

BOTTOM FUR STRIP
FASTENED TO TOP
OF WALL CABINETS

NOTE:

It is usually more convenient to build the soffit before the base cabinets are installed.

FIGURE 15-11 continued

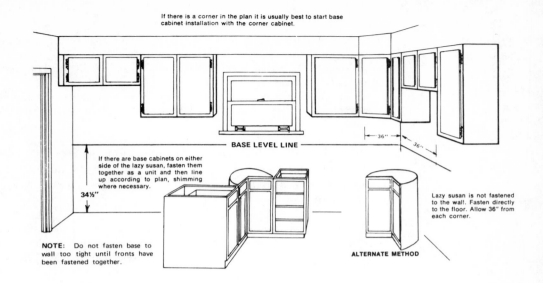

If there is a corner in the plan it is usually best to start base cabinet installation with the corner cabinet.

BASE LEVEL LINE

36"

36"

If there are base cabinets on either side of the lazy susan, fasten them together as a unit and then line up according to plan, shimming where necessary.

34½"

Lazy susan is not fastened to the wall. Fasten directly to the floor. Allow 36" from each corner.

NOTE: Do not fasten base to wall too tight until fronts have been fastened together.

ALTERNATE METHOD

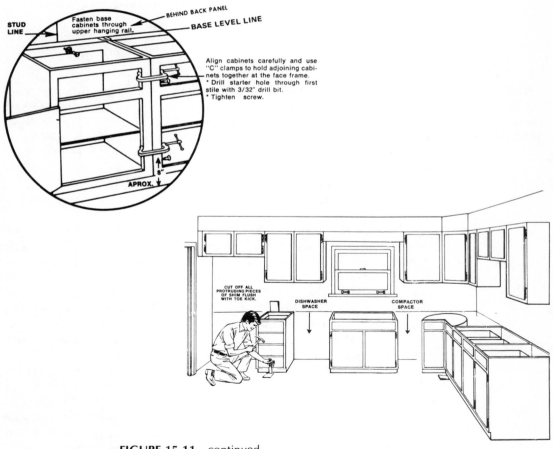

STUD LINE

Fasten base cabinets through upper hanging rail.

BEHIND BACK PANEL

BASE LEVEL LINE

Align cabinets carefully and use "C" clamps to hold adjoining cabinets together at the face frame.
* Drill starter hole through first stile with 3/32" drill bit.
* Tighten screw.

8"

APROX.

CUT OFF ALL PROTRUDING PIECES OF SHIM FLUSH WITH TOE KICK.

DISHWASHER SPACE

COMPACTOR SPACE

FIGURE 15-11 continued

- We shopped for style, quality, and price and then ordered our new cabinets and appliances.
- We read all the installation instructions and stocked up on all the necessary tools and materials.
- We checked our cabinets when they arrived in the store (and found that, sure enough, the manufacturer had filled one piece of the order inaccurately).

Only when all of those advance preparations were checked off our list did we schedule the kitchen job and arrange for the delivery date of cabinets and large appliances. When we circled our calendar, we kept three things in mind:

- That there were no expected conflicts with work or visiting relatives.
- That hardware stores would be open during most of the installation time so we could run out to pick up hardware and tools that we hadn't counted on needing.
- That no fancy company was expected for weeks afterwards, so we wouldn't feel any pressure to take shortcuts to make the job look finished before it really was. (Getting yourself into that kind of box is sure to encourage sloppy work.)

**PUT NEW
SPICE
IN YOUR
OLD
SURFACES**

It's the rare homeowner who can just rip out everything—appliances, cabinets, walls, floor, countertops, and all the trimmings—and plan a new kitchen from scratch. It's expensive and, besides, it's often unnecessary. In kitchens that were planned well to begin with, old cabinets may still give adequate storage space, and old appliances may not only be serviceable but placed correctly for efficient use. Even if there are changes you'd like to see, budget considerations may convince you that you can live with your old kitchen for several more years.

There are still a number of cost-conscious ways to get a new look and more serviceability out of your present kitchen.

Cabinet doors and drawer fronts are among the most-noticed elements of any kitchen. If you're retaining your existing layout and cabinet interiors, you can redo just their visible faces in various eye-catching ways.

A coat of paint is the fastest remodeling around. Be sure to clean the old fronts thoroughly and then steelwool or sand away all gloss from the surfaces. A high-gloss finish is most popular, but some people do prefer semi-gloss. If you're in doubt, stick to glossy. You can always tone it down later with a gentle rubbing with pumice, a mild abrasive stocked at most building supply centers.

If you are willing to remove the doors from their hinges, you can use spray paints. Set outdoors all of the cabinet fronts you're going to paint, don a protective mask, and spray away. Apply coat after coat until you've achieved that shiny, uniform Japanese-lacquer look. Instructions on your spray cans will help you estimate how big a supply of paint to stock up on. When you're done, your doors will look like they were factory-painted.

FIGURE 15-12 The change can be amazing once you cover old walls with spiffy wall covering and old countertops with new Formica-type laminates. For sound cabinet wood, refinishing makes sense; or you can buy new fronts for drawers and doors. (Courtesy Thomas Strahan.)

You can choose other ways to cover old cabinets. Depending on the cut and line of your cabinets, and your decor, you can pick from the likes of:

- Tile
- Formica-type plastic laminates
- Flexible vinyl in woodgrains, solid colors, or prints
- Wall coverings applied with water resistant adhesives
- Fabrics applied with water-resistant adhesives and then protected with clear varnish.

Doors and drawer fronts are now being manufactured precisely for replacement purposes. Check their availability at your local building supply outlets. They come in so many sizes and shapes, you should be able to find some to fit all your cabinets with a minimum of paring-to-size.

A second major focal point in most kitchens is their countertops. If yours are looking seedy these days, you can either replace them entirely or, if they're not nicked or bubbled, cover them up. Several brands of flexible laminated plastic can be turned into do-it-yourself countertops. If you thoroughly wirebrush the surface of your old countertop material, a good brand of contact cement should bond your choice of new top to your old. But test out this procedure on a sample piece before you invest in a large piece of laminate. Some cements don't hold well on some brands of countertop.

Another alternative is to choose some of the prefabricated countertops that are stocked at most building supply centers. You can buy them cut to your own dimensions, even with your sink opening already cut out. But measure carefully, because dealers don't take back cut-to-order pieces. And work with your supplier to plan the most economical and efficient layout for your new countertop. Often, in an "L" or "U" shaped kitchen, you'll need at least one joint with adjoining ends mitered to 45° angles. However, the hardware for joining such edges is flexible, efficient, and easy to use.

When your new countertop arrives, about all you have to do is look in the base cabinets and locate the screws that now hold the old tops on, loosen them, take off the old and lay the new tops onto the exposed base cabinets. Drill pilot holes for your mounting screws, and screw them into place once you've checked to make sure they're level from front to rear and side to side. (The hardest challenge, any cook will tell you, is to measure half a cup of liquid on a countertop that isn't level.)

The third big surface that gives away an old, dingy kitchen is its floor. Before plunging into a major overhaul, study what just a new floor might do to yours. Sometimes simply a combination of new floor, new cabinet fronts, and new curtains will turn a tired old kitchen into a new room. For flooring ideas, consult Chapter 13. Remember that even a wood floor is fine for a kitchen nowadays if it's thoroughly sealed with easy-to-mop, impervious-to-chemicals polyurethane.

The fourth quick-and-easy improvement you can make in a kitchen is to add more fluorescent lighting. Inconspicuous under-cabinet light-strips do a great deal to preserve the patience of cook and cleaner-upper. Position extra lighting anywhere you like, so long as it stops you from working in your own shadow. The improvement is instantaneous.

STRETCH YOUR INTERIOR SPACE

Remember what we said at the beginning of this chapter about the three centers kitchen designers have pinpointed: the food storage center, the food preparation center, and the cleanup center? There's one important point to keep in mind about these categories: they're clues that tell you where to store all the food, pots, pans, strainers, spatulas, potholders, and gadgets galore that every homemaker collects and half of us can't find when we need them most. If you think in terms of function when you begin to figure out how to use the insides of your cabinets and drawers, the efficiency of your kitchen will improve immediately.

We've stored our pots and pans right under our stovetop, and our baking utensils right near the oven. We've got our mixer and blender right at the food preparation center, along with the sugar and flour canisters and all the measuring devices. Our spices are all within easy reach when we stand in front of the stove, since we usually add them to our pots and pans while tasting. Our dishes are stored right above our cleanup counter, with a back door to the cabinet that opens right near the dining table. We've got everything we need right where we need it most, and that's what you ought to aim for.

Sometimes it takes a feat of engineering to cram in all the equipment a modern homemaker needs. But, recognizing this fact of kitchen life, many cabinet makers offer inserts and add-ons that more efficiently utilize interior cabinet space. Foremost is the lazy Susan that tucks into a blind corner, takes up only a few inches of cabinet-front space on each leg of the "L" formed where two rows of base cabinets or hanging closets meet, yet offers up to 8 square feet of easy-to-get-at storage area.

You can purchase pull-out and swing-out spice racks that keep dozens of those pesky little jars in neat, easy-to-find rows. Using the same principle on a much larger scale, some top-of-the-line cabinet makers make entire pantry units that swing or pull out, which can store a hundred or more cans and boxes of food on their narrow floor-to-ceiling shelves. They're not cheap, but they can't be beat for efficient space use and ease of access.

One of the simplest space-savers of all is to simply double up on shelves. If you're going to store cans and boxes in an ordinary cabinet, study their heights and segregate them. A 5-inch-high peanut butter jar has at least 7 inches of wasted space above it if it's stored alongside a 13-inch-tall cereal box. Consider adding shelves and half-shelves, as well as repositioning existing shelves. Divide your space to work for you and you'll conquer the space-squeeze.

Don't stop with the special features offered by your cabinet manufacturer. First of all, there are plenty of other space-savers on the market. When we redid our kitchen, we spent days shopping for slide-in-slide-out hangers, racks, trays, dividers, hooks, stackers, and so forth.

If you're really fanatic about getting the most of everything into the least amount of space—the way we were in designing the interiors of our cabinets for our 6′ × 8′ kitchen—you can build your own simple space economizers. Pegboard fastened to cabinet doors can display dozens of slim cooking and preparation helpers that would otherwise clutter up a whole drawer. The dead air space above the cabinets in most kichens can be built into long-term storage areas by just building a few doors. It seemed a waste to us to spread out all our flat pie plates and cake pans, but we hated to stack them all on top of one another since nothing frustrated us more than knocking them all over in every attempt to pull out just one. So we borrowed an idea from record-cabinet manufacturers and built a network of vertical slots into one cabinet. Now all our baking trays and pans slip upright between the slots. It's amazing what two scraps of pine board and a few pieces of masonite did to improve not just our kitchen's organization, but our output of cakes and pies and cookies.

III
EXTERIOR IMPROVEMENTS

16
Paint Your House Once in Ten Years

If you're like most homeowners, dreading the next time you either shell out a lot of cash to get the outside of your house painted, or go through the mess and agony of doing it yourself, take heart. At last somebody has attacked the problem scientifically. They've accumulated research data on the best way to paint your new or aging castle. And best news of all—the scientists say that a properly done paint job should last for ten years.

They're the guys from the U.S. Forest Products Laboratory (FPL) in Madison, Wisconsin, which is affiliated both with the U.S. Department of Agriculture and the University of Wisconsin. This staff of researchers studies virtually every aspect of wood. Being practical sorts, their indoor and outdoor lab technicians have pinpointed the best paints to protect houses, the reasons for premature paint failures, and even the ideal painting techniques. When they found that most commercial paint materials were lacking in some respects, they developed formulations that are now commercially available. Their hints work not just for wood but for all painted exteriors.

FIGURE 16-1 Outdoor test site at U.S. Forest Products Laboratory in Wisconsin features rows of wooden window frames stained, painted, preserved, and unpreserved to test various formulas for weathering properties. It's results from this lab that led to procedures for painting your home so the job will last.

The primary finding of the lab—which shouldn't surprise most of us—is that moisture is the number one cause of paint failure. So be sure that it won't shorten the lifespan of *your* next exterior paint job. The FPL says that to wrap your home in water-repellancy, a triple coat of paint is needed. That may seem like a lot, but three coats every ten years sure is easier than one coat every year or two.

Figure 16-1 shows what happens when moisture does get under your paint job. Here, the moisture first sneaked in at the siding's edges where two boards meet. The snow, rain, and dew penetrated this lab panel deeply enough to cause unsightly peeling. It's a good precaution to caulk all joints and cracks on your home's exterior to seal out moisture before you slap on any paint. Then your job won't look like the photo.

Even better than paint for protecting against moisture is WRWP,

FIGURE 16-2 Closeup of decayed wooden window frame unit that fell apart after only 6 years' exposure to Wisconsin weather (left) because it was given a standard paint job. The other frame (right) has had 20 years' exposure to the same weather but is still serviceable and could be brought back to like-new condition. This window was protected by the Forest Products Lab's water-repellent preservative. (This and all test photos shown in this chapter, courtesy U.S. Forest Products Laboratory.)

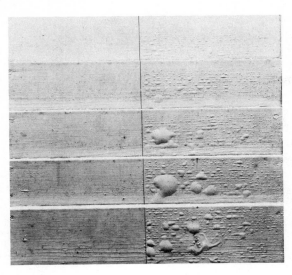

FIGURE 16-3 Moisture accumulating in your walls and creeping through your siding can bubble or blister paint, as you see here, no matter how careful the paint job.

which stands for water repellent wood preservative. Not satisfied with the way ordinary paint deals with moisture, FPL scientists formulated WRWP to contain the ultimate shedder of water, *paraffin wax,* plus *pentachloro-phenol,* a chemical that wards off mildew and other rot. The first coat of anything to touch new wood, or wood that you've stripped, should be WRWP if it's for exterior use. In Figure 16-2, one window had WRWP treatment and the other window didn't. Then they were exposed to wood-rotting Wisconsin winters and summers, after which these amazing photos were taken. Check with paint and building material suppliers for WRWP.

Inside moisture—from showers, drying clothes, cooking, humidifiers, and other sources—can also seep *outward* to destroy your paint job. Newer houses, in which the insulation is equipped with built-in vapor barriers, shouldn't suffer from outward moisture leakage *if* the insulation was installed properly. It shows up mainly in uninsulated older houses or in homes where insulation was blown into walls without thought of creating a vapor barrier. But if you apply vapor-barrier paint or ordinary aluminum paint to your interior walls—especially to those where you've got bubbling on last time's exterior paint job—you'll cut down on that exterior blistering.

A popular solution in the past, to this kind of moisture leakage, has been to put small ventilating louvers into holes that are drilled through to the outside. They *may* allow moisture to escape. FPL architect Gunard Hans says, "We just don't know for sure if they help much. What *does* help is to keep humidifiers turned down to 35 percent and thermostats to 68 degrees."

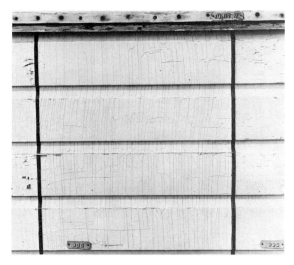

FIGURE 16-4 House paints applied by brush have a grain in the direction of the brush strokes. Paints usually tend to crack along those grain lines. The paints in this photo, however, cracked across the grain. This defect is from *thick paint:* too many coats of paint, or paint gobbed on. About the only remedy for this unsightly mess is to completely strip the paint down to bare wood and start all over from the bottom up. Paint gets thinner as it weathers, but if you paint too often, you'll build up a coating that sooner or later produces cross-grain cracking.

Obviously, you can't apply WRWP over flaking, peeling, chipping, old layers of paint. On the other hand, burning, scraping, or steaming off *all* existing old paint can harm siding. For most situations, that isn't recommended by FPL scientists. Instead, after you've determined why the old paint failed, strip off just all the loose and bubbled spots. We've found that the old-fashioned hand-held scraper works as easily as anything.

Where scraped-off-paint meets not-scraped-off-paint, a rough edge will show through your finished paint job unless you feather it. An electric rasp, which is a perforated steel disc, fits into our electric drill and does the job as neatly and quickly as any other gadget we've tried—and we've tried 'em all. (Since there's likely to be a lot of lead in your old paint, wearing a mask or respirator is a good idea.)

Every paint can we've ever picked up warns you to clean the surfaces before applying paint. Yet three out of four neighbors we watch *don't* scrub down their walls before painting—and they get short-lived paint jobs as a result. Use an old-fashioned hefty scrub brush and plenty of strong trisodium phosphate to clean away all of the dirt, grease, grime, dust, and other surface accumulations that otherwise get between your new paint and your old walls. Then hose away *all traces* of the trisodium phosphate.

FIGURE 16-5 This peeling is caused by failure of the outer coat (or coats) to adhere properly to inner coats. This can be caused by: (1) not washing the siding thoroughly before painting, or (2) applying a second finishing coat too long after the first coat (such as doing one coat in the fall and the final coat in the spring).

Right after you apply WRWP, new wood should be given a primer coat. A nearby illustration shows why. After ten brutal Wisconsin winters and summers, the primed panels on the left survived while the unprimed panels on the right didn't. If you've stripped some areas of an old paint job, those should be spot-primed. If you've done a lot of stripping, it's probably best to begin with a new primer over everything even if it's old wood. Use an alkyd oil-based primer that contains titanium dioxide. The

FIGURE 16-6 Here you see why we recommend primers so strongly. The nice-looking siding was painted with one coat of primer and one coat of a quality exterior house paint, and then exposed to rough Wisconsin weather for 3 years. The other panel was painted with two coats of the same exterior paint as the other panel's final coat, and similarly exposed.

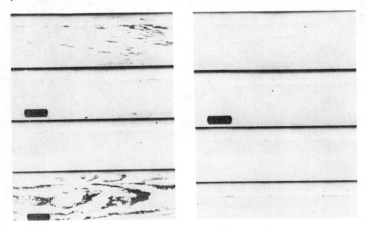

FPL has found that most amateurs spread primer on too thin, so read the instructions, which usually recommend 400 to 450 square feet per gallon.

The FPL's painting advice works whether your siding is wood or nonwood. Just be sure to pick a primer that's made for the material your siding is made of.

The FPL recommends three coats of paint for a complete job: First, use that good oil-base primer. Next, apply two coats of an acrylic latex exterior paint in a flat, semi-gloss, or glossy finish. Generally price is a good indicator of quality. But you don't have to pay for a one-coat-coverage guarantee if you're going to put on two coats anyway. And many local paint factories, especially those frequented by painting contractors, offer lower prices on high-quality paints.

Avoid paints containing zinc oxide pigments if you can, especially if your house has already had many coats of paint. Zinc paints are most likely to break down into the kind of cross-grain cracking shown in Figure 16-4. (The "grain" of paint is the direction you paint in, generally horizontally.)

A second major cause of cross-grain cracking is excessive paint thickness. That's usually caused not by applying too thick a layer at one time, but by repeatedly repainting before the old paint has weathered down to a very thin layer. Therefore, choose a color that you're likely to be happy with for the ten years that *this* paint job should last.

If you think your old paint is in good enough shape to act as a solid base for your new paint, and you plan to skip the primer coat, at least run this test first. After cleaning a test patch thoroughly, paint it with your latex paint. Give it at least 24 hours to dry. Then, onto the test patch, rub a 3-inch-long strip of inch-wide adhesive tape, the kind used to cover a gauze pad over a wound. Pull the tape away quickly. If there's no paint stuck to the tape, your old painted surface is okay; paint away. But if paint has stuck to your tape, you should cover the old paint with a complete coat

FIGURE 16-7 Here's Judi running a tape test to see if our old paint is sound enough to repaint right over it.

FIGURE 16-8 Here's Frank removing paint where the old material wasn't strong enough to endure a new paint job.

of primer. Primers are specially formulated to adhere to problem areas, something ordinary latex finishing-paints are not equipped to do.

Do not apply oil-base paint on a cool wall that will be heated by the sun within a few hours. Follow the sun around your house as you apply primer, or heat blisters may form. (In fact, this is a good policy to follow for latex paints too, even though they "breathe" better than the oil-base.)

Do not wait more than two weeks after priming to apply the top coats. Intercoat peeling of your new paint job may result otherwise. That's what happened to the new paint shown in Figure 16-5.

Don't paint into the evening on cool spring or fall days. Heavy dews can cause waterspots on latex paint and wrinkling or "flatting" on oil-base paints.

Avoid using latex paints if the temperature is likely to fall below 50° overnight. Oil-base paints can be applied even if the air's below freezing.

Unless you're very uncomfortable using one, the fine old-fashioned 6-inch paint brush is the very best tool for applying exterior paint. Most people get the thickest application of paint that way, and in the FPL's expert opinion that's what's most important. They estimate that a thin one-coat paint job slapped up with pad or roller can last as little as a year or two under tough weather conditions, and that the typical two-coat job will probably look good for three years. But a carefully done, brushed-on coat of primer plus two overcoats of latex paint can survive up to ten years on your house. The choice is yours.

17
Facelifts for Older Homes

Every year, over a million homes in the U.S.A. get treated to new siding. The reason, in many cases, is simply that the owners got tired of painting, painting, painting every few years. If you've studied the preceding chapter and feel that your exterior won't respond any more to just a cosmetic job, or if your most pressing need is to get some insulation into those walls, re-siding can be your soundest investment.

There's another reason for re-siding: to redesign the outward appearance of your home. New siding combined, perhaps, with a few changes that alter or camouflage the shape or construction of your home, can turn a be-it-ever-so-dreary tract house into a unique work of art.

Brick, stucco, and stone facades provide special problems for home improvers. In Chapter 19, we'll be discussing how you can handle cement work on your own; much of that information can be applied to patching cracks in these exteriors. Major cracks, however, often remain unsightly even after patching.

If you plan to retain your stone, stucco, or brick, you may be forced to bring in an experienced contractor. The preferred method for bring-

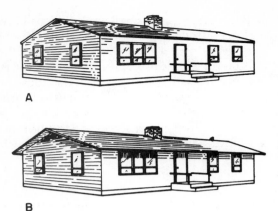

A

B

FIGURE 17-1 Extending the amount of roof
overhang improved the appearance of this house.
(Courtesy U.S. Forest Products Laboratory.)

ing new life to an aged brick or stone finish is sandblasting—beyond the
reach of most do-it-yourselfers. After the blast, however, you should
apply a clear, water-repellant sealer, and *that* is not more demanding than
applying paint.

The standard way of treating unsightly stucco is to scrape off all of
the crumbling material—which generally spreads out more extensively
than your eye sees at first glance—and then to re-stucco it. Your building
supplier can outfit you with all the materials you need, but from the
do-it-yourself stucco jobs we've seen, you may regret tackling the task on

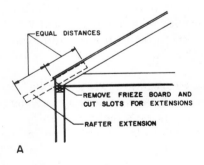

EQUAL DISTANCES

REMOVE FRIEZE BOARD AND
CUT SLOTS FOR EXTENSIONS

RAFTER EXTENSION

A

FIGURE 17-2 Here's one way to
increase the overhang of your own
home. At the eaves (top), extend the
rafters by nailing new pieces onto their
ends. At the gable end (bottom),
cantilever supports to hold up your
overhang. (Courtesy U.S. Forest
Products Laboratory.)

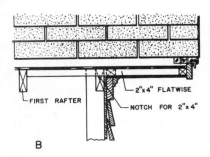

FIRST RAFTER

2"x4" FLATWISE

NOTCH FOR 2"x 4"

B

241

your own. To find out, try just a small area on some backyard corner and multiply that effort by the patience you'll need to get a whole wall looking good.

More and more, people are opting to cover over problem exteriors with one of the modern sidings. That way, if the house needs insulation, a layer of Styrofoam can be easily and inexpensively applied. Sometimes you'll have to erect a web of furring strips under your new siding; often you're spared that job. Study the instructions for the types of siding you're interested in before you choose one. They'll state whether furring is required.

PINPOINT THE PLACES YOU'D LIKE TO SEE CHANGED

If your house is a nondescript box, or a gimcracky collection of trendy features that are reflected in home after home on down the subdivision row, there isn't much you can do to its outward appearance to make it look any worse. You can, fortunately, improve on it. But many older homes have charming features that ought to be retained. Even some postwar house designs have copied styles of the past with some success, capturing the dignity of a two-story Colonial, the quaintness of a Victorian house, the charm of an old English cottage, the look of solid comfort of a Midwestern farmhouse, or the rustic informality of an old-time ranch. If your house looks pretty good when you squint a little, try to keep its character. Re-siding materials should be chosen to complement its style.

When you're planning changes, keep two key elements in mind: unity and simplicity. To achieve unity, make the rooflines and siding as continuous as possible, and use only one or two siding materials. Avoid trim that appears stuck onto the house without any purpose, and remove any old trim that's just there for show. (It'll not only give you more simplicity; it'll lower your maintenance costs.) We don't mean to pull off all that lovely gingerbread from your Scandinavian chalet or your Victorian villa—just to take it off your dome home or your rambling ranch house.

In two-story houses, windows are generally lined up and placed over each other on the first and second floors. Relocating a window so it's out of line could destroy your home's feeling of unity.

For an exceptionally plain house, one of the best places to add interest is at the main entrance. This is the natural focal point for the house. An attractive door, a raised planter, or interesting steps can do a lot for it. But be careful to keep the entranceway in scale and character with the rest of the house, and try to avoid an overly grand appearance.

If your house looks too tall, that can often be improved by adding strong horizontal lines at your porch or carport roof. Painting the first and second story different colors can also produce a lower appearance. But be careful about the colors you choose; we've seen some two-toned houses that ended up looking like they'd been made from halves of two other homes. Your best bet is to use a lighter shade of your bottom-story color for your upper story. To provide unity, paint the trim in one of the shades, a lighter or darker shade of the same family, or one contrasting color for all the trim.

Color can also affect the apparent size of your house. A light color makes a house appear large, whereas a dark color makes it appear much smaller. And if your house is a plain-Jane like our little one-and-a-half-story tract box, don't be afraid to let whimsicality creep in. We chose a bright gold paint for the siding, and softened it by using a light, even brighter buttercup-yellow for the trim. In summer our greenery softens its appearance; on a wintry Wisconsin day it's like our own special sun shining among the three-foot snowdrifts.

Before you select finishing materials for the outside of your house, you should also consider the interior appearance you've tried for. The most convenient materials to apply don't always produce the statement of character you'd like to make. It's usually more pleasing to go from a ranch-house exterior to a relaxed inside environment than to one that's as formal as the White House. Keep unity of effect in mind as you make your plans. (Nearby we've reproduced some illustrations to start you thinking about the kinds of things you can do to improve your home's appearance.)

One of the most common causes of poor appearance is lack of roof overhang. There should be a roof overhang of at least 1 foot and preferably 2 feet all around your house to protect the siding and windows. It keeps rainwater from washing down the face of your walls, creating moisture problems in your siding and trim. In addition, it gives your home a luxurious look. If this overhang is lacking, consider adding one when you're remodeling the exterior.

If you're putting new sheathing on your roof, the sheathing can be extended beyond the edge of the existing roof to provide some overhang. More elaborate overhangs require preliminary framing. (Courtesy, in part, of Forest Products Laboratory, U.S. Department of Agriculture.)

INSULATE AS YOU RE-SIDE

The days of the one-step re-siding project are just about gone. Energy-conscious homeowners want total exterior protection—more insulation, some soffit systems, and lots of storm windows. A maintenance-free exterior is still a primary consideration, but right alongside that one is a concern for upgrading their homes' energy efficiency.

That's why, before adding new siding, folks tack on an outer coat of board-form insulation right over the old house wall. In addition to ease of application, there's actually a significant saving over the cost of blowing in wall retrofit insulation between the skin of your home and its interior walls.

According to its manufacturer, the Dow Chemical Corporation, the installation of Styrofoam insulation during re-siding adds only about 20 percent to the total cost of a standard re-siding project. And it affords thermal protection over 100 percent of the opaque sidewall area—in other words, over everything but the doors and the windows. Even the wall studs are insulated so they can't conduct heat out of your rooms.

FIGURE 17-3   A fairly standard story-and-a-half home like this can become quiet, flashy, or stately depending on *how* you decide to install *which* kind of siding, and *where*. (Courtesy Masonite Corporation.)

But keep in mind that, while Styrofoam type insulation is not very combustible, it must be properly installed to avoid toxic fumes in case the rest of your house catches fire. To do it properly, nail it over your existing exterior sidewall and then cover it completely with your new siding and trim.

WORKING WITH WOOD AND WOOD-LIKE SIDING

The main difficulty in applying new siding over existing siding is in adjusting the window and door trim to compensate for the added wall thickness. The window sills on most houses extend far enough beyond the siding so that new siding should not affect them; however, the casing may be nearly flush with the siding and require some type of extension. If you're also adding exterior insulation board, even the sills may have to be extended. One method is to add additional trim over the existing casing and sill. When this is done, a wider drip cap (the piece of molding over the

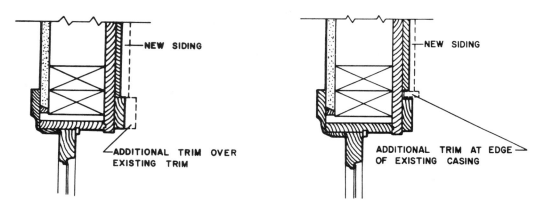

FIGURE 17-4 Here are two ways of extending the trim around doors and windows to match the new siding you apply over old.

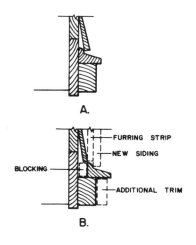

FIGURE 17-5 The drip cap over your doors and windows is vital for keeping moisture out of the trim and off your door. This is how you can extend yours when you install new siding over old. (Courtesy U.S. Forest Products Laboratory.)

top of the window and door) may also be required. The drip cap could be replaced, or it could be reused with blocking behind it to hold it out from the wall a distance equal to the new siding thickness.

Another method of extending the casing would be to add a piece of trim to the edge of the existing casing, perpendicular to the casing. A wider drip cap will also be required. Exterior door trim can be extended using the same technique.

Once you've got your window and door frames figured out, you're ready to get to work. Although any siding material can be used, some are better suited for do-it-yourself facelifting than others. Panel-type siding is probably one of the simplest to install and one of the most versatile. It can be applied over most surfaces, and will help to smooth out unevenness in existing walls. So let's look at it in detail.

Panel-type siding is available in plywood, hardboard, and particle-board, as well as numerous nonwood materials. The most popular of these are probably plywood and hardboard. Always specify exterior type for both, and the hardboard must be tempered. The grade of plywood to choose depends on the quality of finished surface you want.

Plywood panel siding is available in a variety of textures and patterns. Sheets are 4 feet wide and often come in lengths of 8, 9, and 10 feet. Rough-textured plywood is particularly suited to finishing with water-repellent preservative stains. Smooth-surfaced plywood can be stained, but it will not absorb as much stain as rough-textured plywood, so the finish will not be as long-lasting.

Paper-overlaid plywood is particularly good for a paint finish. The paper overlay not only provides a very smooth surface, but also minimizes expansion and contraction due to moisture changes. Most textures can be purchased with vertical grooves. The most popular spacings of grooves are 2, 4, and 8 inches.

FIGURE 17-6   It's important to protect the edges of your siding from the elements. Here's how both interior and exterior corners are protected in traditional lap siding as well as most panel type sidings. (Courtesy U.S. Forest Products Laboratory.)

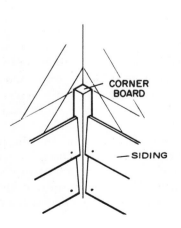

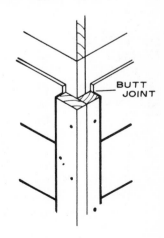

Battens are often used with plain panels. They are nailed over each joint between panels and can be nailed over each stud to produce a board-and-batten effect.

In new construction, plywood applied directly over framing should be at least ⅜ inch thick for 16-inch stud spacing and ½ inch thick for 24-inch stud spacing. But for installation over existing siding or sheathing, thinner plywood can be used. (Most of the available sidings come only in the thicknesses listed above.) Nail the plywood around the perimeter and at each intermediate stud, using galvanized or other rust-resistant nails spaced 7 to 8 inches apart. Use longer nails than are used for applying siding directly to studs.

Some plywood siding has shiplap joints. These should be treated with a water-repellent preservative, and the siding nailed at each side of the joint. Square-edge butt joints between plywood panels should be caulked with a sealant with the plywood nailed at each side of the joint. Where battens are used over the joint and at intermediate studs, nail them with eightpenny galvanized nails spaced 12 inches apart. Longer nails may be required where thick existing siding or sheathing must be penetrated. Nominal 1- by 2-inch battens are commonly used.

Plywood siding can be purchased with factory-applied coatings which are relatively maintenance-free. While initial costs are higher than for uncoated plywood, you may make up the higher cost in freedom from maintenance. These coated sidings are usually applied with special nails or other connectors according to manufacturer's instructions.

Hardboard siding is available in panels 4 feet wide and up to 16 feet long. It is usually ¼ inch thick, but may be thicker when grooved. Hardboard is usually factory-primed, and finished coats of paint are applied after installation. It is applied in the same manner as plywood.

Corners are finished by butting the panel siding against corner boards. Use the boards recommended by your siding's manufacturer. Apply caulking wherever siding butts against corner boards, window, or door casings, and trim boards at gable ends. (Courtesy, in part, of Forest Products Laboratory, U.S. Department of Agriculture.)

DRESS YOUR HOME IN VINYL OR ALUMINUM

Even the manufacturers of vinyl and aluminum siding now pay attention to the demands and skills of do-it-yourself home remodelers. Most of them provide comprehensive booklets to guide you through the entire procedure. They show you how to measure your home, how to estimate how many pieces of siding and corner and trim you'll need, how to begin the job, how to hammer your pieces home, and even how to add the finishing fillips.

Most companies that manufacture and sell the plastic and metal siding components also supply kits for finishing your soffits and overhangs with the same materials. We won't bother to duplicate their instructions here. If you think a pre-finished aluminum or vinyl siding is what you want, check out your local dealers. Collect a bunch of brochures,

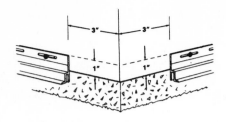

FIGURE 17-7 Here's how vinyl siding is installed over a framework.

study them, calculate the cost of your job, and then decide. We've included a potpourri of sketches from one manufacturer's installation booklet to give you a rough idea of what's involved.

We've found that the installation time for applying vinyl or aluminum siding is about equal to that for other types of siding. The big advantage is ease of maintenance for however many years it takes your siding to start looking dirty or faded; after that, a paint job is a paint job no matter what you paint on. The big disadvantage, of course, is for those of us who like a natural-wood exterior look; only natural wood can provide that.

FIGURE 17-8 When you've followed the detailed instructions that come with the framework, this is how the finished job can look. (Courtesy GAF Corporation.)

18
Getting on Top
of Roof Problems

Home handy folks seem to shy away from working on the roof. It's a shame because the roofing industry has more than its fair share of shady and fly-by-night roofing companies that sock hefty bills to you for shoddy shingling jobs.

Judi shingled our entire roof in Madison in complete safety and with no more instructions than the fifty words and four sketches printed on the paper wrapper around the shingles we bought. Outside of Frank's help in hefting the shingles to the roof, her only assistance came from a son who was 12 at the time, and the roof hasn't blown off—or even leaked—yet. With our several hundred words of advice, and a dozen illustrations, your roof's recladding and maintenance should be a snap.

A wide variety of roof coverings is available to choose from, and most can be used to remodel your roof in the same way that you'd use them on a new roof's sheathing. Sometimes there are local code requirements for fire safety, but your choice of covering will probably be influenced to a large extent by cost. Keep in mind that your roof is probably a major design element of your home, and its covering material should fit in with the overall design. In addition, don't switch to a heavy material like tile or slate unless you're replacing the same material or unless the roof's framing is strengthened to support the additional load. (Tile and slate are tricky to put up; for those materials, you probably have no choice but to hire help. Check to make sure that whoever you contract with has put up several satisfactory roofs before yours.)

The most common way to cover a flat or barely pitched roof is to build up the edges and spread a tar-and-gravel topping.
shingles, or over underlayment applied to sheathing if you're working on a new addition. However, if two layers of shingle exist from previous roofing, it may be a good idea to remove the old roofing before proceeding. Asbestos and metal are more expensive, much less widely used, and require special application not described here.

For very low cost, or over a porch with a relatively low-pitched roof, roll roofing is sometimes used. Judi roll-roofed our garage and it was quick and easy.

The most common way to cover a flat or barely pitched roof is to build up the edges and spread a tar-and-gravel topping.

For a moderate- or low-sloped roof that you're going to cover with

FIGURE 18-1 Ice dams form at the edges of roofs in colder climates. You may be able to prevent them with good ventilation. If you can't, here's how to keep water from leaking through your roofing materials—with wide flashing made of roll roofing. (Courtesy U.S. Forest Products Laboratory.)

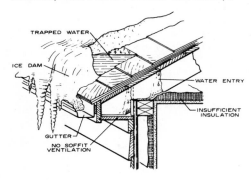

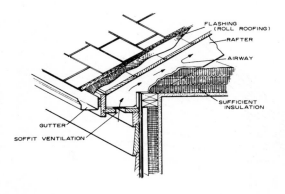

asphalt, asbestos, or slate shingles, or with tile roofing, an underlay of 15- or 30-pound asphalt-saturated felt is used. It's not commonly put under wood shingles or shakes. Where moderate to heavy snowfalls occur, ice dams are a problem. They're formed when melting snow runs down the roof and freezes at the colder cornice area. The ice gradually forms a dam that backs up water under the shingles. If you add a wide flashing at the eave—the lowest edge of your slope—you'll minimize the chance of this water seeping through into your ceiling or wall. For the flashing, use 45-pound or heavier smooth-surface roll roofing along the eave line, extending in width to a point 36 inches inside your warm wall. (Good attic ventilation and sufficient ceiling insulation are also important in eliminating ice dams.)

You will also need roll roofing 36 inches wide for all your valleys. The valley is that inside angle where two sloped roofs come together, such as where a large dormer meets the rest of the roof.

Where you're putting shingles over old wood or asphalt shingles, the shingling industry recommends certain preparations. First, along the eaves and gables, remove the old shingles to the width of about 6 inches, and at these locations nail nominal 1-inch boards. (If you're working over old asphalt shingles, thinner boards may be necessary.) Also remove the old covering from ridges or hips and replace the bevel siding with butt edges up. Place a strip of lumber over each valley to separate old metal

FIGURE 18-2 To estimate the pitch of your roof, stand far enough down the block to get a good clear view of it, then compare your slope to the slopes in this graph. You have greater choice of materials when roofing a high-pitched roof, but you—the roofer—have to be more careful on a higher pitched roof.

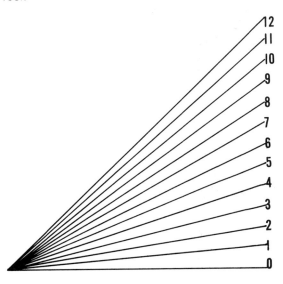

flashing from new. When you begin shingling, put down a double layer for the first course of shingles.

DON'T LET WOOD SHINGLES SHAKE YOU

For a rustic, natural look there's nothing prettier than weathered wood shingles on the roof. If you do-it-yourself, you may find it's easily affordable. Both shingles and shakes aren't hard to apply.

To shop for shingles, select No. 1 grade which is all heartwood, all edge grain, and tapered. The principal kinds of wood used are western red cedar and redwood. Both have heartwood with high decay resistance and low shrinkage. Single widths vary; narrower shingles are most often found in the lower grades. A nearby table helps you choose the best shingle for your roof, depending on its slope and the maximum recommended length of each shingle course that's exposed to the elements.

The following are general rules in applying wood shingles.

1. Extend shingles 1½ to 2 inches beyond the eave line and about ¾ inch beyond the rake (gable) edge.
2. Nail each shingle with two rust-resistant nails spaced about ¾ inch from the edge and 1½ inches above the butt line of the next course. Use threepenny nails for 16- and 18-inch shingles and fourpenny nails for 24-inch shingles. Where shingles are applied over old wood shingles, use longer nails to penetrate through the old roofing and into the sheathing. A ring-shank nail (threaded) is recommended where the plywood roof sheathing is less than ½ inch thick.
3. Allow a ⅛- to ¼-inch space between each shingle for expansion when wet. Space the joints in succeeding courses so that the joint in one course is not in line with the joint above it in the second course, but at least 1½ inches away.

FIGURE 18-3 Guided by this illustration, the nearby text, and the chart that follows, you should be able to figure out just what's involved when it comes to installing wood shingles.

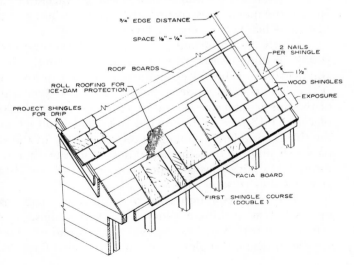

FIGURE 18-4 Recommended exposure for wood shingles.

SHINGLE LENGTH (inches)	SHINGLE THICKNESS (green)	MAXIMUM EXPOSURE	
		SLOPE LESS* THAN 4 IN 12 (inches)	SLOPE 4 IN 12 AND OVER (inches)
16	5 butts in 2 in.	3¾	5
18	5 butts in 2¼ in.	4¼	5½
24	4 butts in 2 in.	5¾	7½

*Minimum slope for main roofs—4 in 12. Minimum slope for porch roof—3 in 12.

4. Shingle away from valleys, selecting and precutting wide valley shingles. The valley should be 4 inches wide at the top and increase in width at the rate of ⅛ inch per foot from the top. Use valley flashing with a standing seam. Do not nail through the metal. Valley flashing should be a minimum of 24 inches wide for roof slopes under 4 in 12; 18 inches wide for roof slopes of 4 in 12 to 7 in 12; and 12 inches wide for roof slopes of 7 in 12 and over.

5. Place a metal edging along the gable end of the roof to aid in guiding the water away from the endwalls. Apply wood shakes in much the same manner as shingles, except longer nails must be used because shakes are thicker. Shakes have a greater exposure to the elements than shingles because of their length. Exposure distances should be 8 inches for 18-inch shakes, 10 inches for 24-inch shakes, and 13 inches for 32-inch shakes. Butts are often laid unevenly to create a rustic appearance.

An 18-inch-wide underlay of 30-pound asphalt felt should be used between each course to prevent wind-driven snow from entering the rough faces of the shakes. Position the underlay above the butt edge of the shakes a distance equal to double the weather exposure. Where exposure distance is less than one-third the total length, underlay is not usually required.

SHINGLING WITH ASPHALT OR FIBERGLASS

Until recently, asphalt shingles had become almost the standard roofing material for all but the most expensive new homes, and the standard replacement shingle for economy-minded owners of old homes. That position is being challenged now by fiberglass shingles. In appearance, the older asphalt shingle and its new fiberglass variation are about identical. In fact, the major construction difference is often just an imbedding of a fiberglass blanket among the layers of asphalt.

There are important practical considerations to bear in mind when you're deciding between the two. Fiberglass shingles are more expensive. But nearly all of them, whether top-of-the-line or lower down, carry Class A fire ratings from Underwriters Laboratory—something that only top-of-the-line asphalt shingles merit. (To earn a Class A rating, the shingle is placed in a 12-mile-an-hour wind and dried wood set on it and ignited. If the fire is completely contained on the surface of the shingle and never passes through to the pine board deck underneath, it warrants a Class A rating.) Also, fiberglass shingles weigh less than comparable asphalt shingles and they're somewhat more durable.

The most common type of asphalt or fiberglass shingle is the square-butt strip shingle, which is 12 by 36 inches, has three tabs, and is usually laid with 5 inches exposed to the weather. When you're storing bundles of these shingles, they should be piled flat so that the strips will

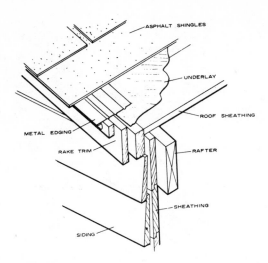

FIGURE 18-5 Here's how to start installing your asphalt or fiberglass shingles. (Courtesy U.S. Forest Products Laboratory.)

not curl when you open the bundles for use. Unless you're working directly over old asphalt shingles, an underlayment of 15-pound saturated felt is often used. (Figure 18-6 shows the requirements in applying underlayment.) In a high-wind area, buy seal-tab or lock shingles.

To apply your roofing, first put a metal edging along the eave line. Double the first course of shingles, extending it downward beyond the edging (or wood shingles, if that's what's underneath) about ½ inch to prevent the water from backing up under the shingles. A ½-inch projection should also be used at the rake. Make several chalklines on the underlayment parallel to the roof slope to serve as guides in aligning the shingles so that tabs are in a straight line. (If you're laying over old shingling and it's straight, you can use its edge-lines as guides.)

To secure your shingles, use manufacturer's instructions, except that in an area where there are high winds it's a good idea to nail each 12 × 36-inch strip with six 1-inch galvanized roofing nails. Where a nail penetrates a crack or knothole, remove the nail, seal the hole, and replace the nail in sound wood. (A hole left unsealed with tar is an invitation to a leak. And a nail that is not in sound wood will gradually work out and cause a hump in the shingle above it.)

FIGURE 18-6 Underlayment requirements for asphalt shingles.

MINIMUM ROOF SLOPE		
5" OF SHINGLE EXPOSED*	4" OF SHINGLE EXPOSED†	UNDERLAYMENT
7 in 12	4 in 12	Not required
4 in 12	3 in 12	Overlap by 2"
2 in 12	2 in 12	Overlap by 19"

*Known in the trade as "double coverage"
†Known in the trade as "triple coverage"

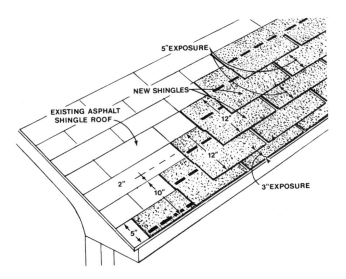

FIGURE 18-7 The way to install new shingles over old for the smoothest possible job. (Courtesy GAF Corporation.)

When you're going to cover square-butt asphalt or fiberglass shingles that have 5-inch exposure with 12 × 36-inch shingles, one manufacturer recommends the following procedure to insure a more uniform thickness of roofing over the entire roof area and a new horizontal nailing pattern that's 2 inches below the old one. By bridging the butts of the old shingles, it will minimize any chance of an uneven appearance in your new roof.

First nail down or remove loose, curled, or lifted shingles and remove loose and protruding nails. Replace badly worn edging strips and sweep the roof clean of all debris.

Then for your starter course, trim a 2-inch strip from the top edge of the new shingles and cut off either their tabs (if their design has tabs) or the entire 5-inch exposure area. What you're left with—approximately 5 inches—should be used for your starter shingles. They should fit exactly over your bottom-most exposed shingle-level. Nail them in place.

Now, for your first course, cut 2 inches from the top of your new full-width shingles and align their edges with the butt edges of the old shingles at the bottom of your roofline. Nail them in place.

For the second course, use a full-width shingle. Align its top edge with the butt edge of the old shingles in the next course. Although this will reduce the amount of shingle that's exposed in the first course, its appearance won't be noticed; it'll probably be concealed by a gutter anyway.

For the third and succeeding courses, use full-width shingles, aligning their top edges with the butts of the old shingles. You'll get an automatically straight shingling job.

When you reach the top of your roofline, you'll find that you've got a row of exposed nails on each side and can think of no way to cover them neatly. Take heart; the industry has several answers to that problem.

The most common method of treating the roof ridge—which is also applicable for hips—is called the Boston ridge. Where asphalt or

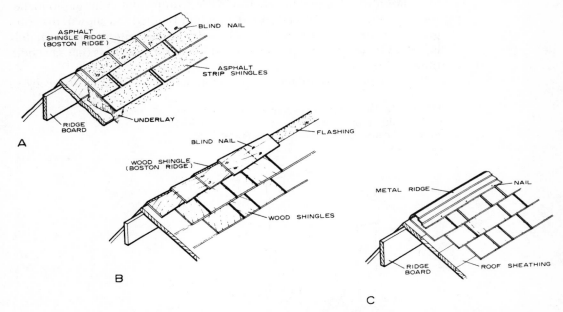

FIGURE 18-8 How to make the peak of your roof both water-repellent and attractive. (Courtesy U.S. Forest Products Laboratory.)

FIGURE 18-9 Down in the valley, take special care—or the water flowing off the joining slopes will seep into your house instead of running off.

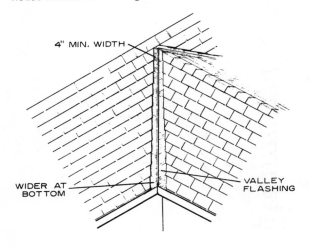

fiberglass shingles are used, cut the 12 × 36-inch strips to 12 × 12-inch sections. Bend them slightly and spread each one in turn across the ridge, lapping one over the other with 5 inches exposed on each one. Hammer your nails where they will be covered by the lap of the next section. A small spot of asphalt cement under each exposed edge will give a positive seal.

For a wood-shingle roof, also use a Boston ridge. Shingles 6 inches wide are alternately lapped, fitted, and blind-nailed. As shown, the shingles are nailed in place so that exposed trimmed edges are alternately lapped. Or you can buy pre-assembled hip and ridge units that save both time and money.

On asphalt, fiberglass, or wood-shingled roofs, a metal ridge roll can

FIGURE 18-10 Take special care around chimneys, or the build-up of torrents of water or slowly melting snow will cause leaks. (Courtesy U.S. Forest Products Laboratory.)

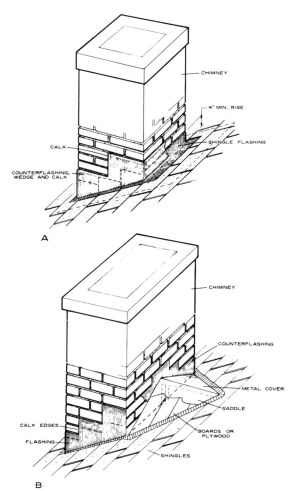

also be used. This ridge is formed to the roof slope out of copper, galvanized iron, or aluminum. Some metal ridges are made to provide an outlet for ventilation—but if you choose one of these, be sure that it prevents rain or snow from blowing in. (Courtesy, in part, of Forest Products Laboratory, U.S. Department of Agriculture; and of GAF Corporation.)

19

Concrete Advice for Your Walks, Steps, and Driveways

If you enjoyed playing with clay when you were a child, you'll love working with concrete as an adult. So don't shy away from pouring your own concrete sidewalks, patios, driveways, steps, and similar improvements. It's as easy as mudpies.

HOW TO TALK IN CONCRETE TERMS TO YOUR SUPPLIERS

All concrete may look alike to you, but beneath the surface there can be important differences. What we call concrete, you see, is actually a mixture of several different ingredients. If the mixture is well suited to the job expected of it, your concrete can hold up for several lifetimes. Otherwise it may crack, crumble, and create havoc within a few years.

The most essential ingredient in a concrete mix is Portland cement. It comes, as a rule, in bags. Each bag contains one cubic foot of cement and weighs 94 pounds. That's a bit hefty for most office workers, but you won't have to handle the bags yourself, as you'll find out shortly.

Portland cement by itself—or even mixed with water—does not make a good concrete. Sand is necessary to give the cement particles something to adhere to so they can form the compact, solid mass you want to end up with. Gravel, too, is an important ingredient which lends strength to the final mixture. In specialized applications, a lightweight aggregate such as cinders or the light mineral vermiculite is substituted for the gravel.

The ratio of cement to sand to gravel is crucial to any successful concrete mixture. One common mixture, called 1:2:4, contains 1 cubic foot of cement, 2 cubic feet of sand, and 4 cubic feet of gravel. Another common mixture, for less arduous applications, is 1:3:5; it contains 1 cubic foot of cement, 3 cubic feet of sand, and 5 cubic feet of gravel.

In addition to getting the proper mixture of solid ingredients, the amount of water is also important. In a 1:2:4 mixture, for example, no less than 6 gallons per bag of cement, but no more than 6½ gallons, is optimum if you are to get maximum strength. The 1:3:5 requires slightly more water per bag of cement.

We've gone through these few mathematical exercises mainly to show you that you can't just toss in a shovelful of this and a pinch of that and expect to obtain professional quality concrete. But once you've learned these ratios, all you need is the proper number of sacks of cement, the proper quantity of sand, the proper quantity of gravel, a hose, and a cement mixer of some sort. You can rent the mixer if necessary, buy the rest, and turn out really fine concrete. We've done it a couple of times—on comfortably small jobs.

Why do we mention the size of the job, if it's all so easy? Because if you're doing a small job, let's say a 10′ × 10′ patio slab that's going to be 4 inches thick, for a 1:3:5 mixture you're only going to need 5½ bags of cement, ⅔ cubic yard of sand, and 1 cubic yard of gravel. You can manage those sizes comfortably, but it really doesn't pay to have a trucker haul in that little bit of material. You will probably find the most economical way to handle such a job is to use bags of pre-mixed cement, sand, and gravel.

On the other hand, if you were planning to pour a 9′ × 50′ driveway, 5 inches thick, you'd need 48 bags of cement, more than 3½ cubic yards of sand, and almost 5½ yards of gravel. If you try it yourself, just storing the stuff till you're ready for it will ruin a lot of your lawn. For those very large jobs, we recommend that you call in a ready-mix truck. This is what most professionals do, and these days most ready-mix companies are perfectly happy to take work orders from amateurs.

How do you deal with the pros? First get your job laid out and your forms in place; we'll tell you how over the next few pages. Then estimate how much concrete your job requires; Figure 19-1 will help you do that. (Notice that the figures show the number of *cubic yards* you'll need. That's the standard unit of measure for concrete work.)

Next phone several local ready-mix concrete companies and get their prices. At the same time try to get a sense of how easy each of them is to get along with. Some may take orders from amateurs only reluctantly while others are outright cordial. We'd be willing to pay a bit more for the cordial treatment, because when you're pouring your first big cement job,

FIGURE 19-1 How to estimate concrete slabs: (1) Lay out your forms first. (2) Measure the thickness of the concrete to be poured into the forms. Measure at several different points and take an average if the figures vary. Circle the thickness along the top of the chart below. (3) Measure the length and width of the project. Multiply those figures to find the area. Round off to the next highest 10-square-feet. (4) If your area figure is printed on the left-hand side of the chart below, circle it. If not, circle several numbers that, when combined, total your given area. (Example: for 560 square feet, circle "500" plus "50" plus "10.") (5) For thicknesses greater than 5 inches, double a smaller figure. (Example: for 7-inch thickness, double the figure for 3½ inches.)

THICKNESS (inches)	3	3½	4	4½	5
AREA (square feet)	(CUBIC YARDS OF CONCRETE)				
10	0.10	0.11	0.12	0.14	0.16
25	0.23	0.27	0.31	0.35	0.39
50	0.46	0.54	0.62	0.70	0.77
100	0.93	1.08	1.23	1.39	1.54
200	1.85	2.16	2.47	2.78	3.09
300	2.78	3.24	3.70	4.17	4.63
400	3.70	4.32	4.94	5.56	6.17
500	4.63	5.40	6.17	6.94	7.71
600	5.56	6.48	7.41	8.33	9.26
700	6.48	7.56	8.64	9.72	10.80
800	7.40	8.64	9.88	11.11	12.35
900	8.33	9.72	11.11	12.50	13.89
1000	9.26	10.80	12.34	13.89	15.43

you won't want a nervous truckdriver standing over you saying, "Hey, get a move on, bud!"

Schedule a delivery to suit your convenience, and then have all the family and friends you can round up ready to help. The truck will arrive loaded with the appropriate amount of pre-mixed concrete; it will back into location and slowly dump the mixture into your forms or into wheelbarrows that you and friends wheel into the right spot and dump, one by one. The company's price includes this "standby time"; when you're getting a cost estimate, also inquire how much standby time they'll accept as reasonable.

The alternative to either mixing concrete yourself or having the ready-mix truck deliver it for you, is to buy bags of pre-mixed concrete mix. Several companies package measured amounts of cement, sand, and gravel in all-in-one bags. They're like cake mixes to which you add just water. You'll find them at most hardware and building supply stores. Bags typically weight 60 to 80 pounds—within the capabilities of one strong person or two good friends, or of a loner with a shopping cart or wheelbarrow. Unlike bags of Portland cement, the pre-mixed bags come with detailed instructions as to how much water to add, how much mixing time is preferred, and so forth. One bag of pre-mixed concrete product is just right for mixing in a wheelbarrow right at your job site.

But even if you're using pre-mix, decide on how much you can competently handle before your time and patience wear thin. To spread concrete on a 9′ × 50′ driveway 5 inches thick, you'd have to mix up about 270 of the 80-pound bags of pre-mix product. That's an awfully tiresome chore, enough to suggest that you might give up by the fortieth bag. On the other hand, for an 8′ × 12′ patio slab 4 inches thick, you need to mix only 48 bags. We'd say that's not an unreasonable undertaking.

CONCRETE TOOLS AND TECHNIQUES

If you're going to mix your own concrete in large batches, you'll need a cement mixer—not necessarily the kind that backs up on a truck, but a small portable hand-operated version of the big job. Shops that specialize in renting small equipment have them for hire in various sizes. A one-bag mixer can handle the amount of sand, gravel, and water needed to mix with one bag of Portland cement. This size is adequate for most home improvement projects, but larger sizes are available. Ask your rental agency for guidance; they're used to handling the needs of small contractors and have usually been able to steer us to proper equipment.

For smaller batches, you can use a wheelbarrow. Of course your wheelbarrow's nice enameled finish probably won't survive intact after it doubles as a mini-mixer, but what's the point of owning one if you drive it only on Sundays?

For larger batches, or more of them, you might consider building a trough about 2 feet wide by 4 feet long out of scrap lumber such as 2 × 6s or 2 × 8s for the sides and ends and plywood for the bottom. Don't worry about making it completely watertight. If you put in the cement and sand first, and pour the water into a well in that mixture as you mix it up, it's like pouring gravy onto mashed potatoes. It shouldn't become soupy until you're ready to pour it out.

The hoe is the traditional tool for mixing concrete. But we've used shovels and other handy implements with fine results.

A wheelbarrow is handy for getting wet concrete from your mixing site to where you want it to reside for the rest of your life, but we've seen people tote the stuff around in pails. Actually, the weight of a pailful is easier for some people to manage than a wheelbarrow. In any case, you'll need a good strong shovel for putting the concrete where you want it to go.

Figure 19-2 shows some of the tools specially made for working with concrete, as well as two kinds of levels that are essential to many jobs. We'll outline the techniques for a concrete job, and that'll show you what each of the tools is used for.

First you must carefully measure the place to be concreted. Drive a stake into each corner of the area and connect the stakes with a taut string. If you're going to build a garage or patio atop the concrete slab, you'd better be sure the corners of the working area are square. You can test your corners with a large square. Adjust your stakes until every corner has a 90° angle.

If you have trouble testing for squareness—most people do have trouble—you can run some extra string lines to assist with the operation. First connect the two pairs of stakes at corners opposite each other; that'll leave you with a big "X" in the middle of your rectangle. Then find the exact midpoint of each of the four outside strings. Connect opposite pairs of midpoints with string. At this juncture you'll have four strings running into your working area: two from the corners, two from midpoints. All four of them should meet at a single point. If they don't, adjust your corner stakes until they do, as shown in Figure 19-3.

Now, if your slab of concrete is going to be *in* the ground, not resting

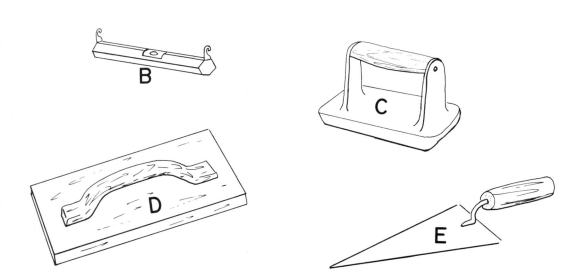

FIGURE 19-2 The major tools of the concrete trade are: (A) carpenter's level; (B) string level, a delightfully handy little tool that hangs over a string that you've stretched from point A to point B, and tells you if the string (and presumably the land in between) is level or slanted; (C) edging trowel; (D) float trowel; (E) pointed trowel. (These illustrations are not to scale.)

FIGURE 19-3 Strings can help you square up the corners of your concrete slab. That's not an important consideration for simple decks, but if you plan to build a garage or porch or covered patio over the slab, your job will go much more quickly and your results look much more professional if the corners are square. Place a network of strings according to advice given nearby in the text. When you've adjusted your corner stakes until the four strings meet at a common point, then the corners are square.

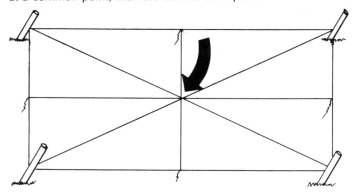

on top of it, you'll have to dig away the dirt inside your rectangle and for enough distance all around it to accomodate your wood forms. Once you get the knack of digging, you'll be able to gauge the depth of your success against some reference point on your shovel. If you want, you can actually paint a colored line on the shovel to show how deep you need to dig.

(A trick for easier digging in dirt is to wet it down thoroughly before you begin.)

Ideal depth varies depending on the project. Concrete in driveways, for example, should be 5 inches deep. Sidewalks and other slabs are often 4 inches deep. In areas with mild winters, you may be able to get away with 3-inch depth, but we suggest that you don't skimp. The extra inch or so is very worthwhile insurance against crumbling, cracking, and general deterioration.

Either before you begin digging, or afterwards, you'll have to account for drainage of rainwater and melting snow. If the slab, sidewalk, or driveway is perfectly level, water will stand on it and you don't want that to happen. But it doesn't have to slope much, so see first if your ground slopes naturally. To find that out, lay a long, straight board across your undisturbed soil and set a level on it.

If your ground doesn't slope, you'll have to create a bit of one by digging deeper on one side than the other, or by laying more cement on the side you want to be higher. Make sure the slope you design tilts *down* from your house or toward an existing driveway or natural drainage feature. In fact, if your ground slopes naturally in the wrong direction, you may want to tilt your slab to correct that.

If all of your strings in your layout have been set at a precise distance above the ground on each stake, then you can find out if your ground is level with a string level, a simple tool shown among the illustrated tools. The string level simply hangs on a tightly drawn string, and shows whether or not the string is level. This is especially helpful if your ground is rocky and uneven.

If the ground you encounter while digging is rather sandy, you can safely pour your concrete directly on top of that. But if you have clay or other sticky soil, you'd better dig out an extra inch or two and bring in sand or gravel to act as your base. In small projects this is not critical, but for sidewalks, garage slabs, driveways, large patios, and such, it's an important step to guarantee maximum durability.

Wooden forms around the edges of your area provide shape and support for your concrete while it hardens. Use cheap 2-inch boards to make your forms. For thinner slabs, 2 × 4s work fine; for thicker ones, use 2 × 6s. Take care how you set your forms. Their tops edges will establish the top of your cement.

Concrete expands and contracts as temperatures increase and decrease. You have to allow for that in large slabs such as for big patios, garages, driveways, and so forth. Redwood 2 × 4s are ideal contraction joints. You can make the redwood boards part of your forms and then leave them in place when the job is done—just be sure they're set far enough into the ground to be flush with your cement. We'll discuss the exact number and kinds of contraction joints you'll need in a later section.

In sidewalks, an additional kind of contraction joint is required about every 4 feet. Since concrete engineers assume that sidewalks and similar structures *will* crack from repeated contraction and expansion, they put in prefabricated cracks that are aesthetically pleasing. Look at any sidewalk and you'll see the scored lines in them about every 4 feet. To make your cracks look as professional as they are, you can use a jointing tool, or you can accomplish the same thing with a common trowel plus an edging tool.

To make an expansion joint this way, simply lay a straight-edged board across your still-wet concrete and draw the point of your trowel along the edge. Be sure to penetrate about a quarter of the way through the depth of your sidewalk. Finish off the joint by running your edger across both sides of the line you've made.

But we've jumped a bit ahead of our job. Let's get back to the point where your forms are in place and you've made sure they're straight. Next pound a hefty stake alongside the forms every 4 feet, outside the area you'll be pouring into. Concrete is very heavy, and without these support stakes the weight of your mixture can force the forms out of line. Hose down the forms and the area inside them, and finally you're ready to pour in your concrete.

Make sure you dump in enough to fill up the forms to the very top, but not so much that it flows all over your grass. You'll learn very quickly the knack of estimating how much to put in at one time.

For deep projects, such as steps, you have to make sure there are no sizeable air bubbles trapped inside the wet mixture. With a shovel, slosh up and down throughout your concrete from one end to the other to force out trapped air.

Next strike off the excess poured concrete, using a 2 × 4 that's longer than the width of your job. On narrow jobs, you can strike off solo, but for a nice-looking finish on a big job you'd better have someone work the other end of your 2 × 4. Slowly seesaw the striking board from one end of the job to the other, leveling off the concrete as you go. Be sure the board is always resting on top of your forms as you move along. You shouldn't progress more than an inch or two forward with each back-and-forth seesaw motion.

By the time you've reached the end of your forms, the surface should be relatively even. If there are any spots that are still lower than the top of your forms, go back and pour in some more concrete there and repeat the striking off in those areas. Once concrete is poured into place, you must move it around as little as possible to obtain the maximum possible strength. On the other hand, you'll also want a level job.

When the striking off is completed, your overall job should be level. But the surface of the wet mixture will be left with a network of shallow ridges made by the striking board. Using a wooden float trowel, firmly smooth out the entire job. Again, start at one end and work toward the other. This floating process serves two purposes: one is to smooth out the surface of the concrete; the other is to embed all the large pieces of gravel *beneath* the surface.

When the floating process is completed, take a pointed metal trowel and slice along the upper inch or two inside the edges of your forms much the way a baker eases a warm cake's edges from its cakepan. You want to be sure the concrete does not adhere to rough spots in the forms. After the surface of your wet concrete has become dull and smooth, and after all of the surface water has evaporated or been absorbed by the concrete, make any necessary contraction joints with pointed trowel and edger the way we described previously. Then run your edger along all the edges of the form. The edger rounds off the corners that will be exposed when the forms are removed, on the theory that rounded corners are less likely to chip off than square ones.

If you want a slick surface on your cement, you'll now have to gently smooth the entire surface with a metal finishing trowel—a flat metal tool about 4 × 12 inches large. Engineers and consumers alike have become convinced that slick surfaces are not usually desirable. They get slippery when wet and give less traction for cars and feet in the wintertime. But if you're going to paint your patio, or you really enjoy that slick look, you may want to use the finishing trowel.

Concrete doesn't reach its maximum strength for almost a month after you pour it. In fact, the first weeks in the life of a new concrete structure are critical, as the Portland cement goes through a strengthening process known as hydrating. To help it hydrate, you must keep the concrete as wet as possible even if you have to go out and hose it down twice a day. Concrete that is kept moist during the first week can be 50 percent stronger than the same job would be if left perfectly dry.

You can remove your forms a day or two after pouring the cement. And you can walk on it at the same time. But don't drive your car over a new driveway until a week after you've poured the concrete.

SIDEWALK STRATEGY

When it comes to sidewalks, most likely you'll be doing more patching than pouring from scratch. An aggressive snow-shoveler, an assertive ice-chopper, and an overactive tree-root may undermine just one small area of a perfectly good walk.

The technique of patching sidewalk—and other concrete structures—is little different from pouring new concrete. One plus is that you won't have to erect new forms since your concrete will be poured between existing concrete and solid earth. Also, you won't have to dig out the earth; it's already dug. What you will have to do is to hammer away all the damaged and crumpled old material before you start to pour in the new. Chips of concrete are incredibly sharp, so be sure to wear protective glasses or a fullface mask while you wield your sledgehammer or comparable tool.

For patching just a few square inches, your best bet is to buy a pre-mixed can of one of the products made specifically for patching up concrete.

To make a new walkway, proceed as we described in the previous section of this chapter. Sidewalks should be a minimum of 3 feet wide. Four feet is preferred if it will get lots of use, but 3 feet is somewhat less conspicuous and costs 25 percent less for concrete. If your ground has not been disturbed recently, you can probably safely pour a 4-inch-thick walk, using 2 × 4s for your forms. But if you've just moved into a development built over a swamp filled up with dirt moved in from somewhere else, the ground is probably still settling. In that case, you'd be wise making a 6-inch thick walkway using 2 × 6s for forms. In areas that endure harsh winters, too, thicker walks hold together longer.

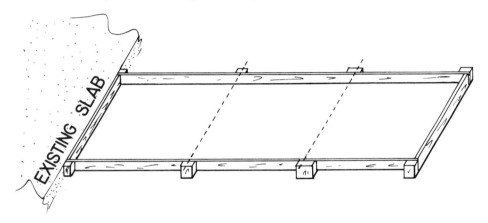

FIGURE 19-4 Forms for a typical small sidewalk. Notice that there's a redwood expansion joint against the existing slab (and *not* nailed to the forms). There are low but strong supports about every 4 feet; they not only hold the concrete within the forms, but serve as a guide when it comes time to create the expansion cracks indicated by the broken lines in this sketch.

Wherever your walkway joins an existing concrete slab, such as another walk, garage, floor, or porch, you should put a redwood expansion joint. That's simply a 2 × 4 made of redwood that you will leave in place at the end of the job. Therefore, don't nail that redwood joint to the rest of your wooden forms.

To protect the safety of people using your walkway, it should not slope more than 5 percent. If your house is considerably higher than the city sidewalk or the other area you're connecting to, check out this point. You can determine if you exceed a 5 percent slope by laying an 8-foot-long straight board where your walk will run. Working at the low end, lay your level on the board and raise that end until your level indicates that the board is level. Then, holding the board up there, measure how far off the ground its end is. If it exceeds 4¾ inches, your slope is more than 5 percent. Nearby we show two ways to build steps into your run of walkway, so that no part of it will exceed the 5 percent limit.

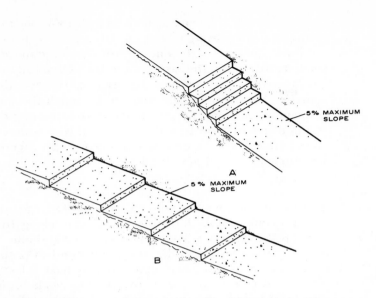

FIGURE 19-5 Two ways to deal with a sloping yard so that your sidewalk will not slope more than 5 percent, the maximum safe tilt. (Courtesy U.S. Forest Products Laboratory.)

If you're eager to make an unusual and attractive walk, you can use something other than ordinary grey concrete. First of all, you can buy dyes that, when added to your concrete mix, will color the walkway permanently. Be careful about this approach, however, since some of the colors end up looking garish. You can also opt to lay down a surface composed mostly of bricks or flagstones. In warm climates, you can set them down on a base of sand or on your sandy subsoil. But in areas where the ground can freeze, you'll need a concrete base.

To set flagstones or bricks into the concrete base, proceed with all of the earlier steps required to lay a concrete walk. Then pour in only enough concrete so that, when each brick or flagstone is laid on top, the

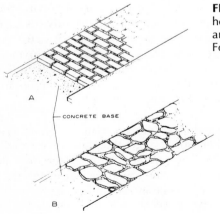

FIGURE 19-6 In the text, we tell you how to create these fancy flagstone and brick walkways. (Courtesy U.S. Forest Products Laboratory.)

upper edge of it will extend about an inch above the top of your wooden forms. Using a twisting motion, force each brick or stone down into the mud until it's level with your forms. They'll sit above several inches of concrete base. After the base has dried, which will take a day or two, you'll have to fill the gaps between the bricks or stones with mortar (which is concrete that doesn't have stones in it), much the way grout is placed between indoor tiles. You can add concrete-coloring dyes to the mortar mix to match or contrast with the color of your stones or bricks. This all takes a great deal more time than laying ordinary concrete, but the results are also a great deal more striking.

DEALING WITH DRIVEWAYS

A driveway may look like nothing more than a large sidewalk, but before you jump into the job, think twice. First of all, a long driveway is probably beyond the patience and stamina of most home improvers—particularly if you've got to dig into the ground to prepare it. Second, it requires a great deal more reinforcing to make it last.

But if you've got a short driveway to tackle or, like us, your land slopes just right so you can get away with minimal digging, here's how to do the job.

First of all, the concrete should be 5 inches thick, so use 2 × 6 boards for forms and bury them an inch. Trowel in expansion joints about every 10 to 12 feet. Use wooden expansion joints wherever the driveway meets another concrete slab, and also every 40 feet along a lengthy driveway.

There's one other reinforcement added to most driveways: steel mesh. At most building suppliers, you can buy rolls of 6 × 6-inch steel mesh. It resembles coarse wire fencing material. We urge you to purchase it. It provides a valuable reinforcement that keeps the concrete from cracking and crumbling under the weight of cars and the stresses of wintertime chilling and summertime sizzling.

After you've prepared your base and forms, lay this mesh down the entire length and width of your driveway. We like to hold it off the bottom by slipping small pieces of 2-inch-thick boards underneath the mesh at intervals of 3 to 4 feet. That way it's *in* and not *under* our poured concrete. An alternate method is to lay down the mesh during the concrete-pouring process, but that gets messier than many novices care to handle.

Where the driveway meets the street it's customary, first of all, to curve the driveway outwards so cars can maneuver more easily into its narrow width and, second, to create a tapered, raised curb along its sides. Contractors use special forms for this. You can create your own curved form if you'll follow this simple procedure:

1. Using a string and sharp stick as a compass, scratch a curve into the ground. Use a 5-foot-long string to get the standard size and shape.
2. Hammer stakes deeply into the ground every foot along the curve.
3. Dig out the ground as you would for a straight form.
4. Curve pre-cut lengths of 6-inch-wide ¼-inch plywood or Masonite along the stakes. You'll have to nail them to the stakes along the way.

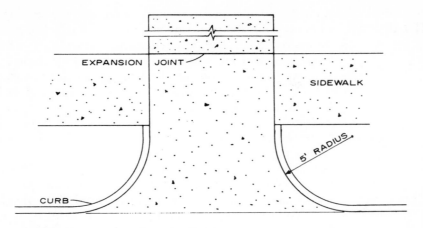

FIGURE 19-7 Here's the official driveway curve that's used on driveways from one coast to the other. But unless your local ordinance requires a curved driveway entrance, you can create any pattern of your own choosing. (Courtesy U.S. Forest Products Laboratory.)

5. After your first layer of plywood or Masonite is in place, go back and add a second and then a third layer, so your resulting form will be 3-ply. That should safely contain the weight of your concrete.
6. Then put reinforcing mesh and concrete into these curved forms as you would into a straight one.

Few local ordinances insist on curved driveway entrances. If you like, you can probably lay straight forms that slant outwards from your 8-foot or 9-foot-wide driveway, ending with an overall width of about 18 or 19 feet. They're a lot easier to construct and just as functional, and with a modern or rustic home they'll look decorative too.

A long driveway can consume an awful lot of concrete. If you're willing to labor more in return for spending less, you can lay one of the ribbon driveways that used to be popular a generation ago. Instead of a solid expanse of concrete 8 or 9 feet wide, this alternative consists of two ribbons of concrete, each 2 feet wide with a space of 3 feet between them. The ribbons are less conspicuous since there's a path of grass down the middle, and they require half as much concrete. But, of course, they'll require twice as many forms.

FIGURE 19-8 Here are the typical dimensions for a ribbon-style driveway. It requires a great deal less concrete, but a great deal more digging and form-making. (Courtesy U.S. Forest Products Laboratory.)

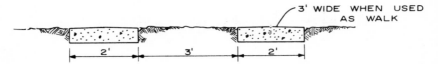

PREPARING PATIO BASES

A patio base, like any large slab of concrete, can be made more easily and with more durability if you include some wooden expansion joints within the overall slab. What's more, designing with the joints in mind will make a large, unwieldy job into one any homeowner can do a piece at a time.

After you've laid out the patio, dug out the soil, and placed your outer 2 × 4 forms into place, fasten some other 2 × 4s inside the forms. Let's assume, for the moment, that your patio measures out to some multiple of four. In that case, an ideal procedure is to make 4-foot squares or rectangles, sectioning them off with expansion joints. You can use redwood, cedar, cypress, or chemically treated pine for the outer forms, as well as for your expansion joints, and you won't need to remove the forms. You can section your patio into multiples of 3 or 5 or whatever makes most sense considering your overall dimensions.

You'll want to hammer support stakes along both sides of the expansion joints as well as along the form, but for this kind of project, hammer them down to at least an inch below the top of your 2 × 4s. That way, they'll eventually be covered by at least one inch of concrete. To keep the expansion joint boards from wiggling loose after a few years of expanding and contracting, drive several galvanized or aluminum nails through each length of board and out of the other side. That way the nails will end up in the concrete to anchor the boards permanently into place.

By making this network of small squares or rectangles, you won't have to pour your entire patio slab at once. You'll be able to work on it square by square.

For a truly fancy patio base, you can use bricks or flagstones over a base of concrete. The technique is the same as that described earlier for walkways.

FIGURE 19-9 For a big concrete patio, here's how you'd lay out the forms and the wooden expansion joints. Use redwood or other rot-resistant wood. The nails will embed in concrete, and these wooden border markers will become a permanent part of your patio.

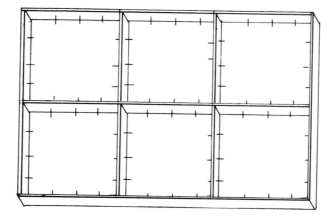

If you've ever tried to shore up rotting, sagging wooden outdoor steps, you'll appreciate the rugged endurance of concrete. The fastest and most surefire way to add concrete steps to your home is to invest in one of the prefabricated step slabs now marketed in most parts of the country. Most companies will deliver their product right to your door, but you might want to save some money by picking one up yourself at the factory. You see, they're hollow—only a few inches thick, at most. (If concrete is manufactured under ideal conditions, it's actually stronger when it's thinner!) One or two people can easily heft a 2- or 3-step slab.

If your steps are not going to be higher than about 2 feet, you can easily pour your own. Here are some of the design considerations you should plan for:

1. Make the landing at least 3 feet wide and 3 feet long.
2. Make each step about 8 inches high.
3. Make each step about 10 inches wide.
4. The steps must be uniform. All the widths *must* have the same dimensions. All the heights *must* have the same dimensions. Otherwise people are sure to trip going up and misstep going down.

FIGURE 19-10   Your forms will look like this when you're about ready to pour a set of concrete steps. Notice how well anchored the side supports are. The higher your step, the tougher these braces must be to withstand the weight of all that concrete.

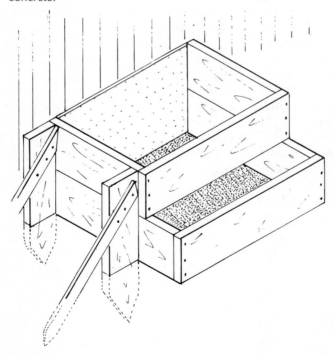

The ideal way to set up outdoor steps is on a footing of concrete that's poured to below the frostline. But since this necessitates digging down several feet in most areas of the country, few people bother with this step. You can take your choice: either dig and pour a footing, or end up several years hence with wobbly steps. (If you want a footing, your town's buildings department will tell you how far down you need it.)

Assuming that you're not beginning with a footing, prepare your ground as for other concrete work; that is, if your soil isn't sandy, set down a layer of sand. Then, using 2 × 8-inch boards, make the form for your bottom step, third step, and on up. Be sure that you cut the boards carefully so that the step forms fit neatly one atop the other. (Your lowest form, front-to-back, will extend the entire depth of your steps; your next form will extend that step's entire depth; and so on.)

Set the set of forms into place and fasten them together on the sides with scrap pieces of 2 × 8s. We like to sharpen one end of each support and hammer it deep into the ground before we nail the forms to it. Then, since concrete is very heavy, we reinforce the supports with additional boards pounded into the ground at an angle and then nailed to our vertical supports.

You'll need to put an expansion joint between your steps and your home or whatever you're adding the steps to. You can buy material that's made expressly for this purpose, or you can simply insert an appropriate-sized piece of Styrofoam insulation against the house and then pour the concrete in against *that*.

There's no need to fill your forms entirely with concrete. You can make up about half the overall volume of your steps with scraps of cement block, stone, brick, and similar materials. Keep the fill material away from the forms, though, so that you end up with at least 4 inches of solid concrete at all sides and at the top.

Before you pour your concrete, apply grease or oil to the insides of your forms so you'll have no trouble later on prying them loose from your finished job. Pour the entire set of steps at once so that you end up with a solid block and not several individual pieces. Be sure to wet down the steps as they cure, and don't pull away your forms for at least two days.

Happy landings!

20
Decks, Patios, Porches: Outdoor Assets

In elegant movies, people sit out on their decks and patios evening after evening, enjoying a cool drink while the meat sizzles on the grill. But those movies never show the insects or the fact that somebody's got to tend the grill and carry the drinks out to the loungers. Movies of the thirties and forties showed folks rocking on the old screened-in front porch, but people have moved to their rear yards for privacy and the deck has replaced the porch.

Though the deck has become as American an institution as apple pie and Mother, many of the ones we've seen have neither the utilitarian value of Mother nor the good taste of apple pie. The deck or patio that's plopped expectantly into the backyard this year is unused and unloved by next year unless it's considered as carefully as any other addition to a home. Before you build one you've got to plan its size, shape, uses, and color in the same way you'd plan new siding, a bedroom addition, or a garage. Your planning should start with serious consideration of the one aspect that's overlooked by too many builders: *use*. If either climate or your busy schedule keeps you from throwing a lawn chair or a blanket on

FIGURE 20-1   You can build modules to help you assemble a deck such as this in a weekend. Hardware and clever designing finish it off with railing, bench, and many other features.

the grass, a deck or patio probably won't get enough use to be worth the investment. If you don't barbecue out-of-doors now, a deck won't change your habits. But if your kids spend half the year playing out in the muddy yard, a deck may be the ideal solution. If the air is cool and the sun is hot, a patio may be for you. If you like to sit out front and watch the world go by, a porch may be just the pick-up you need.

While you're thinking about your particular outdoor needs, let's define our terms. A *deck* is a flat, floored, but roofless area adjoining a home. A *patio* is any kind of open-air area added onto the home's original design; it can be roofed and even screened in. Once you enclose a patio in glass or plastic, you have a porch or a solarium depending on its location. A *porch* is a covered entrance to a home, an integral part of the house's lines. It can be open-air or enclosed with screens, windows, or solid building materials.

BEGIN WITH A PLAN

As with other planning, begin with a list: start by listing the purposes to which your contemplated construction are to be put. Then estimate as closely as you can how much space you really need in order to handle those purposes, and what kind of space it ought to be: sunny or shady; open or screened or windowed; at the front, side, or back of your home; on street level or above it. Beauty should be a consideration, but utility should take precedence. And, we'll repeat, don't plan for a lifestyle that isn't one you've already adopted unless you're certain that the construction will make all the difference.

It helps to estimate your space needs if you actually arrange typical furnishings in some open spot so you can make real measurements for space requirements. (If you don't yet own the furnishings, find a friendly dealer who'll let you do some arranging in his store.) To give you an idea of what you can do with that space, our patio is 12 × 16 feet. On it we have two chaise longues and two other patio chairs, a table and four chairs for outdoor summer dining, a bookcase for the kids to store toys in since they play there on warm rainy days, plus a woodpile to feed our fireplace. It's cozy but it's never seemed crowded, and it serves every function we require of outdoor living space.

In addition to space needs, location is a prime consideration. Many homes have been built with outdoor additions in mind, even to the inclusion of patio doors. The most usual place is right outside the service door, but there's nothing to stop you from putting a deck at the front door or even from building an external access doorway from a dining room or a first-floor master bedroom. You can create a doorway easily out of a window. Starting from scratch is harder, but within do-it-yourself capabilities. (See Chapter 10 for guidance.)

When you've decided on space and location, select a preliminary style. Then it's important to make a sketch showing approximately how the finished addition will affect the overall appearance of your home. This is especially important for a covered or enclosed structure. It will have an impact on the apparent size, shape, and beauty of your house and yard.

In Chapter 1 we showed several ways to achieve three-dimensional sketches. If you have trouble drawing your home's exterior, take a snapshot of it and trace over that. Then sketch in the rough outlines of your proposed alteration. The five views of the same house shown in Figure 20-2 demonstrate how much difference your choice in design can make.

Do consider the impact of other projected additions and alterations when you're designing your outdoor living area. For example, if you know you're going to build a garage onto your two-story house, the best alternative may be to wait and put your solarium atop the garage as shown in the illustration. If you're hoping to put in a pool some day soon, its best placement may help determine where you put your deck.

If you're going to need a walkway from front to side, you could lay down a combination deck-walkway like the one in the illustration. There's a lovely elevated wraparound deck-walkway that lends character to a home near ours. If you're subject to just an occasional buggy evening, you might want a minimal-sized screened-in patio. If you give that a wide overhang, the small structure can also shade part of your deck. On the other hand, a big old shade tree is one of the nicest protections from the sun. In the first of our sketches, that's the only enclosure called for. Sun, shade, rain, wind, and insect protection should be among your considerations.

We don't show views here of decks that are artificially elevated, even though they were a vogue of the 1970s. You can elevate yours if you like; it's not a tough construction job. But it is a design problem. The elevated

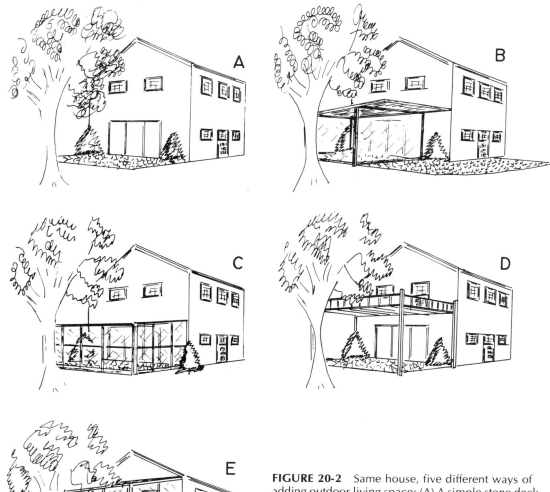

FIGURE 20-2 Same house, five different ways of adding outdoor living space: (A) A simple stone deck outside the patio door. (If no patio door exists, one can be converted from windows; see Chapter 10.) (B) You can extend the deck as sidewalk to the front (or elsewhere). Here, the patio door opens into a small screened-in area. A sun screen substantially overhangs the area, shading inside or outside the screens. Notice how the structure blends in between tree and house. (C) A totally screened-in porch that's low and uses so few visible supports, it's quite inconspicuous. (D) A double-decker, so to speak, in which the 4 x 4s support a deck for the second-story bedroom and the enclosure shades the deck off the first-floor living room. One or the other could be screened in too. (E) If you're adding a garage (or have one now), here's how it can fit into your scheme for outdoor living space.

design looks artificial, blocks your indoor view of the rest of the landscape, uses a lot of expensive lumber, and generally gets less use than decks that splice neatly onto the rest of a family's living area. If you have to climb a ladder or a clumsy stairway to the deck, and then climb down again every time you want a cool drink, you'll begin to think twice about making the climb in the first place. Unless you are particularly in love with the idea of living in a treehouse, avoid erecting an elevated deck even if you win one in a contest.

We suggest that you make deck-designing a wintertime project so that you have plenty of time to put away your preliminary sketches and take them out again for a critical look. By the time spring rolls around, you'll have the best possible design for the money. Order your supplies early, so you can do your building before it gets too hot.

FIGURE 20-3 Turn your entranceway into a deck, as shown here, and you create a luxurious impact. You could extend the roofline to cover this deck.

**CHOOSING
AMONG
FLOORINGS**

Since whatever you build has to have a floor, whether it's a deck, a patio, or a porch, let's examine the choices.

We'll begin with wood, since it's the material used for the majority of decks that are built nowadays. That's probably because lumber yards and lumber manufacturers have done a lot of showing and telling about how to build wooden decks. If you use standard old-fashioned 2 × 4 boards, wood is the least expensive material for erecting most decks. Unfortunately, so many of the instructions we've seen are so needlessly complicated, they preclude your being able to use 2 × 4s. Once you start using 2 × 6s and larger timbers, the cost starts to climb geometrically.

Wood is often chosen for a deck or patio because it has a blend-into-the-trees look. But keeping that natural look in wood that's exposed to the weather requires some planning. If you pick genuine redwood, cypress, or cedar you can get away with a simple finish that protects the wood. Because Mother Nature built in chemical preservatives when she designed those trees, you need only apply three or four coats of varnish that'll preserve the original color. Spar varnish is okay, but we've found that exterior grade polyurethane varnish is best. (In fact, we tested several brands and found that ZAR Imperial is by far our preferred choice.)

Ordinary pine or fir that is to be exposed to the weather requires a chemical treatment to preserve it. Unpreserved it can turn grey and begin decomposing after a year or two in the sun and the rain. You can buy lumber pretreated with preservatives, or you can buy ordinary lumber and treat it yourself with any brand of *penta* wood preservative. (When you work with *penta*, it's important to protect your hands by wearing rubber gloves.) After that, you can either varnish the wood, or treat it with a semi-clear or opaque stain, or paint it. If you're really in love with that redwood look but can't afford the price of genuine redwood, be sure to test out your redwood stain on a sizeable board before applying it to the entire finished deck. Some of the stains do look like redwood; the rest look like hell.

If you want to paint your deck, flip back to our chapter on paint for information on deck enamels and similar finishes.

Brick makes a lovely and durable deck. It costs a good deal more than wood, of course, and may take more time to install, but when it's in there's no maintenance. For a stately old home—especially a brick-faced one—it's an elegant choice. Figure 20-4 shows the range of designs you can build into your deck with bricks.

FIGURE 20-4 Brick makes an attractive deck material—and a durable one. Use your imagination (for instance, leave gaps for trees and planters) and turn ordinary building material into something exotic.

FIGURE 20-5 Here are a few patterns to consider when figuring out how to make your brick patio or walkway.

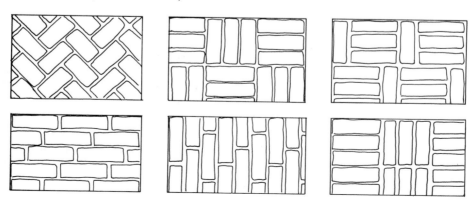

Stone and flagstone make attractive, durable, maintenance-free—and expensive—decking material. But again, if your home's exterior is best complemented by one of these materials, it may be worth the expense. You can economize by making "flagstones" out of concrete. Kits are available by mail order and at many home improvement centers.

You can make your deck entirely out of poured concrete, too. Covered with outdoor carpeting, it loses its institutional look. Outdoor carpeting is almost maintenance-free and now comes in attractive tones of grass-green and earth-brown (as well as bright red, brilliant blue, and other such non-outdoor colors). However, we suggest that unless you lay it inside a covered and enclosed patio, you roll it up and store it away for northern winters.

But here's an alternative: If, realistically, you expect to use your deck only a few times each summer, and own a large driveway that has a bit of privacy, why not buy an outdoor carpet to spread over the driveway whenever you're hosting a cookout? Keep the barbecue pit off the carpet, because hot coals will make holes. And when the cookout's over, shake it out and store it again.

BUILDING THE DECK

For a brick, stone, or concrete deck, consult the previous chapter. If you're making your deck out of wood, read on.

Whether wood or brick, if you're able to lay your entire deck right on the ground (or close to it) then your support problems are minimal. The ground will hold up your deck. If there's a few inches' difference in ground level at the front and back of your wooden deck, or its sides, simply slip wooden or concrete blocks under the lower end to bring the deck to a level position. Keep in mind that any wood that touches the ground, whether supports or the deck itself, must be carefully treated with *penta* wood preservative if it's untreated pine or fir.

In simple layouts, it isn't necessary to fasten your deck directly to your house—although if you're planning to build an enclosure or cover, attaching one end via its horizontal support will lend greater stability. (Incidentally, in a few localities the tax assessment on unattached decks is lower than for attached ones. That's something to check out before building.) In most decks, the 2 × 6 (or other size) support does attach directly to your house. (See Figure 20-7A.)

If your ground slopes precipitously, or if you're building an elevated deck despite our warnings, you'll need a more formal method of construction for your supports. The 4 × 4-inch post has become the standard deck support. Just keep them no longer than 8 feet high and each one will be able to support 6 tons—which is many times more weight than you're ever likely to put on them. And make sure they're well treated with wood preservative.

Figure 20-6 shows how to mount your 4 × 4s into the ground. Be sure that about one-third of each post is sunk into the ground, except that a maximum depth of 3 feet is needed to stabilize any pole of reasonable length. Dig your holes three times the diameter of your posts. For 4 × 4s,

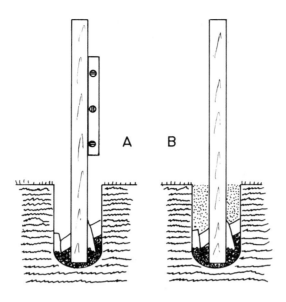

FIGURE 20-6 To set posts, generally 4 x 4s, into the ground to provide support for one or both ends of your deck, dig a hole three times wider than each post and equal in length to one-third of its length—up to 3 feet. Toss in heavy stones or blocks to anchor the post into perfectly vertical position, then fill the hole with concrete.

that'd be a foot wide. Fill the bottom with small gravel or stones, then wedge the post against some heavy stones or bricks to hold it in place while you make sure that it's absolutely perpendicular. Then fill the remainder of your hole with cement. (You need so little cement for the entire job, pre-mixed cement is probably more economical.)

To fasten two pieces of 2 × 6 board to your support posts, follow the nearby illustration. Nail them lightly into place at first, and then make sure that they're absolutely level. You may not have the tops of your post supports exactly at the same height, but you can compensate by placement of your 2 × 6s. (See Figure 20-7B.) Also make sure that the surface of your deck is level from front to rear; you do that by placing an unwarped test board from the support board that you've attached to your house to the two 2 × 6s. Rest a level on the test board that's resting on all three supports, and adjust either the board that's fastened to the house or the other two boards. Finally, be sure that the edges of your deck will be square.

After you're sure that the supports are all as level as you can get them, put your permanent fasteners into place. Use ½-inch by 6-inch lag screws to hold the one support against your house; space them about every two feet. Put two bolts through each joint where post meets 2 × 6 beams; use ½-inch by 8-inch carriage bolts with a washer under each nut.

Here are some weight considerations to keep in mind. In the sample

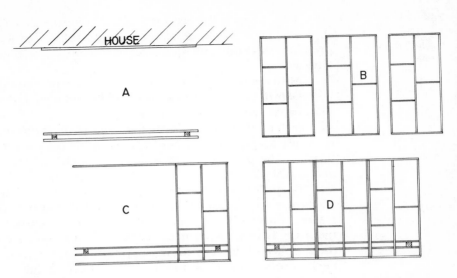

FIGURE 20-7   Pictured here are the steps for building a deck of almost any size from modules. You can use 2 x 4s for most decks; these modules slip easily onto the supports, fasten there, and form a tough base for any outdoor living space. The text explains how to build and work with them.

12-foot-long deck we're erecting in this chapter, we recommended 2 × 6 boards for support beams (such as in Figure 20-7A). The two 12-foot-long beams attached to the two 4 × 4 posts support a total of 1,200 pounds. Since they carry only half the total weight (the other half being on the support that's against the house), this particular deck can safely hold 2,400 pounds. About 700 pounds of that goes to hold up the wood in the deck itself, leaving 1,700 for furnishings, you, and friends. This means that your deck overall can support 17.7 pounds per square foot, which meets most building codes.

If your local code demands more, or if your deck is longer than 12 feet, use 2 × 8s for support beams. A pair of 18-foot-long 2 × 8s can support 1,400 pounds safely. However, for both support and stability, do not space your 4 × 4 supports further apart than every 10 feet. Therefore, very large decks may require three posts per set of 2 × 6 or 2 × 8 beams. And for very wide decks, you may need to erect two complete sets of posts and beams. When in doubt, either get guidance from local building authorities or overbuild.

For deck flooring, we prefer to build the whole thing out of the good old-fashioned 2 × 4, which is about the cheapest building material available. We construct the deck surface in a modular fashion, as shown in Figure 20-7B. Each approximately 2-foot-by-8-foot module weights 220 pounds when completed, which is not too much for handy people to ease into position on the supports. If the width of your deck is not an even number, you'll probably want to make one of the modules only 1 foot wide (unless you can comfortably slide a 330-pound 3-foot-wide piece into place).

The cheapest 2 × 4s come in *stud* length, which is just a few inches shy of being 8 feet long. If you buy the full 8-foot length you'll pay a premium price and end up having to trim off a few inches here and there anyway.

Most people prefer to leave about ¼ inch between the 2 × 4 covering boards. It has a rustic appearance and provides good drainage. If you do that, you'll need 13 2×4s to cover each 2-foot by 8-foot module. As you slide each module into position, toe-nail it to the 2 × 6 beams. Toe-nailing is simply a carpenter's term for driving nails in at an angle. Also nail together the parts of the modules that touch each other, driving a nail about every 2 feet.

People often assess the elegance of structures such as decks by how wide the edges appear. If you want to add elegance onto this economical system, simply nail wide boards along all the outside edges. You can even nail a 1 × 12 or a 2 × 12 on each edge so that about 2 inches extend below the 2 × 4s and the remaining—approximately 5 inches—rises above the deck to serve as part of a fence or enclosure railing.

Using the method described here, you should be able to buy your lumber and erect the entire support and deck structure comfortably in a weekend. You should even have time left Sunday evening to sit on the deck and enjoy it.

Everybody's brother-in-law has a squared-off deck. How would you like one that's a different shape? We've designed a system that utilizes equilateral triangles. Again, the trusty old 2 × 4 is the workhorse. In Figure 20-9 we show how to cut the 2 × 4s for the three-sided base of each 4 × 4 × 4 module and then how to lay out only three 8-foot pieces of 2 × 4 (pieces A, B, and C) for the covering. (If you're willing to put a bit more than ¼ inch space between each, you can use studs instead of 8-footers. Otherwise you need the full 8 feet of length.

First nail boards A, B, and C onto the long end of the triangle, again allowing about ¼ inch of space between them. Saw off the edges and then nail down the second set of three boards. Continue this procedure until each module is completely covered.

FIGURE 20-8 If you're tired of the same old deck construction, here's one based on triangles that can be built in modular fashion.

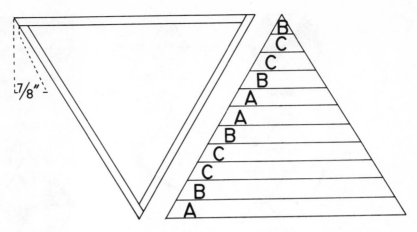

FIGURE 20-9 To create each 4-foot triangle module, you'll need 1½ lengths of 2 x 4 for the frame; cut each end according to the diagram here for the proper angle. Three lengths of 8-foot (or stud length) 2 x 4s are sufficient for covering each triangle. Lay the three 2 x 4s (*A, B,* and *C*) into the appropriate place at the widest part of the triangle, nail, saw them off, then lay them down at the next position and repeat.

You can slide completed modules onto the same framework we described earlier for rectangularly shaped decks. However, you probably will want to make a few modifications.

First, since the three-sided bases all serve as support elements, you should bolt touching pieces together with ½-inch × 4-inch carriage bolts. Use three of them for each 4-foot length. You'll have an easier time during construction if you slide each module into place and have someone hold it while you nail it to supports and adjoining modules. Then drill holes and install the bolts.

Second, unless you want parts of the 2 × 6 beams showing—which is a perfectly acceptable design feature—make the length of your supports match the squared-off portions of your triangular-based decks. Looking at Figure 20-10A, for example, your support beams need be only 4 feet long. That permits a 2-foot overhang on each side, but that 2 feet will be perfectly solid as long as the rest of your deck sits solidly. (We don't advise cantilevering more than 2 feet in any one spot.) Taking Figure 20-10B as another example, this is a deck that's 12 feet long at its center. The beams would be 8 feet long, again permitting 2 feet to cantilever at each end.

For a really large deck built from our three-sided modules, such as Figure 20-10D, you'll need two sets of posts with beams. One set is 16 feet long and runs along the midpoint; the other is 8 feet long and runs along the outside edge. To keep such a large deck from looking chopped-up, bolt together three triangles to form a trapezoid and then use 8-foot-long 2 × 4s to cover it. Since the trapezoid weighs about 575 pounds when finished, you should put the framework almost into its final resting place and *then* cover it with 2 × 4s. You can shove 575 pounds a foot or two for its

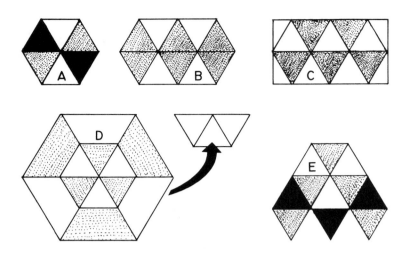

FIGURE 20-10 Here are five formats for unique decks, all based on the equilateral triangles shown earlier. The squared-off portions of (C) are half-modules. The larger trapezoid areas in (D) can be built two different ways, either out of triangle modules or out of frames for three modules fastened together and then covered with long 2 x 4s (8-footers) sawed off to form a trapezoid.

final fit. (If you're a real lightweight, use grease or vaseline on the wood parts that'll rub against other wood.)

These drawings are just a beginning. Let your imagination create a geometric phantasmagoria for your own yard.

FIGURE 20-11 If cantilevering scares you, here's another way to support the outer edges of your various triangular decks. (Courtesy Kant-Sag division of United Steel Products.)

To construct the framework for a roof over your deck, you need simply put up some corner posts and support beams and then construct the same modules you built for your deck (as shown in Figure 20-7). Only don't cover the modules with 2 × 4s. Instead, secure them to your beams and cover them with your roofing material.

If you've planned in advance to erect a roof over your deck, you could simply have used 4 × 4s long enough to reach the 7 or 8 feet of headroom you will need. The 4 × 4s are strong enough to support not only the weight of your deck and your guests, but the roof and snow as well. If you're adding a roof to an old deck, cut away the boards that cover your posts, set extra posts atop the original ones, and secure the new to the old with steel construction plates nailed to join the posts on all four sides. (You'll find them at your building supplier.)

If your existing deck is not supported on 4 × 4s, then you can erect some right alongside the outside edges of your deck. They should be sunk into the ground and cemented as described in the previous section. If you use extra-long 2 × 6 beams sticking out atop your posts, you'll heighten the impact of the exposed posts and beams and give your covered deck the appearance of a pagoda.

To turn your deck into a covered patio, there are several options in design and material. First of all, you can construct an actual shingled roof of whatever shape suits your fancy. Secondly, you can purchase a rigid or roll-up awning that attaches to your house. One economical choice is translucent fiberglass paneling that comes in white as well as a rainbow of colors such as amber, green, brown, yellow, and even stripes. It keeps out the direct sun as well as the rain. Properly supported, it withstands even our testy Wisconsin snow load. The clearest panels admit about 94 percent of the sun's light while the deepest colored ones cut out all but about 20 percent. Before you opt for one of the denser roof panels, we strongly recommend that you take one or two home on trial to see if you really want to block out that much light.

The fiberglass panels we've examined come with reasonably com-

FIGURE 20-12 Profiles of the two major kinds of translucent patio-covering materials. They come in sundry colors and transmit varying amounts of light. Your best bet is to buy one sheet first, test it for a few days in the spot where you plan to install it, and then decide on the type to use for your entire patio cover.

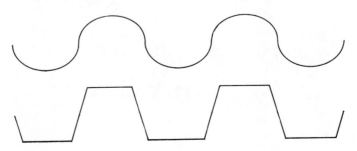

prehensive installation instructions, in lengths that vary from 8 feet up to about 12 feet. In general, you simply lay them over a ceiling support network whose major supports have been spaced 2 feet apart. Then nail them into place with aluminum or coated nails. The best nails incorporate rubber gaskets that seal out the elements. The panels themselves come either corrugated or ribbed (see Figure 20-12). The ribbed kind can be nailed directly onto your supports, but the corrugated panels require redwood crosspieces whose curves match the product's curves. These strips, stocked by most lumber dealers, are inexpensive and easy to install.

For a semi-covered deck that's open and airy, yet blocks the direct rays of the sun, you can build wooden shutters as a roof. Nearby we show one such deck covering. If the shutter boards run almost east to west, the sun will almost never shine directly down through the spaces between the boards. Run them north to south and you've got a lovely decoration but no shutter effect.

The angularity of the sun varies so much from northern states to southern ones that it's impossible to supply you with rules for spacing your patio shutters. Start by spacing them out at twice the width of your boards, making 2 × 4 shutters 8 inches apart and 2 × 8s 16 inches apart. Then test a bit to find out what's the ideal spacing for your location. (The test will be most efficient if you do it in June, when the sun is highest in the sky.) Simply set the boards in place, unnailed, and watch for a whole sunny day to see how well they regulate the shade on your deck. Nail them into place once you're convinced you've got the best positioning. The blind nailing shown nearby is useful for this job; if you have to remove nails to fine-tune your shutters at some later date, only your closest friends will be able to detect the old nailholes.

FIGURE 20-13 Shutters help screen out as much of the sun as you care to screen out. Besides, the wood keeps the entire patio cover rustic and natural-looking. But the open slats do not stop the rain or snow.

If your deck is raised off the ground, you must put a railing on it to keep friends and family from toppling off. Do keep the design and material of your railing in keeping with your deck and your home's exterior design. Our first illustration in this chapter showed a deck with a railing. Figure 20-15 shows how you can build one just like it. Lumberyards stock metal brackets especially designed for adding simple railings to decks. Figure 20-16 shows one of those in use. Traditionally, handrails are from 2 feet 8 inches to 3 feet above the floor, but if you have small children add an additional board about halfway between the floor and the top of your handrail.

Many of the sketches of finished decks in this chapter show furniture and other finishing touches. They suggest homemade benches and planters that should be a snap for you to adapt to match your own decor and

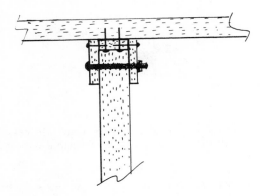

FIGURE 20-14   Here's how you can nail the wooden slats of a sun screen (as seen in Figure 20-13) so the nails are concealed by the supports. That way, you won't hesitate to change the spacing later on if you decide that you want the screen to admit more sunlight or less. (An alternate way of building wooden sun screens is to use the hardware shown at the top of Figure 20-17.)

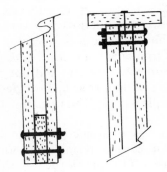

FIGURE 20-15   A railing for your deck is as simple to construct as this. (To see such a railing attached to a deck, refer back to Figure 20-1.) The left-hand apparatus attaches your railing's uprights to the bottom of the deck; the right-hand view shows how to attach the handrail to the uprights.

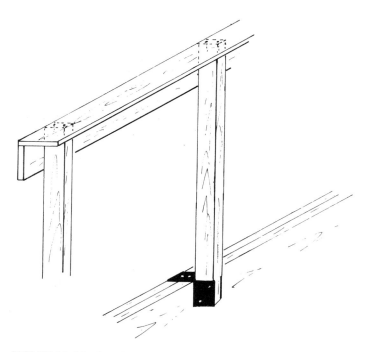

FIGURE 20-16 Here's another handrail system suitable for decks. Brackets like the one shown here (in black) are available at most do-it-yourself centers.

space requirements. To get you started, we've sketched a bench and planter that'll look good on modern wood decks. Each is made with trusty, inexpensive 2 × 4s. Home decoration and do-it-yourself magazines, too, are perpetually filled with novel projects to outfit outdoor living areas: carts, lounges, tables, bars, stools, and more.

FOILING THE INSECTS AND THE ELEMENTS

After you've built that deck and covered it with a patio roof, it's inexpensive and easy to keep out pesky insects by adding screens. Since all the weight of your roof and deck floor is already supported by posts, you can simply nail several vertical 2 × 4s at whatever intervals you like and then staple screening material between all but two of the verticals. There, insert a screen door. Cover up the stapled edges with thin decorative wood strips, finish the new wood to match your deck, and you're done.

Before screening in our patio, we checked out several kinds. We found that, aside from being budget-priced, fiberglass is also the least noticeable. Several times people have walked up to touch a screen to make sure it was really there.

In wintertime we staple clear plastic over our screened-in patio, using cardboard tabs between plastic and staples. (With just a dime-store staple remover, it's easy to take off the plastic the following spring.) We're on our fourth year of using the same plastic and it looks like it's good for another three or four. We could have devised a more sophisticated system

FIGURE 20-17   Here's a potpourri of nifty brackets and supports that'll make easy (and strong) work of building decks, covers for decks, planters or benches for decks, and whatever else you can imagine building. At the display or bin where you find these brackets, look for the company's latest tip-sheets on do-it-yourself projects their designers have concocted. (Courtesy Kant-Sag division of United Steel Products.)

FIGURE 20-18   If you want all-wood planters for your deck, here's one way to construct them out of 2 x 4s. The horizontal cross-pieces overlap; then you nail (or screw) them to the sides that touch them. (An alternate planter plan is seen near the bottom of Figure 20-17.)

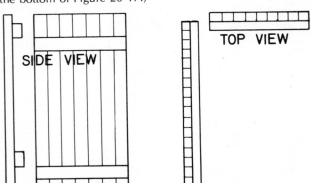

SIDE VIEW

TOP VIEW

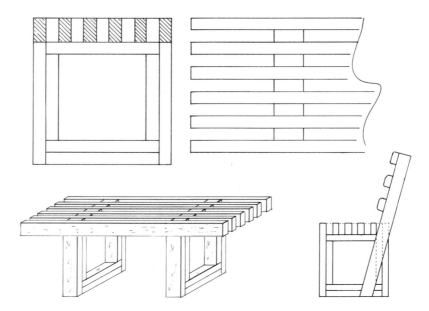

FIGURE 20-19 The bench on the deck in this chapter's first illustration is easy to build yourself from a small stack of 2 x 4s. The bench shown here is about 4 feet long, but this design will hold up for lengths to 8 feet. If you nail only at the sides, virtually every nail in this bench will be concealed. For even greater weather endurance, use lag screws on the outer edges. You can design a back for the bench too, for your less athletic friends. Be sure not to place the bottom crosspiece of the back rest any farther back than shown here. That's where most of the weight is concentrated, and you must keep the weight over the legs or the bench will become tipsy.

for keeping icy winds away from our big glass patio door, but since this one works so well and costs so little, we guess we'll stick to it until the plastic finally gives out.

For a more orthodox method, you can invest in large sheets of rigid clear plastic. Mount them in the aluminum frames designed for do-it-yourself storm window projects and available at large hardware stores and building suppliers. Secure the aluminum frames to your patio's vertical supports with storm window hardware. The initial investment is quite a bit higher than our makeshift arrangement, but the materials should last for the rest of your patio's lifetime.

IV
BUILDING MORE SPACE

21
Add a Dormer
and Raise the Old Roof

Two major problems stop people from living in their attics: too little light and too little headroom. By adding a dormer—a neat bulge in your roof—you can create enough light and headroom for a cozy bedroom or a den. Or how about a second bath? For a few hundred dollars worth of building materials, and your own labor, you can convert a dark, back-bending attic into a comfortable living space.

GABLES, SHEDS, AND OTHER DORMERS

A gabled dormer is peaked like most roofs, but the dormer's peak is set at a right angle to the peak of the existing roof. Gabled dormers work well on either low- or high-pitched roofs.

Some gabled dormers are large enough for the peak of the dormer and the peak of the existing roof to meet. In that case, the front wall of the dormer generally rests on the existing first-floor wall. Peak-to-peak, wall-to-wall dormers are very straightforward to erect. However, such a dormer can be quite large, so you may want to move the dormer peak lower on the roof.

FIGURE 21-1 Inside and outside view of a dormer. Notice how the dormer lends character to the house's roof line by picking up the same type of overhang. In the interior view, see how much roominess and natural light the dormer adds to this otherwise hard-to-use attic.

The shed dormer is probably the simplest of the several basic dormer styles. It looks as if somebody sawed off a piece of the existing roof, raised it, and propped it up with new pieces of wall. Generally there's a window in the new front wall.

The slope of a shed dormer's roof has to be gentler than that of an existing roof. So a low-pitched house roof will make for a flat or nearly flat dormer roof—and that presents problems in shingling it well enough to keep out rain or melting snow.

If your roof slopes at least eight inches vertically for every foot that it runs horizontally (an eight-pitch roof), you can build a shed dormer with a pitch of four. That's adequate for ordinary shingling. You can even get by with a shed dormer pitched at three or two if you double up on shingles or rolled roofing.

A new dormer design has appeared recently: the skylight dormer. Unlike traditional dormer designs, this one rises *above* the peak of your existing roof so the dormer can capture natural light from two directions. The pitch of this dormer's roof is often the same as the pitch of the existing roof, so the two roof lines are parallel.

PLANNING CONSIDER-ATIONS

The number of dormers you choose to add, their locations, and their size should be carefully considered and based on your home's architecture. After all, you'll use the space inside the dormer, but you'll see it from the outside. Your home's architectural style will also probably largely determine which type of dormer you choose.

Even if your attic originally was left unfinished, the joists and other supports had to be designed to sustain a fairly substantial load—30 or 40

SHED DORMER

GABLE DORMER

FIGURE 21-2 Shown are the two classic kinds of dormers: gable dormer on the front of the house, and shed dormer on the rear. A skylight dormer is essentially a shed dormer, except that the roof slopes in the opposite direction from the dormer shown here, and the structure touches the roof's peak. (Courtesy U.S. Forest Products Laboratory.)

pounds per square foot, according to most building codes. So if you turn the attic into a living space, you should not be overloading the house's support system.

Whenever possible, try to place the dormer's front wall over a first-floor outside wall. That provides maximum strength and simple construction. Alternatively, you can place the dormer's front wall over a ground-floor inside wall. If you opt for another arrangement, it's best to take the measurements of your house and attic, including the size and spacing of rafters and floor joists, to your local building department. They should be equipped to offer an opinion on how well your attic floor and downstairs walls can support the extra weight.

Unless you have professional design assistance, it's safest not to make your dormer wider than the distance between six rafters. Put another way, your dormer should not require you to remove more than four rafters from the roof. The space between most rafters is 16 inches, so your dormer can be as wide as 96 inches.

Roofs are designed to hold a lot of snow in most parts of the country. At the very least, they're designed to support safely two burly carpenters. So you can easily remove a rafter or two during dormer construction without fear of the roof collapsing. Because you double up the two rafters bordering the outside walls of your dormer (see drawings nearby), the net loss of rafters during dormer construction will be only one.

Before designing the interior of your dormer, determine how well-supported an attic floor you have. First find out how big the floor joists are in your attic. They'll be anywhere from 2 × 6s to 2 × 12s. Then measure how far those joists have to span your first story walls. For a lived-in upper story, which is what your dormer will give you, the maximum unsupported span for 2 × 6s should be 10 feet, for 2 × 8s, 18 feet; 2 × 10s, 28 feet; and 2 × 12s, 40 feet.

Try to locate your dormer so the live-in area will not span more than 10 feet (in the case of 2 × 6 joists). If you can't, then you must add a beam equal in strength to an interior wall. You may be surprised how much nicer a real wood beam looks than those plastic imitations!

DESIGNING A DORMERED INTERIOR

Ceilings used to be from 8 to 12 feet high in most homes. Newer houses often have ceilings closer to the 7-foot mark. Many people feel comfortable in a well-designed attic-plus-dormer if approximately half of the floor space has headroom of 6′8″ or more. Many local building codes, in fact, specify those figures, but we've found that inspectors tend to be quite lenient about attic living areas in one-family dwellings. Notice that we've said *half* of the area has the 6′8″ ceilings. The other half is under the more severely sloped roof area.

Usually attic rooms are cut off by knee walls well short of the point where the headroom slopes down to nothing. These are typically 4 to 5 feet high. True, most adults can't stand alongside a knee wall, but you can put chests and beds and chairs there. Or you could build in storage drawers.

It's a good idea to make your final decisions about finishing your new space after the dormer's walls and roof are in place. There are so many angles and shapes to deal with, it's difficult to sketch efficient use of the space on paper. You might even dummy up a finished room by stapling butcher paper in the places you think you'd like your knee walls to go before cutting any studs for the walls.

In plotting space for an attic-become-room, forget your old notions about how space in a straight-sided room gets parceled out. For instance, a clothes closet does not have to have the standard 80-inch-high door. A 60-inch door is perfectly adequate. The clothes bar can hang at the 54-inch mark, and the back wall of the closet can be whatever height happens to lie about two feet behind the closet door.

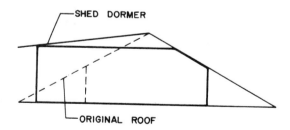

FIGURE 21-3 You can gain space by adding a large shed dormer. For a skylight dormer, about the same arrangement applies. (Courtesy U.S. Forest Products Laboratory.)

BUYING YOUR BUILDING MATERIALS

For dormer walls, use common 2 × 4s (or 2 × 6s for additional insulation space) in whatever lengths fit most economically into your plans. Rafters should be 2 × 6s up to 2 × 12s. Usually 2 × 6s are adequate, but duplicate the size in your existing roof unless you get professional advice to the contrary. The same advice applies to the ridge board.

Space rafters and studs 16 inches apart. Put two studs at the outside corners of your dormer walls for extra support and bracing there. Also put doubled 2 × 4s on the sides and top of a window that's big enough to make you skip one or two studs.

In a skylight dormer, if you have to skip a rafter in order to fit in an extra window or skylight, double up the adjacent rafters. Never do the final framing for a window until you have the unit in hand. That way you can measure the material to fit more precisely.

The skin for your roof and walls will probably be ½-inch "CD" grade plywood, commonly called *sheathing.* Nail the plywood securely to your rafters and studs with 8d common nails. Use 16d nails on all of the structural components such as rafters and studs. And don't forget to insulate the roof and walls of your dormer.

That new floor in your old attic is not just something to walk on. It actually plays a role in strengthening the dormer and the rest of your house. Inexpensive but weak materials such as hardboard and chipboard won't do unless your attic's floor joists are substantially larger than the code requires. The best floor is ¾-inch tongue-and-groove underlayment grade plywood. Ideally, you should glue as well as nail it to the joists. If you plan to install tongue-and-groove finish flooring, you can use cheaper underlayment, however.

A SCHEDULE FOR WORKING HIGH—AND DRY

Schedule your job well in advance, with several alternate dates picked out. Listen carefully to weather reports, and try to choose a time when several sunny days in a row are forecast. You'll have to open part of your existing roof in order to put in the dormer. You might want to pick out a long weekend and start early on the first day to ensure that the job will be enclosed by the time Monday rolls around. Have plenty of plastic tarps and a staple gun standing by so you can build a makeshift tent in case of bad weather.

FIGURE 21-4   How to frame a typical gable dormer.
(Courtesy U.S. Forest Products Laboratory.)

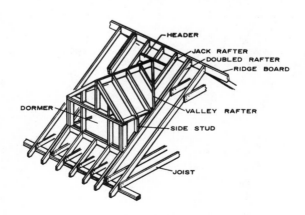

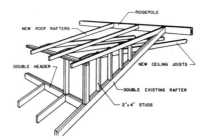

FIGURE 21-5 How to frame a shed dormer. (Courtesy U.S. Forest Products Laboratory.)

The following work schedule should help you get the job done in the least amount of time.

ON ALL
DORMERS:
PRELIMINARIES

1. Determine dormer location from inside attic, based on joist spacing. Drill four holes up through corners of layout; insert four nails.
2. Atop roof, lay out dormer from four protruding nails. Rip away existing shingles 2 inches beyond layout.
3. Saw away existing roof sheathing 1 inch beyond dormer marks.
4. Double up boundary rafters. Nail doubling rafters to ridge boards, joists, and existing rafters.

ON GABLED
DORMERS:
FRAMING

1. Using carefully leveled 2 × 4, measure the precise size of dormer's side walls and angle of dormer rafters.
2. Build dormer's side walls and nail into place atop doubled rafters. Be sure walls are level vertically and horizontally.

FIGURE 21-6 How to install plywood sheathing to the roof of your dormer. (Courtesy U.S. Forest Products Laboratory.)

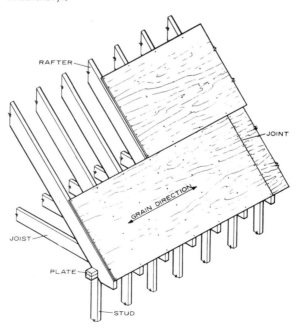

300

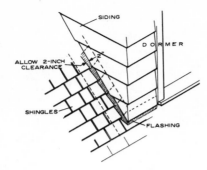

FIGURE 21-7 Don't overlook flashing where the dormer sides join the existing roof, or you may get leaks around the joints. (Courtesy U.S. Forest Products Laboratory.)

3. Install jack (or hip) rafters and dormer ridge.
4. Cut and install dormer rafters.
5. Cut and nail plates and studs for wall.
6. Frame window(s).

ON SHED DORMERS: FRAMING

1. Build front wall. Level horizontally and vertically, then nail into place using temporary supports.
2. Cut dormer rafters and nail to roof's ridge board or dormer's header. Also nail in front wall of dormer.
3. Make final measurements for side walls. Cut and nail studs and plates.

ON SKYLIGHT DORMERS: FRAMING

1. Cut studs for dormer's top wall and nail to ridge board as well as rafters.
2. Cut and nail two side walls after leveling them vertically. Nail them to rafters.
3. Make final measurements for lower dormer wall. Cut studs and plates. Nail to floor and corner studs of side wall.
4. Measure, cut, and nail dormer rafters.

ON ALL DORMERS: ENCLOSING

1. Nail plywood to roof and walls every 6 inches.
2. Where angular part of dormer touches existing roof, overlap boards by 1 inch.
3. Apply roofing felt over plywood, using staple gun.
4. Apply plastic roofing cement liberally to valley where old roof meets new.
5. Nail a 14-inch-wide aluminum valley over strip where old roof meets new. Liberally cover edges and nail heads with plastic roofing cement.
6. On roofs with pitch of four or more, nail shingles according to manufacturer's instructions. For roofs with lower pitch, nail roll roofing over roof before shingling. Overlap roll roofing by 50 percent—so you end up with double layer of roll roofing everywhere. Then shingle.
7. Apply siding of choice.

We listened to weather forecasts for weeks before we opened our roof, and we chose what we thought was the ideal time. We just about had the old roof ripped off when a sudden air shift brought three days of squalls directly over our heads. Weather forecasting is still far from an exact science, so once you begin your job be prepared for anything.

Good luck.

22
How to Finish an Attic

If you've got an attic full of old clothes, old books, old pictures, and old dust, you can turn it easily into one or two new rooms and still hold onto plenty of storage space. In fact, earlier chapters have already revealed almost all of the construction and decoration techniques you'll need.

The previous chapter showed how to add a dormer to increase the airiness and roominess of your attic. Before that, we showed construction and design details for finishing walls, finishing floors, finishing ceilings, installing wiring, installing plumbing, working with windows and doors, and tackling insulation. So now we can concentrate on just the special design problems you'll encounter because these are attic rooms.

SHORTCUTS TO IDENTIFYING YOUR USABLE SPACE

If you have a very steep roof (to find out, check with Chapter 18), you may be able to utilize *most* of your attic for living space with a minimum of structural modification. With lower-sloped roofs, you'll need a dormer or two to make the best use of your area. If your house is two stories plus the attic, you'd better stop right now and check with local building code authorities. Most of them have very strict regulations regarding three-

FIGURE 22-1 If your old attic looks like the one on the left, but you'd like to make more efficient, more aesthetic use of the space, you can convert it easily and economically to something that looks more like the one on the right. (Courtesy Velux-America Inc.)

story homes, and that's what you'll have once you finish your attic. Some ordinances completely forbid them. Others require an outside fire escape. These regulations have been made to protect the safety of the people who will sleep, work, or play in those attic rooms, so please don't try to circumvent the code.

Your next consideration should be headroom. Not many years ago, national building codes required 7 feet 6 inches of headroom above at least half the floor space in any lived-in attic. Later codes modified that rather stringent figure to 6 feet 8 inches, a height that provides comfortable living for most people. We've even heard of some newer local modifications that require a minimum of 6 feet of headroom over half the floor space in a lived-in attic.

We recommend that you refrain from following blindly the minimums recommended by such codes, and it's not only because Frank stands 6 feet 2 inches barefoot. We urge you to select a height that's right for you and your needs, with an eye to resale value unless you're planning to stay put for twenty years. A low ceiling is fine in a children's room or a sleeping loft—but consider the likelihood of future buyers needing a children's room or wanting a sleeping loft. When you have decided on the headroom number for you, insert it wherever you encounter our 6-feet 8-inches figure in this chapter and all your plans will come out correct.

Now, let's see how much of your attic you can really live in. Carefully measure the length and width of your entire attic, plus the headroom at its highest point. Convert those figures to a simple blueprint; it'll resemble a triangle and give you a view of your attic from one end of it. Draw this side-view blueprint to scale, letting ¼ inch equal 1 foot of attic space.

Then draw a floor plan—an aerial view of your attic right to the edges of your house. This will resemble a rectangle. Now put in all obstructions: chimneys, pipes, ducts, wires, and so forth.

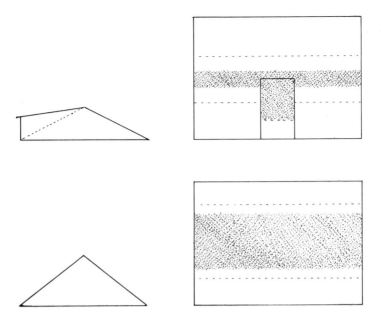

FIGURE 22-2 Here are two different attics, one high-pitched (about 10) and one low (about 6), which illustrate the design factors that enter into maximizing usable space. Both houses are 30′ x 40′. In the low attic, a dormer is absolutely necessary to create a room. With the shed dormer shown, the floor space with 6′ 8″ ceiling above it comes to 504 square feet; with 4′6″ of ceiling above it, 224 square feet. In the other attic, even without a dormer, the area with 6′8″ ceiling room is 560 square feet; with 4′6″, 720 square feet. However, there are 40 feet between the windows at the ends of the attic with pitch 10 roof; add a skylight or dormer midway down one wall, and you'll add light in the room.

Take your side-view sketch and, using a ruler, mark the 6-foot-8-inch headroom cutoff point. (At a scale of ¼ inch, it should be 1¹¹/₁₆, or a hair under 1¾, inches above your base line.) Draw a horizontal dotted line at that 6-foot 8-inch point. Measure it and you'll know how much liveable space you've got in your attic. For example, if it's 8 feet wide to scale, you can count on double that, or 16 feet, of liveable space according to building code requirements.

Dormers, of course, can expand on the amount of useable space. So now's the time to consider whether you want or need a dormer or two. (See previous chapter for construction information.)

Transfer your headroom information to your floor plan, drawing dotted lines to show where the 6-foot 8-inch dividing lines are. They'll form two boundaries; within them the headroom will all be over 6 feet 8 inches; outside of them, there'll be less headroom. Once you take into account all your projected (or existing) dormers, the dotted lines will probably form an irregular shape. Nearby illustrations show typical attic layouts and may help guide your planning.

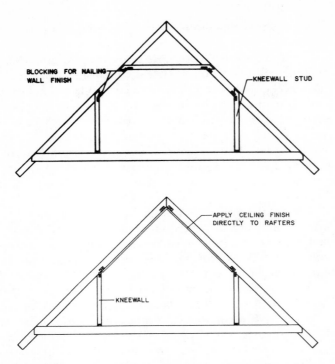

FIGURE 22-3 Here is the layout for knee walls and possible ceiling rafters in both the garret and cathedral-style attic. Length of the studs for knee walls depends on whether you decide to finish off the edges at 5', 4'6", or some other height. (Courtesy U.S. Forest Products Laboratory.)

Now there's another headroom dividing line that should be drawn onto your floor plan. In general, any space with less than a 4-foot 6-inch headroom above it is of little living-space use. (It's fine for storage.) Therefore, locate where the 4-foot 6-inch headroom ends on your side view and transfer that line to your floor plan. (We suggest that you avoid confusion by drawing this line in another color or in some other way separate it from your 6-foot 8-inch line.)

After all these preliminary calculations are made, you should have a pretty good idea of the shape of your projected living space. Now you can decide the best way to utilize it. You may find that you can create as much as two new rooms plus a bathroom. Do take into consideration the placement of your attic stairway and consider whether it ought to—and can —be relocated. Most do-it-yourselfers sidestep the building of stairs. They are somewhat tricky to get right, but fortunately many building supply outlets can make you an entirely pre-built stairway to order if you simply provide a comprehensive set of dimensions. They'll draw up the stairway, cut the boards, and even assemble as much of it as you ask them to. (Codes generally require 6-foot 8-inch headrooms above the entire stairway, and stairs that are at least 3 feet wide. However, local authorities often relax these rules now that more and more people are turning attics into sleeping alcoves.)

Spiral staircases cost more than straight stairways, but they have the advantage of being able to fit into much smaller areas—even into a space that's 4 feet in diameter. They can be purchased in kits from lumberyards and by mail order for do-it-yourself installation. Doors aren't easy to engineer at the top and bottom of these staircases, so what most people end up with is an open stairwell that lets noise, warm air, and people move from one floor to the other without any barriers. And have you ever tried to carry a sofa up a spiral staircase? Unless you've an alternate way of getting furniture and large suitcases up and down, you may have to forget the idea.

Windows are easily installed in the straight end-walls of your attic, but they may not provide enough light and ventilation, especially if you plan to make several rooms. You may want to add windows along one or both sloping sides. Dormers are the oldfashioned solution. If you have a high-pitched roof, you can install a skylight. Nowadays, the fancier models are every bit as convenient as windows; they even open for ventilation. Some come with built-in shades, venetian blinds, or shutters.

But before you dot your attic with windows, be sure to reread our chapter on energy (Chapter 5). Windows not only let in light, they let out heat all winter. If your new attic living space will be used for bedrooms, they'll get minimum use during daylight hours. Decide whether you really need lots of light, or just air circulation. If it's the latter, have a look at the blowers and fans that, installed in an outside wall, can be closed tight when

FIGURE 22-4 Skylights are a good way to get light into attics, turning them from dingy storage places into delightful living areas. Notice that you can even use curtains and venetian blinds with modern skylights. (Courtesy Velux-America, Inc.)

they're not needed. The ones we've seen are not very attractive, but we haven't looked at them all.

Another convenient way to move air is with a window fan. Ours is installed all summer. On hot days, we pull air from the attic room—and up out of the lower level to help keep that area cool. At night, just a few minutes' blowing not only pulls the warm air up and out, but sucks in the cool evening air down on the first floor and right up into the bedroom. We have a central air conditioner, but we've had to turn it on only when temperatures have climbed above 85° outdoors.

Your next design consideration is whether to leave a vaulted ceiling in the new rooms or to make more traditional garret ceilings—flat at the center and sloping at the sides. The cathedral effect requires less framing with 2 × 4s but a bit more finishing material such as paneling or gypsum board. Vaulting helps to make a small room look airier.

However you finish your ceiling, be sure to allow plenty of room for insulation. While an uninsulated attic rarely gets chilly in winter since heat rises into it from the downstairs living areas, it can get awfully hot in the summertime since it's right up there under the roof. Install as much fiberglass or rockwool insulation between the rafters as space permits. If you have 8-inch rafters, that should be sufficient. If you have only 6-inch rafters, think seriously about putting a layer of Styrofoam insulating board over the fiberglass. Then be sure to protect the Styrofoam from fire with gypsum board or paneling that has a fire rating that meets local building and fire codes.

Also allow for ventilation above the insulation. (See Chapter 18 for more information.)

HOW TO MAXIMIZE ATTIC-ROOM SPACE

You really have to shake off a few deep-rooted notions about home design before you can make the best use of the most space in what used to be almost an unused attic. About the only thing that seems to come naturally is the positioning of furniture, since most of us place ours against our walls.

In attics, since the adequate headroom must be reserved mostly for walking around, sitting and storing pieces should all stand in those under-6-foot-8-inch areas. For instance, if your attic is about to become a bedroom, an ideal arrangement is to place the bed against one knee-wall where headroom is minimal, since people seldom stand up in bed. For dressing tables and chairs, low walls are ideal: people use these pieces sitting down. Chests of drawers belong against knee-walls too, since they extend out from the walls quite a bit. The net result is to put lots more than 5 feet of headroom above the person who's using them. In fact, in our custom-made bedroom-loft attic, the wall against which Judi's dresser sits was pared down to 4 feet to pick up more living area. Since she's 5 feet 2 inches tall, she's got ample headroom.

Closets offer room for the greatest alteration from our traditional concepts of design. Our attic bed-loft has a 10-foot-long closet on one

FIGURE 22-5 Careful placement of furniture maximizes the usable space you'll enjoy in your attic *cum* bedroom, den, sewing room, guest bedroom . . . Desks, chests, beds, and such require very little headroom.

knee-wall. It stands just 5 feet 6 inches high on its front face, and we've finished it with nearly 10 feet of cut-down louvred doors. We've put the clothes rod at 4 feet 6 inches from the ground, and that's a fine height for everything but the few formal gowns that can be stored elsewhere since they're not among our everyday needs. We have no shelf above the rod the way most closets do—but short Judi usually can't reach those shelves anyway. And instead of a cluttered shoe-filled closet floor, we've built a separate shoe closet into another knee-wall.

Built-in dressers and cedar-lined drawers are other luxury features you can add.

Just because you're turning the attic into living space doesn't mean having to do without all that dead storage space you once enjoyed. Behind your knee walls, under the attic slope, you still have may cubic feet of space. By using flush doors that are disguised as part of our walls, we have easy access to three separate storage areas without breaking up our living area with lots of doorway moldings.

When you're wiring the attic so that it can be lived in, be sure to wire up a light inside each storage area with a switch or pull-cord right near the entrance to it. It's tough to go searching for Junior's old boxing gloves with a flashlight in one hand.

23
How to Turn Your Basement into a Living Room

That damp, dreary, dismal thing over which your house may be sitting—your basement—can become your ticket to an easy expansion of family living space. People who think immediately of finishing an attic or adding a room out back often forget that the basement might be put to far better use than for dead storage, laundry room, and a place to shoo the kiddies to.

If your basement is like so many others, you wouldn't think of entertaining your friends there, or of sleeping down there, and you find it hardly a good place to relax. But dreariness and even dampness can be easily corrected.

HOW TO TAKE THE BASENESS OUT OF YOUR BASEMENT

If you're lucky enough to have a house on a hillside, you have no basement problem—you're probably making full use of every level. If you've bought a split-level home, you're also making full use of your lowermost rooms even though you're not on a hill; split-levels seem to have been designed with imaginary hillside surroundings in mind. People who own either of these types of home associate no unpleasantness with relaxing in their low-down rooms because they never think of them as basements. In large part, that's because those rooms have full-sized windows.

One solution to a dark or dreary basement, then, is to install large windows. If you live in an area where the builder bulldozed a small hill onto three or four sides of your home after bulldozing the acreage flat for the foundation—effectively covering over all but the few top inches of your basement—all you have to do is to bulldoze the dirt out of the way again. It's not exactly a do-it-yourself project (although a friend of ours did rent a small bulldozer to landscape his own large yard), but a small contractor should be able to handle the job for you at a budget price.

Once you've got the high dirt away from part of your house, decide where you want your windows. Then, for each, just knock out part of the concrete or cement-block foundation with a large star drill and a hammer, frame in the space with wood (see Chatper 10), caulk up the spaces between your framing and the concrete around it, and put in your windows.

If your home doesn't have an artificial hill, you can still add windows to your basement. As a corollary, you'll have to live with a sunken garden—but sunken gardens, landscaped well, are rare and lovely additions to any home. Again, it involves bulldozing a good-sized portion of land deep enough down to expose about the upper 4 feet of your basement. Build a retaining wall around your sunken land to keep the rest of your property from collapsing into it. Then knock your holes in your foundation and add full-sized windows. The last step is to do something about draining your sunken garden or you'll end up with an indoor swimming pool whenever it rains. Three approaches are most used.

The first way is to drain your garden with a pipe that connects

FIGURE 23-1 One way to create basement windows is to make a sunken garden outside. (Courtesy U.S. Forest Products Laboratory.)

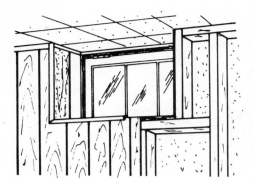

FIGURE 23-2 With a sunken garden outside, you can frame in your new basement window, decorate brightly, and end up with a *living* room.

directly to your house's sewer line. It's easy—but it's prohibited in some parts of the country.

The second method is to drain off your garden into a pipe that runs off into the unbulldozed ground and to some distant spot that's lower than your sunken garden's ground level; that way, gravity will drain away the problem water.

In areas with adequately porous soil, you can simply let rainwater soak into the ground—but for safety, into the ground furthest from your home. You can achieve that by sloping the sunken garden so that water runs away from the house, and then building into the retaining wall plenty of ground-level spaces between its stones or logs. The spaces will pipe the rainwater directly into the surrounding ground.

You can use this techique, however, even if your soil isn't porous. Bulldoze away several extra cubic yards of earth and then haul in at least a truckload of gravel fill. Dump it on the ground right behind your sunken garden's retaining wall. You can cover the gravel with dirt and the dirt with grass and still enjoy your subterranean gravel catchbasin that will funnel away your sunken garden's excess water.

Before you open up the ground around your basement, check with your local building codes. They vary greatly and change constantly, but we can summarize the most common restrictions:

• If you intend to use any part of your basement for living, eating, cooking, or sleeping, the new ground level against the exterior of that part of the basement should be no higher than 4 feet above the level of your finished floor.

• Many codes specify a ceiling height of no lower than 6 feet 9 inches *on average* in habitable rooms. (If some spots are higher than 6 feet 9 inches, others can be lower.)

• You may be required to provide a fire exit that leads directly from your basement to the outdoors. If your code is as flexible as most, however, one of those handy sloped areaway entrances, a bit like the old cellar doors, is considered perfectly acceptable and can be placed in a part of the basement that you plan to retain as storage area. Let's hope you'll never

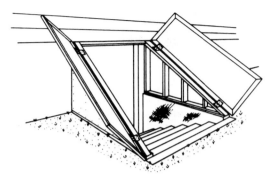

FIGURE 23-3 One way to add a fire exit to your basement is with an area-way type of opening such as this one. It meets most fire codes, and is also handy for bringing hefty tools into the basement for storage. (Courtesy U.S. Forest Products Laboratory.)

need to use it for more than dragging in bikes and lawnmowers; still, in case of fire, it's a perfectly adequate fire escape.

If there's no way to put real windows in your basement, don't give up. Take a tip from the model room decorators in large department stores: put up some real curtained windows on your interior walls and hang fluorescent lights behind them. If you use translucent glass, that's all you need do. If you use transparent glass, hang murals behind them with your favorite outdoor views. It's amazing how much you can fool even yourself with a little *trompe l'oeil.*

BASEMENTS DON'T HAVE TO BE DAMP

Are you one of those people who wonder how those underground homes you read about can stay warm and dry when just your 4 feet underground oozes wetness continually? The fact is, below-ground rooms don't have to be cavelike. Pinpoint the source of your dampness and correct it.

Basement dampness comes from one (or both) of two sources: seepage through concrete walls, or condensation of humidity when the warm inside air strikes the cold foundation walls. To see what's at fault in your case, you can run a quick test. Cut off a piece of ordinary aluminum foil about 1 foot square. Tape it securely along all four edges to one of your basement walls. Leave it there for several days, and then remove it. If the side facing the wall is wet, you have seepage; if the other side's wet, you have condensation problems. If both sides are wet—yup, you've got both.

To stop seepage, first you must plug up all the cracks in your concrete blocks and in the mortar between the blocks, then apply a specially formulated masonry waterproofing sealer. So examine all your mortar joints, not just the ones where leaking is obvious. Don't overlook

FIGURE 23-4 If your basement walls look like this, you'd better read carefully the text on moisture. It's possible to stop seepage by patching cracks right down to where the walls meet the floor, and then "painting" with a special masonry wall sealer. (Courtesy United Gilsonite Laboratories.)

the joint where your walls meet floor, a common source of seepage. Chisel away any loose mortar you find, but avoid the temptation to end up with v-shaped indentations. If you must chisel out a substantial amount of old mortar, square off the working area so that your patches will be at least ¾ inch thick.

Fill your cracks and holes with hydraulic cement, so named because it's designed to expand as it sets and thus dam up the flow of water. The better hydraulic cements set in a few minutes. Use the same product to bead the spot where wall meets floor.

Before applying sealer, clean your concrete walls thoroughly. All old paints must be scraped or wire-brushed away unless you're sure that they contain a base of Portland cement. (Sealers contain Portland cement.) Be sure to remove any white or light-gray crystals that you find on the surface of the walls. Known as efflorescence, these crystals are salt compounds that have been drawn out from the concrete onto its surface by the water seepage. Left there, they'll keep your waterproofing paint from sticking to the walls.

Some of the companies that make concrete sealing paint also sell acid compounds that remove efflorescence. You can use one of these products or you can scrub the walls with a 20 percent solution of muriatic acid. (To make the solution, put on rubber gloves and protective goggles and then slowly pour 1 part of acid into 4 parts of water. DO NOT POUR WATER INTO ACID.) Whether you're scrubbing with your homemade product or the store-bought one, do wear protective goggles and rubber gloves. (Before mixing, the muriatic acid is no more dangerous than a liquid drain cleaner; mixed, both products are somewhat less dangerous—but you ought to wear goggles and gloves when you use drain cleaners, too!)

Once the surfaces of your walls are shipshape, apply a good brand of masonry waterproofing paint. If you don't intend to cover that with something fancier, you can ask your paint dealer to add tint to the sealer, which comes in white. Best results are obtained if you apply it with a brush, at least for the first coat.

If most of your seepage is near the bottoms of your walls, apply a

FIGURE 23-5 Here's a surefire way to keep condensation from forming on walls. First treat them with waterproof sealer, next install foamed insulation board such as Styrofoam, then finish with gypsum board, plywood paneling, or other fire-rated material. (Courtesy U.S. Forest Products Laboratory.)

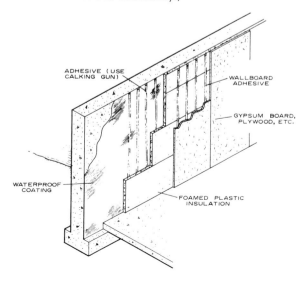

preliminary coat of sealer to the bottom one-third of your walls. When that's set, apply a second coat top-to-bottom. After your sealer has been on the walls for a few days, examine the job. You may find that water is still seeping through a few pinholes. Repaint those areas.

Condensation can be controlled by improving air circulation in your basement. If you're converting it to living space, the addition or enlargement of basement windows will solve the problem so long as they're opened once in a while. If you can't open windows, install a small fan. If your area of the country has humid air at times during the year, you may need a dehumidifier.

Another way to avoid condensation is by insulating your walls. If you're in a cold climate, whether or not you use your basement, you'd better insulate those walls anyway. But if seepage is a problem, seal before you insulate.

FIGURE 23-6 Carpet your basement, panel its walls, and live in it. With the dampness controlled and the windows enlarged (or good lighting added), it can look like this. (Courtesy Masonite Corporation.)

BEAUTIFYING BASEMENT WALLS

The fastest and least expensive way to beautify old concrete-walled basements is to glue Styrofoam insulation right onto them using an adhesive that won't harm the insulation but will adhere to the concrete. Then glue paneling onto the Styrofoam. (With luck, the same adhesive will work for that too.) Be sure to select a paneling that has a fire rating high enough to protect the Styrofoam in case of fire. Fortunately, panel manufacturers now provide so many variations on the old familiar grooved wood designs that you're sure to be able to create a look that says something other than "finished-basement." With the help of the tips in Chapter 12, you can have all your walls finished in a day's work.

The alternative to the preceding "one-two" method takes more time and more materials, but is still a simple enough job for nearly any do-it-yourselfer. First erect a false wall against the concrete by using 2 × 4s spaced at 24-inch intervals and by nailing them up with masonry nails. Then you can staple fiberglass insulation with a built-in vapor barrier to the 2 × 4s. Any relatively flame-resistant material can be applied directly to the wood 2 × 4s. For other finishes, first install gypsum board according to Chapter 12's directions; then you can finish with wallpaper, tile, carpeting, glue-on imitation brick or stone, or whatever else you'd like. Once you've licked your moisture problem, any finish is acceptable.

NEW FLOORS FOR OLD BASEMENTS

Though most people think first about finishing their walls and only later about putting down flooring, it's probably best if you work the other way round. That's because, although the fastest way to finish a basement floor is with durable brightly colored floor paint suitable for use on concrete, finishing yours that way will make it feel like a basement no matter how expertly you decorate your walls.

Some kinds of carpet, tile, and wood flooring can be put right on dry concrete floors. When you shop around, be sure to specify to the dealer

FIGURE 23-7 Here's an x-ray view of what the floor on a well-covered basement will look like. Floor tile is at upper part of this sketch, and wooden flooring is at lower part. (Courtesy U.S. Forest Products Laboratory.)

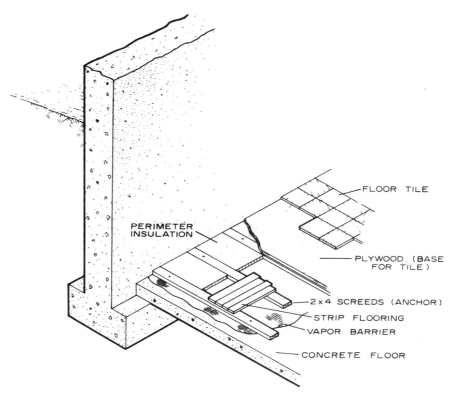

FLOOR TILE

PERIMETER INSULATION

PLYWOOD (BASE FOR TILE)

2 x 4 SCREEDS (ANCHOR)

STRIP FLOORING

VAPOR BARRIER

CONCRETE FLOOR

that you need a product that you can install easily below grade on concrete and that will hold up well under this use. See Chapter 13 for our hints, and be sure to follow manufacturer's instructions for use on concrete basement floors.

If your concrete floor is full of ridges or little hills or it's beset by dampness, build a raised floor over it.

- First lay down a good vapor barrier such as a sheet of polyethylene plastic.
- Then use masonry nails to secure a network of 2 × 4s to the floor. Space them 16 inches apart unless you plan to install ceramic tiles over plywood; in that case space them at 12-inch intervals.
- If your basement floor is less than 3 feet below ground level, lay down some Styrofoam or fiberglass insulation around the entire perimeter where the floor meets walls. Very little cold enters through the floor, but a great deal can enter from the walls and then be transmitted via the concrete through the outside edges of your floor.
- Nail wooden floorboards to the 2 × 4s or cover them with ½-inch exterior grade plywood.
- Then apply whatever finished floor you've chosen. Assuming that you've licked all your moisture problems, you can select any flooring material your heart desires. So you might want to build this false floor even if your concrete flooring is sound.

FIGURE 23-8 Start thinking about how you can turn your basement into a real room. (Courtesy Masonite Corporation.)

In most basements, you can't just nail up gypsum board, slap on a coat of paint, and forget about your ceilings. Up there is a network of pipes, cables, and other features that you may have to get to the next time something plugs up or shuts down.

There are several solutions. One is to install a suspended-ceiling system; if you need the headroom, you can put it right up close to your ceiling beams. (If you add several flourescent ceiling lights, they'll instantly turn any basement into a daylight-bright room.)

Another way to provide access is with a paneled ceiling—only instead of nailing all the paneling to your beams, screw in the panels that may, at some later date, need to be removed. Match the panels' color as closely as you can with your screws and they'll never be noticed. For example, with wood paneling, purchase brass screws.

If the ceiling you want finished has just a few pipes or wires in it and you think it's unlikely you'll want access to them in the conceivable future, you can nail up gypsum board the way you would with any other ceiling, as we described in Chapter 12. But first we suggest that you mark, somehow, the sites of those wires or pipes. Five years from now, when you need quick

FIGURE 23-9 Here's how to nail furring strips to overhead joists in your basement so you can blind-staple ceiling tiles. (Courtesy U.S. Forest Products Laboratory.)

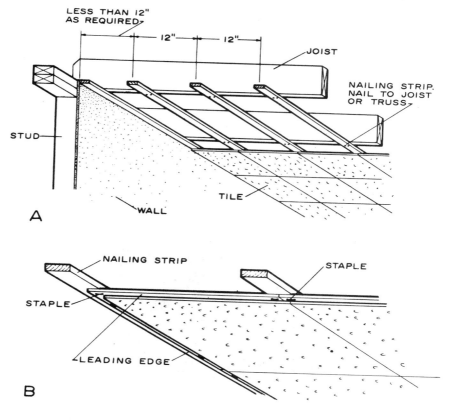

access, you're not going to remember even which side of the room they're on. Patching up a piece of gypsum board ceiling is not a difficult project, but patching up ten holes you've made to locate the right place is a project we wouldn't want to be called in on.

We would like to hear about your improvements. Write to us in care of our publisher and tell us about them. Send a photo, and maybe we can include it in our next book. Till then, may your every project bring you pleasure.

Index